DICEY + 100

DICEY + 100

Albert Venn Dicey: A Centennial Commemoration

Edited by
Andrew DICKINSON
Timothy ENDICOTT
Wolfgang ERNST

Assistant Editor
Sophie RYAN

INTERSENTIA
Cambridge – Antwerp – Chicago

Intersentia Ltd
8 Wellington Mews
Wellington Street | Cambridge
CB1 1HW | United Kingdom
Tel: +44 1223 736 170
Email: contact@larcier-intersentia.com
www.larcier-intersentia.com

Distribution for the UK and
Rest of the World (incl. Eastern Europe)
NBN International
1 Deltic Avenue, Rooksley
Milton Keynes MK13 8LD
United Kingdom
Tel: +44 1752 202 301 | Fax: +44 1752 202 331
Email: orders@nbninternational.com

Distribution for Europe
Lefebvre Sarrut Belgium NV
Hoogstraat 139/6
1000 Brussels
Belgium
Tel: +32 (0)2 548 07 13
Email: contact@larcier-intersentia.com

Distribution for the USA and Canada
Independent Publishers Group
Order Department
814 North Franklin Street
Chicago, IL 60610
USA
Tel: +1 800 888 4741 (toll free) | Fax: +1 312 337 5985
Email: orders@ipgbook.com

Dicey + 100. Albert Venn Dicey: A Centennial Commemoration

ISBN 978-1-83970-426-0
D/2024/7849/8
NUR 820

British Library Cataloguing in Publication Data. A catalogue record for this book is available from the British Library.

IN MEMORY OF
ALBERT VENN DICEY K.C.
BORN 1835 DIED 1922
VINERIAN PROFESSOR OF ENGLISH LAW
FOR 27 YEARS
M.A. HON. D.C.L. OXFORD
HON. LL.D. CAMBRIDGE GLASGOW EDINBURGH
FELLOW OF ALL SOULS COLLEGE OXFORD
HON. FELLOW OF TRINITY AND BALLIOL COLLEGES
JURIST – POLITICAL PHILOSOPHER – PATRIOT
HE WAS HONOURED AND LOVED AS A GREAT TEACHER AND A
TRUE FRIEND
"HE BEING DEAD YET SPEAKETH."
HEBREWS XI.IV

EDITORS' PREFACE

Albert Venn Dicey died at his home on Banbury Road in Oxford on 7 April 1922, at the age of 87. Three days later, he was buried at St Sepulchre's Cemetery, off Walton Street (see photograph at p. 108). His wife of 50 years, Elinor, survived him by 19 months and is buried alongside him.

Almost 100 years later, one of us (a student of the conflict of laws) ventured to the Cemetery in search of Dicey's resting place. The site has been carefully tended in recent years by volunteers, but many of the gravestones understandably show signs of age. In Dicey's case, this is something of a metaphor, for his reputation as a legal scholar and political thinker has encountered heavy weather in recent times. Dicey, no doubt, would have accepted some of this commentary as fair – as an individual, he was conscious of his own fallibilities and not averse to acts of self-criticism. In some part, however, he has been disadvantaged by a modern inclination to pass judgement according to contemporary facilities, knowledge, and standards, and a tendency to highlight failings in the midst of achievements. As editors, we are in no doubt that the dedication to Dicey as having been 'honoured and loved as a great teacher and a true friend' was truly deserved. The honest and earnest dedication with which he approached his life's work shines from the page, and his two most important works on *The Law of the Constitution* and *The Conflict of Laws* live on as testaments to his academic endeavour.

That visit prompted the idea that the centenary of Dicey's death ought to be marked by an event in Oxford, where he had studied (at Balliol College) and spent much of his life (as a Fellow of Trinity College and, later, as Vinerian Professor of English Law and a Fellow of All Souls College). Happily, that idea garnered support and the three of us had little difficulty in persuading colleagues to take part. The conference took place over two days, on 3 and 4 October 2022, at All Souls College and St Catherine's College. The speakers reflected on a wide range of topics inspired by Dicey's body of work and lifetime's accomplishments, venturing in and beyond the legal subject areas with which he is most closely associated, providing an opportunity to examine his professional life, political engagement, and literary passions. Many of the papers presented on that occasion have been refined and are collected in this small book.

We are extremely grateful to all of those who have contributed to this project. In particular, we would like to express our thanks to our authors, the Fellows and staff members of All Souls and St Catherine's College, the Faculty of Law for financial and logistical support, Tarquin Holmes for advice on funding matters, Michelle Robb and Clare Oxenbury-Palmer for helping with the conference website and social media, and Asang Wankhede and Sophie Ryan, who ensured that the event ran smoothly. This publication would not have been possible without Sophie, our Assistant Editor, whose many contributions we have greatly valued and with whom it has been a pleasure to work. Intersentia have been very supportive of the proposal, and we would like to thank Rebecca Moffat, Francesca Ramadan and other members of their team who have helped to bring it to fruition.

Andrew Dickinson
Timothy Endicott
Wolfgang Ernst
(Editors)
All Souls' Day, 2023

CONTENTS

PART II. DICEY AND THE CONSTITUTION

PART III. DICEY AND THE CONFLICT OF LAWS

LIST OF CASES

LIST OF LEGISLATION

LIST OF CONTRIBUTORS

Professor Andrew Dickinson (Editor)
Professor of the Conflict of Laws and Fellow of St Catherine's College, University of Oxford

Professor Timothy Endicott (Editor)
Vinerian Professor of English Law and Fellow of All Souls College, University of Oxford

Professor Wolfgang Ernst (Editor)
Regius Professor of Civil Law and Fellow of All Souls College, University of Oxford

Sophie Ryan (Assistant Editor)
Rhodes Scholar and DPhil in Law candidate at Magdalen College, University of Oxford

Dr Roxana Banu
Associate Professor and Fellow of Lady Margaret Hall, University of Oxford

Professor Sally Bushell
Professor of Romantic and Victorian Literature, Lancaster University

Professor John W. Cairns
Professor of Civil Law, University of Edinburgh

The Rt Hon Lord Collins of Mapesbury
Professor of Law, University College London and formerly a Justice of the United Kingdom Supreme Court

Dr Hasan Dindjer
Associate Professor and Fellow of Balliol College, University of Oxford

Dr James Kirby
Barrister, Ten Old Square

Dr Marc Mulholland
Associate Professor and Fellow of St Catherine's College, University of Oxford

Professor Mark D. Walters
Professor of Public and Constitutional Law, Queen's University

Professor Alison Young
Sir David Williams Professor of Public Law and Fellow of Robinson College, University of Cambridge

PART I

DICEY IN HIS TIME AND OUR TIME

DICEY AT OXFORD

John W. Cairns

1. INTRODUCTION

On 28 May 1909, Lord Curzon wrote to A. V. Dicey remarking that he had been 'seriously distressed' when Dicey had told him of his intention to resign the Vinerian Professorship at Oxford. He said he understood Dicey's reasons, which were honourable, and reflected his sense of public obligation. Curzon hoped, however, that, 'as Chancellor of the University at the moment of your retirement', he might be permitted 'to send ... a brief line of sincere and grateful recognition of the preeminent contribution that [Dicey had] made ... to the life, the learning and the public distinction of Oxford'; his 'name and works' had 'shed a lustre upon the University'.[1] On election as Chancellor, Curzon had personally nominated Dicey to receive the degree of D.C.L. *honoris causa*. The professor stands out in the list of honorands gaining this degree, mainly distinguished politicians and military men, the only other lawyers being the Lord Chancellor and the Lord Chief Justice of England.[2] This is powerful testimony to Dicey's quality and the recognition he had achieved. He was touched by the *laudatio* given by his colleague Henry Goudy, who, as Professor of Civil Law, had the

[1] Lord Curzon to A.V. Dicey, 28 May 1909, Glasgow University Library, MS. Gen. 508/55. Dicey was troubled by his increasing deafness, diminishing memory, and reduced energy: R.S. Rait, *Memorials of Albert Venn Dicey: Being Chiefly Letters and Diaries*, Macmillan & Co., London 1925, pp. 200–01.

[2] 'University Intelligence' (5 Jun. 1907) 25 *Oxford Magazine*, p. 383.

onerous task of giving a Latin oration for each of the graduands. That for Dicey he gave extempore, such was his knowledge of his colleague and the affection he felt for him.[3] Goudy apostrophised Dicey, not unjustly, as '*vir eloquentissime, in forma et consuetudine nostrae civitatis versate, nec non Hiberniae domi retinendae acerrime adsertor*'.[4]

Dicey's resignation of the Vinerian Chair did not end his links with the University. In October 1909, he proposed to deliver a set of lectures on Conflict of Laws (aimed at those intending to be examined for the degree of B.C.L.) and another on Special Points in the Law of Contract.[5] In the same month, he was elected Professor Emeritus.[6] In November he was elected as a Fellow of All Souls.[7] The next year he was appointed to a Lectureship in Private International Law, giving an inaugural public lecture on the study of the topic at Oxford on 21 October 1910.[8] In this he stressed the importance of making the subject a regular part of legal study at Oxford.[9]

Dicey's appointment to a Lectureship in Private International Law is no surprise. The topic was even described in *The Times* as 'his own special subject'.[10] His interest in it had earlier led to his seeking the Chichele Professorship of International Law at Oxford in 1874.[11] This was rumoured in the *Daily News* on 1 June 1874.[12] A letter to his former tutor and friend Mark Pattison in 1879 – enclosed with a presentation copy of his *Law of Domicil as a Branch of the Law of England*, a treatise on Private International Law – confirms the candidacy. He wrote to Pattison that he came to study the topic because of the latter's advice that he should 'stand for the International Law Chair' which led 'at least indirectly' to the writing of the book.[13] A year later he wrote to Oliver Wendell Holmes asking if he

---

3 A.V. Dicey to E. Dicey, 27 June 1907, in Rait, above n. 1, p. 194.

4 'The Encaenia at Oxford' (27 Jun. 1907) *The Times*, p. 14; perhaps: 'most eloquent man, skilled in the constitution and custom of our polity, while the most vigorous champion of retaining Ireland as part of the homeland'.

5 'Notice of Lectures by Dr. Dicey' (8 Oct. 1909) 40 *Oxford University Gazette*, p. 37.

6 'University Intelligence' (13 Oct. 1909) *The Times*, p. 12.

7 'University Intelligence' (2 Nov. 1909) *The Times*, p. 9.

8 'General University Notices' (19 May 1910) 40 *Oxford University Gazette*, p. 323; 'University Intelligence' (15 Oct. 1910) *The Times*, p. 9.

9 'University Intelligence' (22 Oct. 1910) *The Times*, p. 6.

10 'Oxford: Summer Term' (28 Jun. 1910) *The Times*, p. 9.

11 See M.D. Walters, *A. V. Dicey and the Common Law Constitutional Tradition: A Legal Turn of Mind*, Cambridge University Press, Cambridge 2020, pp. 78–79, fn. 143.

12 (1 Jun. 1874) *Daily News*, p. 3. This was picked up in evening newspapers: (1 Jun. 1874) *Edinburgh Evening News*, p. 3; (1 Jun. 1874) *Pall Mall Gazette*, p. 6.

13 A.V. Dicey to M. Pattison, 30 June 1879, pasted into A.V. Dicey, *The Law of Domicil as a Branch of the Law of England: Stated in the Form of Rules*, Stevens & Sons, London 1879, copy in Stanford University, Royal Law Library. Most of the letter has

could find him 'at Harvard a well paid Professorship'. Its subject was to be 'the Conflict of Laws'.[14] If the approach to Holmes was jocular, the choice of subject was serious. In the same year he was elected as an Associate of the *Institut de Droit International*; in five years he was duly elected a full member.[15] Dicey continued to be interested in the *Institut*, attending its meetings in Paris in 1910 and Oxford in 1913, even though his increasing deafness made participation difficult.[16] Conflict of laws was a major interest of the *Institut*. Dicey's *Law of Domicil* was later developed into his *Digest of the Law of England with Reference to the Conflict of Laws*.[17] Hanbury described this as 'really his greatest book'.[18]

Other than among specialists in private international law, Dicey is best remembered, however, for his work on the theory of constitutional law. This was the focus of the studies of his two recent biographers, Cosgrove and Walters.[19] It is easy to explain this emphasis. Dicey first published *Lectures Introductory to the Study of the Law of the Constitution* in 1885; a second edition appeared in 1886.[20] By the date of his death in 1922, a further six editions, under the revised title *Introduction to the Study of the Law of the Constitution*, had appeared, along with a French translation.[21] It is telling that Walters has an entire section devoted to this work in his listing of Dicey's publications, while all the other monographs are listed together as 'other books'.[22] It is easy to trace citation of the work in Parliament; Gladstone – one imagines with a certain relish, given Dicey's strong opposition to Home Rule – cited it in a debate on the Government of Ireland in 1886, not long after its publication.[23] Indeed, when John Kirkpatrick, Professor

---

been scanned by Google Books and is accessible on Internet Archive. It is quoted in Walters, above n. 11, pp. 78–79, fn. 143.

14 Walters, above n. 11, p. 69.

15 'The Institute of International Law' (8 Sep. 1880) *The Times*, p. 9; 'The Institut de Droit International' (10 Sep. 1885) *The Times*, p. 6.

16 Rait, above n. 1, pp. 208–09, 219.

17 Dicey (1879), above n. 13; A.V. Dicey, *A Digest of the Law of England with Reference to the Conflict of Laws*, Stevens & Sons, London 1896 ('*Digest*').

18 H.G. Hanbury, *The Vinerian Chair and Legal Education*, Basil Blackwell, Oxford 1958, p. 101. Its descendant remains in publication.

19 R.A. Cosgrove, *The Rule of Law: Albert Venn Dicey, Victorian Jurist*, University of North Carolina Press, Chapel Hill 1980; Walters, above, n. 11. T.H. Ford, *Albert Venn Dicey: The Man and His Times*, Barry Rose Publishers, Chichester 1985, was more curious than helpful.

20 Walters, above n. 11, p. 412.

21 ibid., pp. 411–12.

22 ibid., pp. 412–13.

23 'House of Commons' (9 Apr. 1886) *The Times*, p. 6. Macmillan advertised the work for sale in October 1885: 'Column of New Books' (15 & 21 Oct. 1885) *The Times*, p. 12.

of Constitutional Law and History, presented Dicey for the degree of LL.D. *honoris causa* at the University of Edinburgh in April 1886, though all his works were mentioned, he particularly singled out the 'masterly lectures' on the *Law of the Constitution* with its recent citation in the House of Commons.[24] Dicey wrote extensively on the constitutional position of Ireland in popular monographs, periodicals, and the newspapers, while later in life he became interested in questions posed by the Union between England and Scotland.[25] His obituary in *The Times* specifically picked out his work on constitutional law.[26] Harold Laski described Dicey as having 'won for himself [a position] as a constitutional lawyer [that] was remarkable'.[27] Laski understandably described the *Introduction* as a 'classic'.[28] The clarity of writing made it 'masterly'.[29]

The *Lectures Introductory* did not purport to be a comprehensive account of the relevant law. Dicey stressed in his preface that the work only focused on 'two or three guiding principles' to provide a manual that students could use to help them understand other works, such as that of Blackstone. He also emphasised the danger in emphasising the history over the law. He acknowledged the consequence of the work's origin in lectures, stressing again that it was an account of principles, not a detailed textbook.[30] One can indeed trace the origin of the book in his lectures. Dicey was elected to the Vinerian Chair on 5 December 1882.[31] His first classes were those on Elementary Principles of the Law of Contract in the Trinity Term, scheduled to start on 23 April 1883, which he taught again in the Michaelmas and Hilary Terms of 1883–84.[32] It was not until the Trinity Term of that academic year that he offered, alongside a specialised course on Contract, one on the Law of the Constitution, starting on

24 'University of Edinburgh. Graduation Ceremonial' (22 Apr. 1886) *The Scotsman*, p. 7.

25 A.V. Dicey and R.S. Rait, *Thoughts on the Union between England and Scotland*, Macmillan & Co., London 1920.

26 'A Great Jurist' (8 Apr. 1922) *The Times*, p. 14.

27 H. Laski to O.W. Holmes, 17 April 1922, in M.D. Howe (ed.), *Holmes-Laski Letters: The Correspondence of Mr. Justice Holmes and Harold J. Laski, Volume 1: 1916–1925*, Harvard University Press, Cambridge MA 1953, p. 421 ('*Holmes-Laski Letters*').

28 H. Laski to O.W. Holmes, 25 May 1924, in *Holmes-Laski Letters*, above n. 27, p. 621.

29 H. Laski to O.W. Holmes, 23 Oct. 1923, in *Holmes-Laski Letters*, above n. 27, p. 553.

30 A.V. Dicey, *Lectures Introductory to the Study of the Law of the Constitution*, Macmillan & Co., London 1885, pp. v–vii.

31 'General University Notices. Vinerian Professorship of English Law' (8 Dec. 1882) 12 *Oxford University Gazette*, p. 191.

32 'Notices of Professors … Law' (6 Mar. 1883) 12 *Oxford University Gazette*, p. 352; 'Notices of Professors … Law' (12 Oct. 1883; 18 Jan. 1884) 13 *Oxford University Gazette*, pp. 19, 224.

30 April 1884, to consist of 'six lectures on some fundamental principles of Constitutional Law'. He also delivered a public lecture entitled the 'True Nature of (so-called) Constitutional Law'.[33] In the next academic year, he taught both Contract and the Law of the Constitution, described as 'Rights of Citizens' in the Hilary Term.[34] He did not again touch on questions of constitutional law until the Trinity Term of 1886–87, when he scheduled six lectures on, for the first time, Comparative Study of the Constitution, a quite different course from the *Lectures Introductory*.[35]

2. LAW TEACHING AT OXFORD, 1883–1909

Dicey was elected to the Vinerian Chair just as major reforms became effective in Oxford.[36] Acts of Parliament in 1850 and 1877 had established Royal Commissions that had introduced significant changes. Oxford was, of course, not alone in being the object of reform. All British universities in this era were undergoing major restructuring through the mechanism of Commissions established by Acts of Parliament to propose and oversee change through detailed regulation. These changes affected curricula and teaching.[37] While different problems were identified in different institutions, the general ambition was to develop, modernise, and expand university education. Reforms in legal education at the universities were also related to reforms proposed by the legal professions, which, in the various jurisdictions of the United Kingdom, controlled admission as a lawyer, whether barrister, advocate, or solicitor.[38]

---

33 'Notices of Professors ... Law' (18 Apr. 1884) 13 *Oxford University Gazette*, p. 386.

34 'Notices of Professors ... Law' (10 Oct. 1884) 14 *Oxford University Gazette*, p. 18.

35 'Notices of Professors ... Law' (8 Mar. 1887) 17 *Oxford University Gazette*, p. 352. See A.V. Dicey, *Comparative Constitutionalism*, J.W.F. Allison (ed.), Oxford University Press, Oxford 2013, pp. xi–xii. Based on study of Dicey's MSS, Allison dates the lectures from 1895–1900 and again just to before Dicey's retirement in 1909. But he obviously started to develop them rather earlier.

36 L.W.B. Brockliss, *The University of Oxford: A History*, Oxford University Press, Oxford 2016, pp. 347–95; A.J. Engel, *From Clergyman to Don: The Rise of the Academic Profession in Nineteenth-Century Oxford*, Oxford University Press, Oxford 1983, pp. 257–85.

37 J.W. Cairns, 'The Early Historiography of the Lex Aquilia in Britain: Introducing Students to the Digest' in P.J. du Plessis (ed.), *Wrongful Damage to Property in Roman Law: British Perspectives*, Edinburgh University Press, Edinburgh 2018, pp. 7–8.

38 P. Polden (partly with M. Lobban) 'The Education of Lawyers' in W. Cornish, S. Anderson, R. Cocks, M. Lobban, P. Polden and K. Smith (eds.), *The Oxford History of the Laws of England*, vol. XI, Oxford University Press, Oxford 2010, pp. 1175–1211;

Lawson has sketched out the reforms in teaching law at Oxford in this period. In 1850, a School of Law and Modern History was established, study in which was to follow that of *Literae Humaniores* (a practice later abolished), in order to gain the degree of B.A.[39] An ordinance of 1857 provided for the conversion of fellowships at All Souls to support chairs in law and modern history.[40] The new Chichele Professorship of International Law and Diplomacy was duly filled in 1859 and that in Modern History in 1862.[41] In 1867, it was finally agreed that the Codrington Library in All Souls should pay 'special attention to law and history', and a new reading room was built to accommodate the readers.[42] In 1869, Corpus Christi College established a Professorship of Jurisprudence specifically for Henry Maine. The professor was given wide scope in his teaching, though it generally came to be understood as involving historical jurisprudence.[43] The next year Dicey's good friend James Bryce was appointed to the Regius Chair of Civil Law.[44] The Vinerian Chair of Common Law, held by J. R. Kenyon, appears to have become inactive at the end of the 1870s, the Professor last offering lectures on the 'Common Law of England' in June 1879,[45] but in 1867 it had been decided that a Vinerian Readership should be established until the Chair became vacant. The Readership was held by three individuals: K. E. Digby, who often taught Roman law as well as English; T. E. Holland, who was elected in 1874, but in the same year was chosen Chichele Professor; and finally Sir William Anson, who held it until elected Warden of All Souls in 1881.[46] In 1878, Sir William Markby, who had just retired from the bench in Bengal, was made Reader in Indian Law, reflecting the importance of training candidates for the Indian Civil Service.[47]

J.W. Cairns, 'A History of the Faculty of Advocates to 1900' in T.B. Smith and R. Black (eds.), *The Laws of Scotland: Stair Memorial Encyclopaedia*, vol. 13, Butterworths/Law Society of Scotland, Edinburgh 1992, pp. 499–536.

39 F.H. Lawson, *The Oxford Law School, 1850–1965*, Clarendon Press, Oxford 1968, pp. 20–33.

40 J.S.G. Simmons, 'All Souls' in M.G. Brock and M.C. Curthoys (eds.), *The History of the University of Oxford: Volume VII, Nineteenth-Century Oxford, Part 2*, Clarendon Press, Oxford 2000, pp. 210–13.

41 Lawson, above n. 39, pp. 30–31.

42 Simmons, above n. 40, p. 212.

43 A.W.B. Simpson, *Reflections on The Concept of Law*, Oxford University Press, Oxford 2011, pp. 18–24.

44 Lawson, above n. 39, p. 29.

45 'Law' (3 Jun. 1879) 9 *Oxford University Gazette*, p. 408.

46 Hanbury, above n. 18, pp. 92–97.

47 Lawson, above n. 39, pp. 50, 74.

From 1870 onwards, steps were taken to divide History and Law into two separate Sections for examinations, each with its own Board of Studies.[48] On 21 April 1871, Congregation passed an Act to this effect.[49] A few days later this was amended to rename them as Schools.[50] Over the next year, the reform worked its way through Congregation with votes and amendments. The name of the proposed new School became that of Jurisprudence, and the composition of the Board of Studies and the subject of the examinations were determined. Finally, on 2 June 1871, Convocation approved and passed the relevant statute.[51] In July 1871, the Board of Studies gave notice of the examinations in the new Honour School, thereby providing a syllabus.[52] The Board of Studies in Jurisprudence was also to serve as the Board of Studies for the degree of B.C.L.[53] These reforms also reveal the renaming of the Vinerian Chair to be in English rather than Common Law. These new provisions came into effect in 1872.[54] Teaching was carried out under the auspices of the Board of Studies by the professors and readers, with the classes of the combined college lecturers also advertised.[55] In 1883, the Boards of Studies were replaced by Boards of Faculties that possessed relatively wide powers.[56]

By statute, the examinations in the Honour School of Jurisprudence were to cover Jurisprudence, History of English Law, 'such departments of Roman Law, and – if the Board think fit – such departments of English Law as the Board of Studies may specify', and some 'department' of International Law.[57] Lawson reports that this remained in force essentially unchanged until 1948.[58] The important shift in the era with which we are

48 'Congregation of the University' (8 Mar. 1870) 1 *Oxford University Gazette*, p. 7; 'Congregation of the University' (22 Mar. 1870) 1 *Oxford University Gazette*, pp. 6–7; 'Congregation of the University' (29 Mar. 1870) 1 *Oxford University Gazette*, p. 10.

49 See, e.g., 'Congregation … Agenda' (21 Mar. 1871) 2 *Oxford University Gazette*, pp. 79–80.

50 Its progress may be traced through the *Oxford University Gazette*.

51 'Convocation … Statute' (2 Jun. 1871) 2 *Oxford University Gazette*, pp. 210–11.

52 'University Examinations' (13 Jun. 1871) 2 *Oxford University Gazette*, p. 242; repeated 'University Examinations' (8 Jul. 1871) 2 *Oxford University Gazette*, p. 260.

53 'Voting on Statutes' (28 Nov. 1871) 2 *Oxford University Gazette*, pp. 365–66; 'Convocation' (12 Dec. 1871) 2 *Oxford University Gazette*, p. 387.

54 H. Hall, 'Jurisprudence' in A.M.M. Stedman (ed.), *Oxford: Its Life and Schools*, Methuen & Co., London 1889, p. 274.

55 'Combined College Lectures' (24 Jan. 1882) 12 *Oxford University Gazette*, p. 220; 'Combined Lectures. Law Lectures' (12 Jan. 1883) 13 *Oxford University Gazette*, p. 245.

56 Lawson, above n. 39, pp. 61–66; C. Harvie, 'From the Cleveland Commission to the Statutes of 1882' in Brock and Curthoys, above n. 40, p. 93.

57 Hall, above n. 54, p. 276.

58 Lawson, above n. 39, p. 36.

concerned was the development of the teaching of English law. In 1877, the first special subject in English Law was specified as 'Principles of the English Law of Contract', which was, as we have seen, the first subject to be taught by Dicey.[59] In Trinity Term of 1886, new examination statutes, decided in 1884, became operative. Lawson rightly described the changes in Roman Law and English Law as 'substantial'.[60] Because the changes in the Honour School and the B.C.L. were to have a major impact on Dicey's teaching, it is important to set out briefly here those with which he was concerned. English Law was now to cover: (1) the law of contract; (2) the law of succession, testamentary and intestate, to real and personal property; (3) real property, in so far as not covered in succession; and (4) the law of the constitution, for which candidates were 'expected to have mastered the leading principles of existing Constitutional Law' but also to show a knowledge of: (i) the legislative power of Parliament; and (ii) the prerogatives of the Crown, the privileges of the Houses of Parliament, and the constitutional position of the Privy Council, the ministers of the Crown, the courts of law, and the armed forces. The B.C.L. degree retained a strong focus on Roman law, but in English Law, as well as standard fare of property, common law, and equity, it had several special subjects, one of which was to be selected by each candidate. These included agency, sale, and specific performance. In International Law, candidates were to be examined either on the general principles of private international law or on the law of neutrality.[61] This remained standard through Dicey's time.[62]

Dicey was elected just as the University was fine-tuning the new regulations for the organisation of teaching through the Boards of the new Faculties that were to replace the old Boards of Studies.[63] The change became effective in the first half of 1883, the new Faculty Boards being asked, for example, to produce schedules of their lectures for publication.[64] On 13 April 1883 the first such set of schedules of lectures for each Board of Faculty was published as a supplement to the *Oxford University Gazette*.[65] Thereafter this practice was routine for each term. Following the structure

59 Hall, above n. 54, p. 280; see above, text at nn. 31–32.

60 Lawson, above n. 39, p. 66.

61 Hall, above n. 54, pp. 280–85. Hall also sets out the requirements for the pass degree.

62 R. Hale, 'The Teaching of Law at Oxford University' (1926) 12 *American Bar Association Journal* 702, 702–07.

63 Lawson, above n. 39, p. 47, fn. 4.

64 'Boards of Faculties' (13 Feb. 1883) 13 *Oxford University Gazette*, p. 310.

65 'Schedules of Lectures Issued by the Boards of the Faculties of Theology, Law, Natural Science, and Arts (Oriental Languages and Modern History), for Easter and Act Terms, 1883' (13 Apr. 1883) 13 *Oxford University Gazette*, pp. 403–10.

of the new statute, the lectures were classed, with only occasional variation, into Roman Law, English Law, International Law, and Jurisprudence, with 'Indian Law' added at the end. From January 1889 onwards, there is the additional heading of 'Subjects of Preliminary Examination'.[66] For much of the period at issue, it was a regular practice in the Michaelmas Term to produce, in a Supplement to the *Gazette*, a summary statement of the lectures, organised by the traditional hierarchy of Faculties, given in the previous academic year.[67]

This practice not only allows us to trace Dicey's basic teaching, but also to relate it to that of his colleagues. Thus, in the Michaelmas Term of 1888, Dicey was lecturing on the Law of Contract, but so were his colleagues, J. C. Wilson (Exeter), A. A. Prankerd (Brasenose), J. B. Moyle (New College), and H. Duff (All Souls). Constitutional Law was to be taught by Anson (All Souls), A. C. Hamilton (University), and F. York Powell (Christ Church). Some individuals taught across English Law, Roman Law, and Jurisprudence.[68] One assumes that the Board of the Faculty co-ordinated the lectures to ensure the syllabus for both the Honour School and the B.C.L. would be covered for the examinations. For completeness, it is worth mentioning that students could also be taught by tutors in their colleges, and the 'Unofficial Notices' in the *Oxford University Gazette* contained advertisements from individuals offering their services as law teachers.[69]

Most issues of the *Oxford University Gazette* also contained notices inserted by professors and readers, under the heading 'Professors' Notices'. These would announce a public lecture or some change to a class.[70] But at the start of each term there was always a section in the *Gazette* headed 'Professors' Notices for the Hilary Term' (or Michaelmas or Easter and Trinity Terms as appropriate). It settled into a standard pattern in the 1880s, containing details of the classes of professors and readers, organised by the Faculty, again following the traditional university hierarchy.[71] At the end

66 'Faculty of Law' (21 Jan. 1889) 19 *Oxford University Gazette*, p. 227.

67 See, e.g., 'Summary Statements of Lectures, 1887–8' (20 Nov. 1888) 19 *Oxford University Gazette*, pp. 133–40 (Law is at p. 134).

68 'Faculty of Law' (15 Oct. 1888) 19 *Oxford University Gazette*, p. 27.

69 To pick one: 'T. Radford Potts, D.C.L., Barrister-at-Law, will be glad to read with Gentlemen for the B.C.L., Honour and Pass Law, and Law Preliminary Examinations' (24 Oct. 1893) 24 *Oxford University Gazette*, p. 80.

70 'Professors' Notices' (12 Feb. 1889) 19 *Oxford University Gazette*, p. 272 (James Bryce announcing commencement of set of lectures).

71 See, e.g., 'Professors Notices for Michaelmas Term' (12 Oct. 1888) 19 *Oxford University Gazette*, pp. 11–18.

of each term, there was an advance notice of the lectures in the next.[72] The 'Professors' Notices' for the forthcoming terms were considered likely to be more accurate than the lists of lectures provided by the Boards, no doubt as more up-to-date.[73]

2.1. DICEY'S CLASSES, 1883–98

Dicey spent the Michaelmas Term of 1898 in the United States lecturing at Harvard Law School and the Lowell Institute in Boston.[74] In his absence, W. M. Harrison (later Graham-Harrison), a Vinerian Scholar and Fellow of All Souls, delivered the first part of his course of lectures on the Law of Contract.[75] Harrison, later to be a noted Parliamentary Draftsman, was an obvious choice. He had already assisted Dicey's colleagues Anson and Digby with their scholarly work on contract and real property.[76] Dicey's time at Harvard, however, provides a caesura in his teaching. Though beyond halfway in his period of active teaching at Oxford, which lasted until 1913, it can be seen as marking a change. When he returned to Oxford for the Hilary Term of 1899, he resumed teaching Contract with his Second Course, while in the Easter and Trinity Term he lectured on Comparative Constitutions.[77] These were subjects he had taught since the 1880s, but thereafter his classes were to be more varied than they had been before the time at Harvard.

Dicey had always been impressed by the teaching at the leading United States law schools. After his visit to the United States with James Bryce in 1870, he used an essay on the aims of the newly founded Legal Education Association to provide not only a scathing account of the current education

---

72 See, e.g., 'Professors Notices for Hilary Term, 1889' (4 Dec. 1888) 19 *Oxford University Gazette*, pp. 171–77.

73 'Professors' Notices for Michaelmas Term' (10 Oct. 1890) 20 *Oxford University Gazette*, p. 15.

74 Cosgrove, above n. 19, pp. 170–71.

75 'Schedule of Lectures ... Faculty of Law' (17 Oct. 1898) 29 *Oxford University Gazette*, p. 40; 'Notices of Professors' (18 Oct. 1898) 29 *Oxford University Gazette*, p. 55.

76 J. Tomes, 'Harrison, Sir William Montagu Graham (1871–1949), Parliamentary Draftsman', *Oxford Dictionary of National Biography* <https://www.oxforddnb.com/view/10.1093/ref:odnb/9780198614128.001.0001/odnb-9780198614128-e-33509>.

77 'Schedule of Lectures ... Faculty of Law' (23 Jan. 1899) 29 *Oxford University Gazette*, p. 247; 'Schedule of Lectures ... Faculty of Law' (24 Apr. 1899) 29 *Oxford University Gazette*, p. 425.

of the English bar, but also a paean to the teaching at US law schools.[78] This is important, given that it was in about this period that Dicey started to think seriously of following Bryce into a university chair in law.[79]

In the Trinity Term of 1899, Dicey advertised a public lecture on 'Legal Education at Harvard'.[80] It was published as an essay in November. Here it is necessary to focus only on one aspect, which Dicey described as 'the most salient and original feature in the Harvard method of instruction'. This was the way that 'tuition is in the Law School grounded in the study of cases, and is in its form catechetical'. Dicey explained how this worked as 'the Socratic method applied to law', bringing out the principles of the cases discussed. He expressed the view that some 'branches of the law', notably contract and torts, lent themselves 'with special facility to the catechetical method', while others such as real property were less suited.[81]

Between 1883 and 1898, Dicey gave lectures on Contract more frequently than on any other subject, usually in the Michaelmas and Hilary Terms. We have seen that in the Trinity Term of 1883 he taught 'Elementary Principles of the Law of Contract'.[82] He did so again in the next academic year starting in the Michaelmas Term, continuing these classes in the Hilary.[83] In the Trinity Term, however, as well as offering six lectures on Constitutional Law, he offered classes on 'The Law of Contract (Statute of Frauds)'.[84] In the next academic year, this offering on Contract continued, but in the Trinity Term, he offered six lectures on Agency.[85] In 1885–86, his class on Contract was described as 'Law of Contract exhibited in the form of Rules'.[86] With some exceptions, he taught this course under this name over these two terms every academic year until that of 1895–96.[87]

---

78 A.V. Dicey, 'Legal Education' (1871–72) 25 *Macmillan's Magazine* 115, 112–27. On the Association, see Polden (partly with Lobban), above n. 38, pp. 1185–90.

79 Walters, above n. 11, pp. 76–79.

80 'Notices of Professors' (8 May 1899) 29 *Oxford University Gazette*, p. 464.

81 A.V. Dicey, 'The Teaching of English Law at Harvard' (1899) 76 *Contemporary Review* 742, 750–52.

82 Text above nn. 31–35.

83 'Notices of Professors ... Law' (12 Oct. 1883; 18 Jan. 1884) 14 *Oxford University Gazette*, pp. 19, 224.

84 'Notices of Professors ... Law' (18 Apr. 1884) 14 *Oxford University Gazette*, p. 386.

85 'Notices of Professors ... Law' (10 Oct. 1884; 16 Jan. 1885; 17 Apr. 1885) 15 *Oxford University Gazette*, pp. 18, 226, 397.

86 'Notices of Professors ... Law' (16 Oct. 1885; 22 Jan. 1886) 16 *Oxford University Gazette*, pp. 19, 267.

87 'Notices of Professors ... Law' (15 Oct. 1886; 14 Jan. 1887) 17 *Oxford University Gazette*, pp. 10, 201; 'Notices of Professors ... Law' (14 Oct. 1887) 18 *Oxford University Gazette*, p. 10; 'Schedule ... Faculty of Law' (16 Jan. 1888) 18 *Oxford University Gazette*, p. 237; 'Notices of Professors ... Law' (12 Oct. 1888; 18 Jan. 1889) 19 *Oxford University*

In 1887–88, the course expanded into the Easter and Trinity Term when six further lectures were given.[88] This may be because other commitments had led to fewer lectures in the Michaelmas and Hilary Terms.[89] In 1889–90, he used this slot of two terms to lecture instead on 'Points of Special Importance in the Law of Contract'.[90]

The use Dicey made of the final, Easter and Trinity, Term, which he often used for short, specialised topics, reinforces the perception that, before he left to visit Boston and Harvard, most of his teaching had been in the field of contract. If in 1884 he offered classes on the Statute of Frauds,[91] in 1885 the offering was six lectures on Agency in Contract; this was repeated in 1886, 1889, and 1891.[92] In 1890, he announced that he would lecture either on 'Agency in Contract' or on 'Contracts in Writing with special reference to contracts within the 4th and 17th sections of the Statute of Frauds'.[93] In 1892, he announced he would lecture on both.[94] Agency was, of course, a special topic for the degree of B.C.L.

Given Dicey's admiration for United States legal education, it is no surprise to find that – at least initially – he offered what he described as 'a Catechetical Lecture on the subjects included in the Lectures of the week' on a Saturday.[95] He offered such 'catechetical' classes again in the

Gazette, pp. 12, 211; 'Notices of Professors ... Law' (10 Oct. 1890; 16 Jan. 1891) 21 *Oxford University Gazette*, pp. 10, 222; 'Notices of Professors ... Law' (16 Oct. 1891; 5 Feb. 1892) 22 *Oxford University Gazette*, pp. 15, 228; 'Notices of Professors ... Law' (14 Oct. 1892; 20 Jan. 1893) 23 *Oxford University Gazette*, pp. 12, 221; 'Notices of Professors ... Law' (11 Oct. 1895; 24 Jan. 1896) 26 *Oxford University Gazette*, pp. 13, 212.

88 'Notices of Professors ... Law' (14 Oct. 1887; 20 Apr. 1888) 18 *Oxford University Gazette*, pp. 12, 374; 'Schedule ... Faculty of Law' (16 Jan. 1888) 18 *Oxford University Gazette*, p. 237.

89 In the Michaelmas Term he was offering lectures on Public International Law and in Hilary on the Rights of Citizens. According to the 'Summary Statement of Lectures' he also taught a 'Discussion of Difficult Points in the Law of Contract' (20 Nov. 1888) 19 *Oxford University Gazette*, p. 134.

90 'Notices of Professors ... Law' (11 Oct. 1889; 17 Jan. 1890) 20 *Oxford University Gazette*, pp. 12, 197.

91 Text, above n. 84.

92 'Notices of Professors ... Law' (17 Apr. 1885) 15 *Oxford University Gazette*, p. 397; 'Summary Statement of Lectures ... 1885–6' (23 Nov. 1886) 17 *Oxford University Gazette*, p. 130; 'Notices of Professors ... Law' (26 Apr. 1889) 19 *Oxford University Gazette*, p. 360; 'Schedule ... Faculty of Law' (20 Apr. 1891) 21 *Oxford University Gazette*, p. 399.

93 'Notices of Professors ... Law' (25 Apr. 1890) 20 *Oxford University Gazette*, p. 342.

94 'Notices of Professors ... Law' (29 Mar. 1892) 22 *Oxford University Gazette*, p. 372.

95 'Notices of Professors ... Law' (13 Apr. 1883) 13 *Oxford University Gazette*, p. 396. The class in fact was on a Tuesday: 'Professors' Notices' (24 Apr. 1883) 13 *Oxford University Gazette*, p. 431.

Michaelmas and Hilary Terms of academic year 1883–84, but not thereafter.[96] In the Michaelmas and Hilary Terms of 1883–84, he also offered 'to form a Class for the study of the leading cases in the current Law Reports'.[97] This offer was repeated each year through to 1886–87, sometimes for one term only, with slight variations in the wording, such as 'study and discussion of reported Cases' or 'study of the cases bearing on the rules as to the formation of contract'.[98] He offered a version of this again in academic years 1892–93 and 1896–97, as well as 1897–98, when it was described in the Hilary Term as 'a Class for the Discussion of Cases illustrating the law of Contract'.[99] This course, in whatever version, only features twice in the Board's Schedule of Lectures, suggesting he may, at least sometimes, have given it in addition to his statutory duties when enough students expressed interest.[100]

On 28 April 1884, Dicey advertised a public lecture on the 'True Nature of (so-called) Constitutional Law'. This marked the start of his teaching the topic at Oxford, as two days later he started his six lectures on the Law of the Constitution, covering 'some fundamental principles of Constitutional Law'.[101] He taught the subject again in the Michaelmas Term of the following academic year, describing its focus as on 'Rights of Citizens', in which he covered the subjects discussed under the 'rule of law'.[102] It was to be nearly ten years before he returned to the subject, in 1893–94, when he taught it over the three terms. He covered 'Sovereignty of Parliament' and 'Rights of Citizens', finishing the latter with two lectures in the Trinity Term.[103]

---

96 'Notices of Professors … Law' (12 Oct. 1883; 18 Jan. 1884) 14 *Oxford University Gazette*, pp. 19, 224.

97 'Notices of Professors … Law' (12 Oct. 1883; 18 Jan. 1884) 14 *Oxford University Gazette*, pp. 19, 224.

98 'Notices of Professors … Law' (10 Oct. 1884; 16 Jan. 1885) 15 *Oxford University Gazette*, pp. 18, 226; 'Notices of Professors … Law' (16 Oct. 1885) 15 *Oxford University Gazette*, p. 19; 'Professors' Notices' (26 Oct. 1886) 16 *Oxford University Gazette*, p. 57.

99 'Notices of Professors … Law' (14 Oct. 1892; 20 Jan. 1893) 23 *Oxford University Gazette*, pp. 12, 221; 'Notices of Professors … Law' (22 Jan. 1897) 27 *Oxford University Gazette*, p. 221.

100 'Schedule of Lectures … Faculty of Law' (23 Jan. 1893) 23 *Oxford University Gazette*, p. 237; 'Schedule of Lectures … Faculty of Law' (25 Jan. 1897) 27 *Oxford University Gazette*, p. 237. R.G. Tatton of Balliol offered a course on 'Leading Cases in the Law of Contract in 1885': 'Schedule of Lectures … Faculty of Law' (19 Oct. 1885) 15 *Oxford University Gazette*, p. 35.

101 'Notices of Professors … Law' (18 Apr. 1884) 14 *Oxford University Gazette*, p. 386.

102 'Notices of Professors … Law' (10 Oct. 1884) 15 *Oxford University Gazette*, p. 18. He lists the topics in 1896: 'Notices of Professors … Law' (16 Oct. 1896) 27 *Oxford University Gazette*, p. 19.

103 'Notices of Professors … Law' (13 Oct. 1893; 12 Jan. 1894; 20 Apr. 1894) 24 *Oxford University Gazette*, pp. 13, 233, 382; 'Schedule of Lectures … Faculty of Law' (16 Oct. 1893) 24 *Oxford University Gazette*, p. 35.

Before his visit to the United States, he taught the subject twice more, in the Hilary Term of 1894–95, and the Michaelmas and Hilary Terms of 1896–97.[104] In the Hilary Term of 1897, he proposed to hold 'a class for the Discussion of Questions of Constitutional Law every Monday'.[105] It is tempting and entirely plausible to relate the pattern of classes to the publication of the editions of Dicey's *Law of the Constitution*, the first three being issued by Macmillan between 1885 and 1889, and the fourth and fifth in 1893 and 1897 respectively, with his interest being alternately exhausted and intrigued by working on the book. The subject was also regularly covered by other teachers, notably Anson.

If Dicey taught the Law of the Constitution relatively infrequently, he often taught the class on Comparative Study of the Constitution. Thus, in 1890–91, when his time was largely taken up with teaching contract, he also proposed to give a 'Course of Four Public Lectures on the Comparative Study of the Constitution'.[106] As already noted, he had first taught the subject in the Trinity Term of 1887, and then alongside his classes on contract in the Hilary Terms of 1889 and 1890.[107] He was able to do this because the course was relatively short, initially consisting of only six lectures; in the 1890s, he taught it in the Trinity Term, expanding it from six to eight, and finally to ten lectures before he left for his visit to Boston.[108]

It can be no surprise that Dicey, given his interest, was keen to offer a course on Conflict of Laws, or Private International Law. From 1886, it was a possible option for the degree of B.C.L., but it seems to have been rarely taught. In October 1887, Dicey advertised that he would be obliged if those thinking of 'attending his Lectures on Private International Law' would let him know. The class was listed in the Board's Schedule of Lectures as 'Rules of English Law concerning the Conflict of Laws (Private International Law)'.[109] He thereafter offered the class from time to time, as in 1891–92,

---

104 'Notices of Professors ... Law' (18 Jan. 1895) 25 *Oxford University Gazette*, p. 241; 'Notices of Professors ... Law' (16 Oct. 1896; 22 Jan. 1897) 27 *Oxford University Gazette*, pp. 19, 221.

105 'Notices of Professors' (2 Feb. 1897) 27 *Oxford University Gazette*, p. 266.

106 'Notices of Professors ... Law' (10 Oct. 1890) 21 *Oxford University Gazette*, p. 16.

107 'Notices of Professors ... Law' (8 Mar. 1887) 17 *Oxford University Gazette*, p. 320; 'Notices of Professors ... Law' (18 Jan. 1889) 19 *Oxford University Gazette*, p. 211; 'Notices of Professors ... Law' (17 Jan. 1890) 20 *Oxford University Gazette*, p. 197.

108 'Notices of Professors ... Law' (14 Mar. 1893) 23 *Oxford University Gazette*, p. 350; 'Notices of Professors' (30 Apr. 1895) 25 *Oxford University Gazette*, p. 463; 'Notices of Professors ... Law' (24 Apr. 1896) 26 *Oxford University Gazette*, p. 392; 'Notices of Professors ... Law' (30 Apr. 1897) 27 *Oxford University Gazette*, p. 428.

109 'Notices of Professors ... Law' (14 Oct. 1887) 18 *Oxford University Gazette*, p. 12; 'Schedule of Lectures ... Faculty of Law' (18 Oct. 1887) 18 *Oxford University Gazette*, p. 45.

when he advertised that he wished 'to form a class', and again in 1894–95, when he advertised that he would teach it 'as part of the law of England'.[110] It is worth noting that the report on lectures given in 1891–92 does not list a class in Conflict of Laws.[111] In 1896, he published the first edition of his *Digest of the Law of England with Reference to the Conflict of Laws.*[112]

Dicey also taught a few other courses in this period, presumably reflecting changing needs to cover the syllabus for the Honour School of Jurisprudence. Thus, in the Hilary Term of 1886 he taught the 'Law of Succession to Real and Personal Property';[113] he taught this again the following year.[114] In 1895–96, he gave a set of six lectures for neophytes on 'Introduction to the Study of the Law of England'.[115] This was an innovation that he repeated two years later.[116]

Most interesting is the set of six lectures he gave in the Trinity Term of 1898. They covered the 'Development of English Law since the Beginning of the Century'.[117] He obviously took the opportunity provided by the Trinity Term to try out an early version of the lectures he was to give at Harvard in the autumn, having already agreed the topic with Charles Eliot. He may have revised them in Boston, but they had substantially been written before he left, contrary to what has been suggested.[118]

2.2. DICEY'S CLASSES 1899–1909 AND THE FINAL YEARS

When Dicey returned from the United States, he taught two familiar courses for the remainder of the academic year: his second course on the Law of Contract and that on the Comparative Study of Constitutions.[119]

---

110 'Notices of Professors ... Law' (14 Oct. 1891) 22 *Oxford University Gazette*, p. 15; 'Notices of Professors ... Law' (12 Oct. 1894) 25 *Oxford University Gazette*, p. 19. The differing wording may be significant. The lectures are listed in the Board's Schedule in 1894, but not in 1891: 'Schedule of Lectures ... Faculty of Law' (19 Oct. 1891) 22 *Oxford University Gazette*, p. 37; 'Schedule of Lectures ... Faculty of Law' (15 Oct. 1894) 25 *Oxford University Gazette*, p. 41.

111 'Summary Statement of Lectures ... 1891–92' (17 Nov. 1892) 23 *Oxford University Gazette*, p. 136.

112 Dicey, *Digest*, above n. 17.

113 'Notices of Professors ... Law' (22 Jan. 1886) 16 *Oxford University Gazette*, p. 267.

114 'Notices of Professors ... Law' (14 Jan. 1887) 17 *Oxford University Gazette*, p. 201.

115 'Notices of Professors ... Law' (11 Oct. 1895) 25 *Oxford University Gazette*, p. 13.

116 'Notices of Professors ... Law' (15 Oct. 1897) 27 *Oxford University Gazette*, p. 17.

117 'Notices of Professors ... Law' (15 Mar. 1898) 27 *Oxford University Gazette*, p. 359.

118 Cosgrove, above n. 19, p. 171.

119 'Schedule of Lectures ... Faculty of Law' (23 Jan. 1899; 24 Apr. 1899) 29 *Oxford University Gazette*, pp. 247, 425.

He had lectured on the latter topic at the Lowell Institute in Boston, and the slight change in title may reflect this and, according to Allison, a change in content.[120] It continued to consist of the ten lectures it had reached in 1897; it later returned to eight lectures, the name reverting to 'Comparative Study of the Constitution'.[121]

Aspects of Dicey's teaching remained much the same after his American sojourn, notably contract. Thus, in the autumn of 1899, in 1901, and again in 1902 (this time in association with Edward Jenks, the Reader in English Law), he proposed to hold a 'Class for the Discussion of Cases on the Law of Contract'.[122] Over the Michaelmas and Hilary Terms of 1900–01 and 1902–03, he gave the two courses on the Law of Contract 'exhibited in the form of Rules' that had been such a staple of his teaching.[123] Between 1901 and 1908, he also taught courses on 'Special Topics' or 'Special Points' of contract, as well as explicitly in some years on agency in contract and tort, and conditional contracts.[124]

He offered courses on the Conflict of Laws in 1901–02, 1904–05, and 1908–09. That in 1901–02 was explicitly intended for those studying for the degree of B.C.L.[125] He obviously had difficulty attracting a class in the subject. In 1908 he was reduced to stating in the Michaelmas Term that he would lecture on Conflict of Laws in the next term 'provided even a small class can be formed'. J. H. Beale of Harvard, subsequently Dean of Law at Chicago, later described him as never getting 'more than half a dozen students for the Conflict of Laws at Oxford'.[126] Dicey published

[120] J.W.F. Allison, 'Editor's Introduction to Volume II' in Dicey, above n. 35, p. xii.

[121] 'Notices of Professors ... Law' (18 Apr. 1905) 35 *Oxford University Gazette*, p. 468.

[122] 'Notices of Professors' (31 Oct. 1899) 30 *Oxford University Gazette*, p. 94; 'Notices of Professors' (29 Oct. 1901) 32 *Oxford University Gazette*, p. 103; 'Notices of Professors ... Law' (17 Jan. 1902) 32 *Oxford University Gazette*, p. 253.

[123] 'Schedules of Lectures ... Faculty of Law' (15 Oct. 1900; 21 Jan. 1901) 31 *Oxford University Gazette*, pp. 41, 265; 'Schedules of Lectures ... Faculty of Law' (20 Oct. 1902; 19 Jan. 1903) 33 *Oxford University Gazette*, pp. 45, 255.

[124] 'Notices of Professors ... Law' (17 Jan. 1902) 32 *Oxford University Gazette*, p. 253; 'Notices of Professors ... Law' (16 Oct. 1903; 22 Jan. 1904) 34 *Oxford University Gazette*, pp. 20, 264; 'Notices of Professors ... Law' (14 Oct. 1904; 22 Jan. 1905) 35 *Oxford University Gazette*, pp. 19, 260; 'Notices of Professors ... Law' (13 Oct. 1905; 22 Jan. 1906) 36 *Oxford University Gazette*, pp. 21, 256; 'Notices of Professors ... Law' (12 Oct. 1906; 18 Jan. 1907) 37 *Oxford University Gazette*, pp. 19, 268; 'Notices of Professors ... Law' (11 Oct. 1907; 17 Jan. 1908) 38 *Oxford University Gazette*, pp. 20, 274.

[125] 'Notices of Professors ... Law' (11 Oct. 1901) 32 *Oxford University Gazette*, p. 23; 'Notices of Professors ... Law' (20 Jan. 1905) 35 *Oxford University Gazette*, p. 260; 'Notices of Professors ... Law' (23 Apr. 1909) p. 535.

[126] J.H. Beale, 'A Digest of the Law of England with Reference to the Conflict of Laws (Book)' (1923) 36 *Harvard Law Review* 766, 766.

a second edition of his work on the topic in 1908.[127] In preparing it, he had corresponded with Arthur Berriedale Keith of the Colonial Office, later of the University of Edinburgh, graduate of both Edinburgh and Oxford and acknowledged expert on matters relating to the Colonies, their constitutions, and their relationships with the government in London.[128] Keith not only assisted on specific issues, such as Indian divorces, for which he was specifically thanked in the preface, but commented more generally on the text.[129]

One obvious aspect of Dicey's pattern of teaching towards the end of his tenure of the Chair was his continuing development of the lectures on Law and Public Opinion in the nineteenth century. He taught this course in 1899–1900 (over the Michaelmas and Hilary Terms), in 1900–01 in the Trinity Term (seven lectures), in 1901–02 in the Michaelmas and Trinity Terms, and in 1902–03 in the Trinity Term.[130] The advertisements sometimes give details of the individual topics he intended to cover, and one can see he was working towards the publication, in 1905, of his book.[131] In his final year before retiring from the Chair, his main class was 'Introduction to the Study of the Law of England', which he taught over all three terms.[132] As well as adding a class on Conflict of Laws to this subject in the Trinity Term, he then gave a course of seven lectures in 1909 comparing the government of France and England.[133]

Dicey ended his academic career as he had hoped to begin it, as a teacher of Conflict of Laws – his 'own special subject'. As Lecturer in

---

127 A.V. Dicey, *A Digest of the Law of England with Reference to the Conflict of Laws*, 2nd ed., Stevens & Sons, London 1908.

128 Keith has benefited from a detailed biography: R.F. Shinn, *Arthur Berriedale Keith, 1879–1944: The Chief Ornament of Scottish Learning*, Aberdeen University Press, Aberdeen 1990.

129 See the correspondence, 1905–07, in R.F. Shinn and R.A. Cosgrove (eds.), *Constitutional Reflections: The Correspondence of Albert Venn Dicey and Arthur Berriedale Keith*, University Press of America Inc., Lanham 1996, pp. 1–24; Dicey, above n. 127, p. vi.

130 'Notices of Professors ... Law' (15 Oct. 1899; 19 Jan. 1900) 30 *Oxford University Gazette*, pp. 19, 220; 'Notices of Professors ... Law' (12 Mar. 1901) 31 *Oxford University Gazette*, p. 421; 'Notices of Professors ... Law' (11 Oct. 1901; 25 Apr. 1902) 32 *Oxford University Gazette*, pp. 22, 433; 'Notices of Professors ... Law' (24 Apr. 1903) 33 *Oxford University Gazette*, p. 429.

131 A.V. Dicey, *Lectures on the Relation between Law and Public Opinion in England During the Nineteenth Century*, Macmillan & Co., London 1905, pp. vii–viii.

132 'Notices of Professors ... Law' (9 Oct. 1908; 15 Jan. 1909; 23 Apr. 1909) 39 *Oxford University Gazette*, pp. 19–20, 291, 535.

133 'Notices of Professors ... Law' (23 Apr. 1909) 39 *Oxford University Gazette*, p. 535.

Private International Law, he taught the topic each year until his three-year lectureship came to an end in 1913.[134] He was not thereafter idle. He continued to work on new editions of his books. The effort he put into working on them is easily revealed. For the eighth edition of his *Study of the Law of the Constitution*, published in 1915, he again corresponded extensively with Keith.[135] The latter was touched by the warm acknowledgment he again received in the preface.[136] When Dicey received a letter from the publishers requesting a new edition of his work on *Conflict of Laws* he once more turned to Keith to request assistance.[137] Keith agreed.[138] Dicey praised his assistance.[139] The surviving materials collected for this edition give a sense of Dicey's careful methods.[140] Dicey received a copy shortly before his death.[141]

His interest in the question of the Union with Ireland inevitably raised the question of England's Union with Scotland. Cosgrove suggests that Dicey thought that Ireland should be treated like Scotland.[142] The approach of the 200th anniversary of the Union of Scotland and England further stimulated his interest. This may have been developed by the work of R. S. Rait, a Fellow of New College, on the Scottish Parliament before the Union of the Crowns.[143] Cosgrove suggests that Dicey read Rait's work in 1906 and only then became interested in Scotland. Dicey, however, already in the Trinity Term of 1905, had devoted to the Scottish constitution one of the eight lectures in his course on the Comparative Study of the Constitution.[144] In that year C. S. Terry had published *The Scottish Parliament: Its Constitution and Procedure, 1603–1707*, providing Dicey with further material.[145] On the 200th anniversary of the Union, he

134 Rait, above n. 1, p. 205.

135 See the extensive correspondence edited and printed in Shinn and Cosgrove, above n. 129, pp. 1–150. The letters reveal the extent of the assistance Keith gave the aging Dicey.

136 A.B. Keith to A.V. Dicey, 18 January 1915, in Shinn and Cosgrove, above n. 129, p. 151.

137 A.V. Dicey to A.B. Keith, 25 March 1915, in Shinn and Cosgrove, above n. 129, pp. 154–56.

138 A.B. Keith to A.V. Dicey, 27 March 1915, in Shinn and Cosgrove, above n. 129, pp. 156–57.

139 A.V. Dicey to R.S. Rait, 25 June 1921, in Rait, above n. 1, p. 282.

140 Edinburgh University Library, Coll-238, MSS Gen. 531–541*.

141 Rait, above n. 1, p. 288.

142 Cosgrove, above n. 19, pp. 116–17.

143 R.S. Rait, *The Scottish Parliament Before the Union of the Crowns*, Blackie & Son, London 1901.

144 'Notices of Professors … Law' (18 Apr. 1905) 35 *Oxford University Gazette*, p. 468.

145 C.S. Terry, *The Scottish Parliament: Its Constitution and Procedure, 1603–1707*, MacLehose, Glasgow 1905.

advertised a set of four lectures to be given in the Trinity Term;[146] at the same time he gave notice that in Comparative Study of the Constitution there would be special reference to the Acts of Union between Scotland and England and Great Britain and Ireland.[147] The next year he again included the 'Scottish Constitution and the Act of Union' as the topic of one of the eight lectures in Comparative Study of the Constitution.[148] In 1906, Dicey had already proposed to Rait a collaboration on a study of the Union of Scotland and England.[149] He continued to be busy on a variety of projects, however, so work was postponed until after Rait had become Professor of Scottish History and Literature at Glasgow in 1913, and no doubt was further delayed by Rait's work at the war trade intelligence department in London.[150] Their study was eventually published in 1920.[151]

3. CONCLUSION

It is difficult at this remove to assess Dicey as a teacher. He was evidently conscientious and interested in his students. His 'catechetical' classes and those examining cases and law reports indicate a desire to engage with them to aid their learning. He advertised times when he would be available to students to discuss their studies.[152] In the early years, he gave notice of when he would be in the Library at All Souls in July to help students preparing in the summer for examinations in the Honour School of Jurisprudence.[153] In 1908 he lent his support as an honorary member to a recently formed 'Society ... for the discussion of legal questions useful for undergraduates interested in Law'.[154] In April 1908, however, he commented to his wife that his 'lectures have been not successful this academic year'.[155] He does

146 'Notices of Professors, &c' (23 May 1907) 25 *University Magazine*, p. 348.
147 'Notices of Professors ... Law' (26 Apr. 1907) 37 *Oxford University Gazette*, p. 507.
148 'Notices of Professors ... Law' (24 Apr. 1908) 38 *Oxford University Gazette*, p. 519.
149 Rait, above n. 1, p. 207.
150 D.M. Abbott, 'Rait, Sir Robert Sangster', *Oxford Dictionary of National Biography* <https://www.oxforddnb.com/view/10.1093/ref:odnb/9780198614128.001.0001/odnb-9780198614128-e-35655>.
151 Dicey and Rait, above n. 25.
152 See, e.g., 'Notices of Professors ... Law' (16 Oct. 1885) 16 *Oxford University Gazette*, p. 19; 'Notices of Professors ... Law' (16 Oct. 1903) 34 *Oxford University Gazette*, p. 20.
153 'All Souls College' (3 Jun. 1884) 14 *Oxford University Gazette*, p. 535; 'College Announcements' (10 Jun. 1885) 3 *University Magazine*, p. 284.
154 'Society for Discussion of Legal Questions' (19 Nov. 1908) 27 *University Magazine*, p. 96.
155 A.V. Dicey to E. Dicey, 12 April 1908, in Rait, above n. 1, p. 197.

not explain why, but whatever the often self-deprecating Dicey meant, it does suggest a concern that his classes be good. He is often reported as an excellent public speaker.[156]

In his assessment of Anson, Dicey made a distinction between the work of a lecturer and that of a tutor. He wrote that the 'professorial system tends towards the production of good lectures, probably to be embodied in books, the tutorial system tends towards the teaching of individual pupils'.[157] Much of Dicey's teaching did end up as books. His major academic publications were developed through and out of his classes. This reflects the significant theme in his inaugural lecture of 1883 that university lecturing in English law would help produce better law books.[158] He stressed that he drew no distinction between the 'function of a professor as a teacher, and his duties by way of investigation, research, or authorship'. This was because there was 'no opposition'.[159] His account of Anson as a law teacher divided teaching into oral and written; both were linked professorial duties. Dicey later told Rait that when he returned to Oxford as Vinerian Professor he 'had been working in one form or another assiduously on the subject of Conflict of Laws'. He thought that if he completed the book, he could place himself 'at the head of modern English authorities on the subject'. He thought it would take him three years; in fact, it took a further 14. But he justified the slow progress as having been beneficial.[160]

Of course, part of the detour on the way to completion of his work on conflicts was the writing of the *Lectures Introductory* that made him famous, here revealed as an interruption. Dicey wrote to Bryce in 1909, remarking that he had just given his last public lecture, that on Blackstone. He added that he would 'like to see if [he] could force on the study of the Conflict of Laws'.[161] This he did. After he demitted the All Souls Lectureship in Private International Law, a new lecturer was appointed for the next three years.[162] In 1951 this Lectureship became a permanent Readership in the Conflict of Laws.[163]

---

156 See, e.g., 'Notes and News' (13 Jun. 1894) 12 *University Magazine*, p. 383.

157 A.V. Dicey, 'Law-Teaching, Oral and Written' in H. Henson (ed.), *A Memoir of the Right Honourable Sir William Anson*, Clarendon Press, Oxford 1920, p. 88.

158 A.V. Dicey, *Can English Law be Taught at the Universities? An Inaugural Lecture, Delivered at All Souls College*, Macmillan & Co., London 1883, pp. 24–29.

159 Dicey, above n. 158, p. 24.

160 Rait, above n. 1, p. 285.

161 A.V. Dicey to J. Bryce, 13 June 1909, in Rait, above n. 1, p. 203.

162 Lawson, above n. 39, p. 120.

163 ibid., p. 150.

In 1868, Dicey's friend Goldwin Smith had considered whether legal education should develop in Oxford. He thought it should. Practical aspects would still need to be learned in London, but he claimed that the 'lawyers generally testify that law ought to be studied more scientifically … and that no place is so proper for this purpose as the University'.[164] By the date that Dicey retired, the University of Oxford had risen to become a noted centre of legal education and scholarship. Smith's 'scientific' legal education was available. Dicey had played a notable part in this, as Lord Curzon had recognised. Finally, it is worth noting that, in his letter to the *Harvard Law Review*, Dicey singled out as significant the establishment of the new lectureship in Private International Law, and the role of the subject in the degree of B.C.L. He promised to 'study with his pupils the various sides of a subject to which as a writer … he has for years devoted attention'.[165]

164 G. Smith, *The Reorganization of the University of Oxford*, James Parker & Co., Oxford 1868, pp. 28–29.

165 A.V. Dicey, 'The Extension of Law Teaching at Oxford' (1910) 24 *Harvard Law Review* 1, 5.

DICEY ON HIGHER AND LEGAL EDUCATION

Andrew DICKINSON

1. DICEY THE PROFESSOR

On Saturday 21 April 1883, a little over four months after his election as Vinerian Professor of English Law,[1] A. V. Dicey delivered his inaugural lecture in the Hall of All Souls College, under the title 'Can English Law be Taught at the Universities?'[2] He gave a strongly affirmative answer to his titular question. Not only was the setting of a university suitable for the teaching of principles of English law, but the subject and the legal profession could, in Dicey's view, flourish only if a professional professoriate were entrusted with the task of identifying, encapsulating,

1 *Oxford University Gazette* ('*Gazette*'), Supplement to vol. XIII, No. 437, 8 December 1882, 191.

2 *Gazette*, vol. XIII, No. 451, 13 April 1883, 396. The lecture was originally scheduled for 24 February (*Gazette*, vol. XIII, No. 440, 12 January 1883, 233) but postponed (*Gazette*, vol. XIII, No. 445, 13 February 1883, 308).

recording and disseminating legal principles for the benefit of those who wished to study law in order to pursue a career in legal practice.[3]

In Dicey's view, the provision of legal education through the universities would secure the following advantages, when compared with the prevailing method of aspiring barristers reading in chambers:[4]

1. Teaching law as a whole with each part related to the others.
2. Inculcating the habit in students of analysing and defining legal concepts.
3. Encouraging students to look upon law as a series of rules and exceptions, and to carefully mark off the exact limits of ascertained principles.
4. Bringing about much needed reform of legal literature.

For Dicey, the principal engine driving this change would be the small but growing class of university law professors. In his view, it was not necessary to distinguish the functions of a university professor as a teacher and 'his'[5] responsibilities with respect to investigation, research or authorship, for 'there exists no opposition'. The qualities necessary to achieve the pedagogical aims set out above were qualities 'fostered by the necessity for clear exposition of actual law, and are also characteristics which ought to be found in authors who wish to produce monumental works of literature'.[6]

---

3 A.V. Dicey, *Can English Law be Taught at the Universities? An Inaugural Lecture Delivered at All Souls College*, Macmillan & Co., London 1883 ('*Inaugural Lecture*').

4 ibid., pp. 10–24. Dicey did not trouble himself here with the education received within the other branch of the legal profession, although he had himself taught at the Incorporated Law Society in the early 1870s.

5 Dicey's writing here and elsewhere reflects his lived existence in which the teachers and the taught ('men') were male. On this subject, however, there is evidence that he held and advocated views that were more enlightened than many of his contemporaries. During his first visit to the United States, in 1870, he recorded the amusement of his host, Dr Charles W. Eliot, President of Harvard Law School, 'about our zeal in investigating the subject of women's education', adding that '[o]ur desire to know female professors specially amused him' (R.S. Rait, *Memorials of Albert Venn Dicey: Being Chiefly Letters and Diaries*, Macmillan & Co., London 1925, p. 61). Elsewhere, his biographer records that Dicey 'never slackened in efforts to improve educational opportunities for women' (R.A. Cosgrove, *The Rule of Law: Albert Venn Dicey, Victorian Jurist*, University of North Carolina Press, Chapel Hill 1980, p. 57). His wife, Elinor (née Bonham-Carter), a noted proponent of women's education, was likely influential in shaping his views. Both were active in the foundation of Newnham Hall in Cambridge (G. Sutherland, *Faith, Duty, and the Power of Mind: The Cloughs and their Circle, 1820–1960*, Cambridge University Press, Cambridge 2006, pp. 95–96).

6 Dicey, *Inaugural Lecture*, above n. 3, pp. 24–25.

In his choice of, and approach to, the topic of his inaugural lecture, Dicey opened himself to criticism from a number of directions. First, from those inclined to disagree with his views, whether defending the traditional role of the professional bodies in legal instruction or seeking to preserve educational tradition within the universities, and in particular in Oxford. Prior efforts at reform of legal education, with which Dicey was closely familiar, had shown no shortage of recruits in each camp.[7] Secondly, to questions as to the soundness of his judgment in choosing to make his mark as Vinerian Professor in this way.[8] Thirdly, to the accusation that in presenting his own manifesto, he did not sufficiently credit the work and achievements of others, in particular his Oxford colleagues, Sir Henry Maine (Chair of Historical and Comparative Jurisprudence, 1869–77), Dr James Bryce (Regius Professor of Civil Law, 1870–93), Thomas Erskine Holland (Chichele Professor of International Law, 1874–1910), and Sir William Anson (Warden of All Souls, 1881–1914), in driving change. Fourthly, to the charge that his lecture was thinly reasoned. On this last point, we may note the relatively short time period, less than three months, that passed between his appointment and the date originally fixed for the lecture, and that Dicey began his first series of public lectures, on 'The Elementary Principles of the Law of Contract' only two days after delivering his inaugural address. For a man who later would admit to being 'by nature a slow worker',[9] the pressure of time may have told on the quality of his reasoning.

Perhaps more damningly, Dicey's vision of the nature of legal education and of the role of the 'law professor' within that pedagogical model seems

---

7 See W. Cornish, S. Anderson, R. Cocks, M. Lobban, P. Polden and K. Smith (eds.), *The Oxford History of the Laws of England*, vol. XI, Oxford University Press, Oxford 2010, pp. 1175–92; F.H. Lawson, *The Oxford Law School, 1850–1965*, Clarendon Press, Oxford 1968, ch. 2; L.C.B. Gower, 'English Legal Training' (1950) 13 *Modern Law Review* 10, 139–44; G. Hawtin, 'The Mid-XIXth Century Debate Concerning Legal Education', Bulletin (Haldane Society of Socialist Lawyers) NS, (1972) vol. 2, 19 and (1973), vol. 3, 24; B. Nicholas, 'Jurisprudence' in M.G. Brock and M.C. Curthoys (eds.), *The History of the University of Oxford: Volume VII, Nineteenth-Century Oxford, Part 2*, Clarendon Press, Oxford 2000, pp. 385–86. See further Section 3 below.

8 It is reported that friends advised Dicey that his choice of subject matter was 'wanting in dignity' (M.D. Walters, *A.V. Dicey and the Common Law Constitutional Tradition: A Legal Turn of Mind*, Cambridge University Press, Cambridge 2020, p. 114). The lecture was criticised in the *Oxford Magazine* as 'a work of supererogation' (Lawson, above n. 7, p. 65).

9 Rait, above n. 5, p. 285.

wanting not only in detail, but also in ambition. Even if we accept the need to put the lecture in its historical context, and are willing to set aside the elitist[10] vision of 'law professors' as the producers and distributors of legal nectar, an account which envisages law as 'a series of propositions which are both intelligible and in correspondence with the decisions of the courts and the opinions of practising lawyers'[11] seems unduly reductive. That is a meritorious goal in a book whose principal purpose is to guide practitioners, but it seems inadequate in a lecture or other teaching aid, the principal purpose of which is to train aspiring lawyers to think, clinically and critically, about the nature and functions – as well as the content – of legal institutions and rules. Here, Dicey, whose reputation as a legal scholar rested in large part upon two works written principally for a practitioner market,[12] involving the collation of material into the 'rules' and 'exceptions' in a way that is now seen as a hallmark of his work,[13] may have been (subconsciously?) cutting his coat according to the available cloth in order to advance his professorial credentials.

We should not, however, be overly critical in our judgment of the professor or of his lecture. Dicey's appointment to the Vinerian Professorship, although it pleased him,[14] also evoked disappointment at the closing of doors to his political and judicial ambitions.[15] His innate modesty,[16] and lifelong self-doubt,[17] coupled with his self-imposed sense of responsibility for the restoration of the reputation of the Vinerian Chair, after an unhappy period in its history,[18] all no doubt contributed to overwhelming desire on Dicey's part to make a good first impression.

---

10 Dicey and his professorial colleagues were not above suspicion of snobbery (Lawson, above n. 7, p. 115).

11 Dicey, *Inaugural Lecture*, above n. 3, p. 25.

12 A.V. Dicey, *A Treatise on the Rules for the Selection of the Parties to Action*, Maxwell & Son, London 1870 and *The Law of Domicil as a Branch of the Law of England: Stated in the Form of Rules*, Stevens & Sons, London 1879.

13 Dicey's best known work (A.V. Dicey, *A Digest of the Law of England with Reference to the Conflict of Laws*, Stevens & Sons, London 1896) followed the same model, a tradition which continues in its recently published 16th edition (Lord Collins of Mapesbury, J. Harris and others (eds.), *Dicey, Morris and Collins: The Conflict of Laws*, 16th ed., Sweet & Maxwell, London 2022).

14 Walters, above n. 8, pp. 113–14.

15 Cosgrove, above n. 5, pp. 45–47.

16 Lawson, above n. 7, p. 71, fn. 1.

17 Cosgrove, above n. 5, pp. 63–64.

18 Cosgrove, above n. 5, p. 47; H.G. Hanbury, *The Vinerian Chair and Legal Education*, Basil Blackwell, Oxford 1958, ch. 6. Dicey's contributions as Vinerian Professor are described in detail in chs. 7–8 of the latter work.

Through his choice of topic, Dicey associated himself with the first and most illustrious of his predecessors, who, in his own introductory lecture, had sought to advance the cause of legal education in the universities.[19] Moreover, by providing an account of good professorial practice which closely fitted his own skills and aspirations, Dicey would have been able to distinguish himself from his immediate predecessors in post.[20]

2. DICEY THE JOURNALIST

To gain a less veiled perspective of Dicey's views on legal education, and higher education more generally, it is necessary to move from the summit of his career[21] to the foothills. In the 1860s, after working (with mixed success) as a tutor in both Oxford and London,[22] and while struggling to make his mark as a barrister[23] and working on his first treatise,[24] Dicey found the time to write on a variety of topics. In October 1869, he secured publication in *Fraser's Magazine*[25] of a review of Mr Mark Pattison's work, *Suggestions on Academical Organisation.*[26] In the course of his book review, engaging with Mr Pattison's arguments and proposals, Dicey scrutinised

19 W. Blackstone, *A Discourse on the Study of the Law being an Introductory Lecture*, Clarendon Press, Oxford 1758, pp. 26–34. Dicey also chose to pay tribute to Blackstone in his valedictory lecture, at the end of his long tenure in the Chair (see A.V. Dicey, 'Blackstone's Commentaries' (1909) 54 *The National Review* 653, reproduced in (1932) 3 *Cambridge Law Journal* 286). See text at nn. 86–87 below.

20 As Cosgrove notes, '[w]hatever the reservations Dicey privately may have held concerning the professorship, once the position was his he strove mightily to restore its prestige': Cosgrove, above n. 5, p. 50.

21 For later contributions, comparing legal education in England and the United States, see A.V. Dicey, 'The Teaching of English Law at Harvard' (1900) 13 *Harvard Law Review* 422 and 'The Extension of Law Teaching at Oxford' (1910) 24 *Harvard Law Review* 1.

22 Cosgrove, above n. 5, pp. 20–22, 30. For later roles, see Walters above n. 8, pp. 76–77.

23 Cosgrove, above n. 5, pp. 28–30.

24 See text accompanying above n. 12.

25 A.V. Dicey, 'Suggestions on Academical Organisation' (1869) 80 *Fraser's Magazine* 407.

26 M. Pattison, *Suggestions on Academical Organisation with Especial Reference to Oxford*, Edmonston and Douglas, Edinburgh 1868. Pattison served as Rector of Lincoln College from 1861 until his death in 1884. For discussion of Pattison's work in its historical context, see C. Harvie, 'Reform and Expansion, 1854–1871' in Brock and Curthoys, above n. 7, pp. 718–22; A.J. Engel, *From Clergyman to Don: The Rise of the Academic Profession in Nineteenth-Century Oxford*, Oxford University Press, Oxford 1983, pp. 134–36, also pp. 189–92.

defects in and possible reforms to 'the University system'. His focus, like that of Pattison, was on the situation at his own alma mater, the University of Oxford.[27] The choice of topics, and Dicey's views, summarised below, suggest that in the academic world, as with so many things, *plus ça change, plus c'est la même chose.*

2.1. DICEY ON ACADEMIC SALARIES AND CASUALISATION

Dicey shared Pattison's strong criticisms of the University's commitment of its financial resources,[28] in large part, to scholarships and fellowships for students, rather than to the employment of academic staff or the promotion of research.[29] Dicey bemoaned that:[30]

> Not only the professors technically so called, but all the persons engaged in the profession of teaching are underpaid. For no one can maintain that a professor, who always ought to be and often is a man of eminence, is adequately remunerated by a salary which often falls short of, and rarely exceeds, 600 [pounds] a year.

Dicey suggested that 'a professor of history who is not utterly unfit to fill his chair ought … to receive at least the 1000 [pounds] a year which is not too much to pay for the routine duties of a clerk of assize'.[31]

Nevertheless, professors were well-rewarded by comparison with their more junior colleagues who, in Dicey's view, were 'worse paid for good

---

27 Dicey had studied (at Balliol College) for a Bachelor of Arts Degree from 1854–58, placing in the First Class in Honour Moderations and in the final exams for the *Literae Humaniores* school. He secured a pass in his second school, Law and History.

28 For these purposes, they did not distinguish the central University from its colleges (see Dicey, 'Suggestions on Academical Organisation', above n. 25, 408–09).

29 ibid., 408–10.

30 ibid., 410. See Engel, above n. 26, pp. 122–29.

31 ibid., 410. The comparison is an intriguing one. According to the Bank of England's inflation calculator (<https://www.bankofengland.co.uk/monetary-policy/inflation/inflation-calculator>), £600 and £1,000 in 1869 were worth approximately £54,400 and £91,000 respectively in May 2022. The post of Crown Court Clerk at Aylesbury Crown Court was recently advertised with an upper salary range just above £27,000 and that of Delivery Manager at Lancashire Crown Courts with an upper salary range of around £34,500. The Professorship of the Philosophy of Law in Oxford was advertised last year with a salary of around £105,000 (subject to contract). On this measure, the professoriate has not fared too badly.

work than any man in England' with a salary of up to 300 pounds a year.[32] Nor did lecturers or tutors have a clearly marked career path:[33]

> [A tutor] may spend the best part of his life in the zealous discharge of duties which only men of talent[34] can discharge, and yet as he advances in age he will find himself with no chance either of a professorship or of any other reasonable reward for his labours ... Thus it happens that Oxford, with all her emoluments and with all the attractions offered by the studious ease of a college life, can hardly retain the best and most promising teachers.

Dicey concluded that 'teaching is not at Oxford in any sense a profession',[35] adding:

> It is essential to a profession that it should give persons who embrace it at least the hope of rising, and also some prospect of a fair support and independence.

With respect to the relationship of teaching with research, Dicey appeared sympathetic to Pattison's view that the University ought to be 'a place where a body of men, pre-eminent in all branches of knowledge, might at once pursue their inquiries, and disseminate among their pupils the result of their studies'.[36]

2.2. DICEY ON PEDAGOGY

At this point, Dicey turned his attention to the role of examinations in university education. He posed the question, '[c]an any person who knows Oxford say that there is not a risk of examinations becoming an evil?', which he answered as follows:[37]

> ... University life consists of alternatively preparing for examinations, of going through examinations, and recovering ... strength after examinations. The kind of pressure under which [the student] is kept may be necessary but it causes great evils. It entails in the first place a waste of time and of intellectual strength. It further gives an unfortunate bias to studies. [Students] inevitably study not

---

32 Dicey, 'Suggestions on Academical Organisation', above n. 25, 410–11.
33 ibid., 411.
34 As to the exclusively masculine terminology, see above n. 5.
35 Dicey, 'Suggestions on Academical Organisation', above n. 25, 411.
36 ibid., 412, but see text to nn. 53–55 below.
37 ibid., 414. The text here has been adjusted to remove masculine nouns and pronouns. See also Engel, above n. 26, pp. 139–45.

> what they think best worth investigation but those subjects which are of most importance for success in examinations. … In other words, [students] learn in order to be examined instead of being examined in what they have learned.

For Dicey, this complaint was borne of personal experience. His own time at university had been affected by struggles with his physical health[38] and he completed his degree with the regret that he had regarded literary study only as a means to an end (the passing of examinations) and not for its own sake.[39]

Dicey followed these observations with a withering look at the (still predominant at this time) class of students taking pass degrees, of whom 'the typical representative … is a person of slender ability … who ought never to have come to the University'.[40] He was, however, more willing to defend, against Pattison's challenge, the education received by those taking honours. In Dicey's view:[41]

> [T]he toils of a succession of University reformers have been repaid by a brilliant success. An English University has been stirred up to active intellectual life. You may criticise the Oxford training as you will, but the fact remains that at a time when even educated Englishmen seem dead to all speculative enquiries and when the energy of the respectable middle classes seems gradually more and more devoted to the sordid pursuit of position and success in life, the University has become a centre of speculative activity and has succeeded in sending forth students interested in all the theories of the age and 'moulded towards a high ideal'.

Dicey regretted, nonetheless, that the key to success in examinations lay as much in the ability to write 'in English which would suit the columns of a leading newspaper' as in the pursuit of scientific knowledge.[42] As he put it:[43]

> The effect complained of in the Oxford training, when it is said not to be scientific … [is] that little trouble is taken to force or induce [students] to study carefully the principles of any branch of knowledge.

---

38 Rait, above n. 5, p. 25; Cosgrove above n. 5, pp. 10–11; Walters, above n. 8, pp. 36–37.

39 Cosgrove, above n. 5, p. 12.

40 Dicey, 'Suggestions on Academical Organisation', above n. 25, 415.

41 ibid., 416–17.

42 ibid., 417–18. Dicey recounts (ibid., 418) the tale of a lecturer who is reported to have told his students: 'Take care in the examinations that you are not dull – you had much better be flippant than dull'.

43 ibid., 418, with minor adjustments.

In Dicey's view, a major cause of this defect was the system by which fellowships and prizes 'are almost wholly given as a reward for the possession of general information and literary skill, and are not, with some rare exceptions, to be gained by special knowledge'.[44]

2.3. DICEY ON LEGAL EDUCATION

Writing after the reform, in 1866, which had made proficiency in a single school sufficient to obtain a degree in Oxford, thereby removing the requirement for all students to sit for the *Literae Humaniores* school, but before the division, in 1870, of the Law and History School into separate faculties,[45] Dicey lamented the fact that 'it is extremely difficult to obtain at Oxford a really good instruction in the scientific side of the liberal professions'.[46] Within the legal profession, talented students who had studied for a university degree started on their career paths later than those who had moved directly into the professions, without the compensation of a legal education that would serve them well in their professional careers. Legal study in Oxford, in Dicey's view (possibly drawing upon his own personal experience), often leads a student to acquire 'a taste for generalisation that makes him an admirable critic of the defects … of English law writers' but which hinders immersion in the day-to-day activities of the legal profession.[47]

2.4. DICEY ON ACADEMIC APPOINTMENTS AND SECURITY OF TENURE

In the latter part of his review article, Dicey turned to consider the elaborate proposals advanced by Pattison for the reform of the University's structure.[48] A central element in these reforms was the appointment of a

---

44 ibid., 419.

45 Lawson, above n. 7, pp. 27–28, 34–36; Nicholas, above n. 7, pp. 386–91.

46 Dicey, 'Suggestions on Academical Organisation', above n. 25, 419.

47 ibid.

48 These included a proposal to recast the college system into groups of institutions with a specialism in a particular discipline (for example, 'in that of the faculty of law, All Souls, Queen's and Oriel are given up to the support of this faculty': ibid., 423). Dicey chose not to express an opinion on this specific aspect of the package. Dicey's former tutor, Benjamin Jowett, was notable in his opposition to such a reform when touted in the 1870s (see Lawson, above n. 7, pp. 46–47).

new class of professors 'who would be primarily men devoted to learning, and only secondarily teachers'.[49] These appointments, in Pattison's scheme, would be made by a centralised selection panel. Dicey was especially critical of this element of the scheme. His attack was two-pronged. First, the exercise in patronage was, in Dicey's opinion, highly unlikely to result in appointment of the best-qualified candidates.[50] Secondly, it offered no guarantee that the professors, when appointed, would do their work, and in particular that they would undertake their commitment to teach.[51] These two flaws were, in Dicey's view, interconnected for:[52]

> As long as professors are expected to teach, there exists a check, though not an efficient check, on the appointment of men utterly incompetent to be teachers. This check is at once removed by any scheme which encourages professors to lead a life which might be a life of learned leisure, but which might also be a life of unlearned indolence.

For Dicey, although energetic teaching was sometimes overrated, 'it is still possible to form a most exaggerated and artificial opposition between learning and teaching'.

In Dicey's view, Pattison had fallen into a grave error of seeking to place in opposition the university as a place of education and the university as a place of scientific endeavour. In his view, echoed in his inaugural lecture,[53] the two objectives were not opposed. While it was, on the one hand, desirable to avoid a situation in which 'the teachers are so occupied in teaching that they have no time to learn, or where teaching is so ill remunerated that men of first-rate ability will not as a rule remain teachers', it was also, on the other hand 'quite possible to give a learned man too much as well as too little time for study'.[54] To avoid these evils, those provided with central funding to enable them to devote themselves to research, 'should also be compelled to devote a large portion of their energies to teaching'.[55]

---

49 Dicey, 'Suggestions on Academical Organisation', above n. 25, 419.
50 ibid., 427.
51 ibid., 428.
52 ibid., 429.
53 Text accompanying above n. 6.
54 Dicey, 'Suggestions on Academical Organisation', above n. 25, 429–30.
55 ibid., 430. In our own time, that sound advice has been overlooked in the design of the mechanisms for the funding of teaching and research in higher education, and in the specification and oversight of senior professorial rules.

3. DICEY THE POLITICAL ACTIVIST

At about this time, Dicey became involved in long-standing efforts to centralise and professionalise legal education[56] through an association with the Legal Education Association, formed in 1867 and led in the early 1870s by Sir Roundell Palmer (later Lord Selborne).[57] Dicey was one of the signatories to the petition presented by Palmer to the House of Commons seeking a Charter for the establishment of a National School or University of Law. In 1871, he penned an article in *Macmillan's Magazine*, which can perhaps best be described as an op-ed piece in support of the Association's aims.[58] It conveys, more vividly and sharply than his later writing, Dicey's views on legal education and is deserving of attention for that reason.

Dicey pulled no punches from the outset. The mischief that he identified was that a man[59] could gain the privileges of a barrister 'by eating or affecting to eat a score or so of bad dinners, and paying in the shape of fees and otherwise from between £100 to £250', and 'may indeed have read through Coke or Stephen, but he may quite as likely have qualified himself for advocacy by devoted study of Trollope, Dickens, or the *Sporting Life*'.[60] The path to legal insight 'is a curious and tortuous road which a student finds it a difficult task to follow' without professors or teachers or a recognised systematic course of reading to guide students.[61] The Association sought, for admirable reasons, to address these evils by founding a university or school of law, to ensure both that those admitted to legal practice had a sufficient framework of legal knowledge and that those wishing to study legal principles in detail had the opportunity to do so.[62]

These aims were, Dicey recognised, distinct – the former could be achieved more straightforwardly by the professional bodies establishing an examination framework, without the formal structure of a law school.[63]

---

56 See *The Oxford History of the Laws of England*, vol. XI, above n. 7, pp. 1180–90; Hawtin (1973), above n. 7, pp. 27–30.

57 *The Oxford History of the Laws of England*, vol XI., above n. 7, pp. 1180–90; Hawtin (1973), above n. 7, pp. 29–30.

58 A.V. Dicey, 'Legal Education' (1871–72) 25 *Macmillan's Magazine* 115.

59 As to the exclusively masculine terminology, see above n. 5.

60 Dicey, 'Legal Education', above n. 58, 115.

61 ibid., 116.

62 ibid., 117.

63 ibid.

As he recognised, 'examination is not instruction, and instruction does not imply examination'.[64] Indeed, he ventured so far as to suggest that:

> if the status of a barrister is to be attainable without study of the law, it would be better to abolish the status altogether, and let any man who pleased style himself barrister-at-law and get such practice as his abilities or supposed abilities might command.[65]

As Dicey put it:[66]

> There is, in short, much to be said for treating the trade of the law as an ordinary trade governed by the maxim caveat emptor. There is also much to be said in favour of restricting the practice of the law to men who have shown themselves qualified to be lawyers, and who have been admitted to a degree or status which is a sign that they understand their profession; but there is nothing to be said in favour of first giving men a degree which marks them out as lawyers, and then taking no precautions to secure that the persons so marked out shall have the least knowledge of the law.

Dicey was no less pugnacious when he turned to consider the utility of the system of reading in chambers as the principal means of acquiring legal knowledge, describing it as 'haphazard' and 'eccentric',[67] overburdening the student with useless knowledge, and being self-defeating in exposing the student to legal practice 'without providing them with the instruction which makes study in chambers worth having'.[68] For Dicey, this had a seriously detrimental effect upon standards in the profession:[69]

> A man who learns law by practising law, inevitably tends to learn only just as much law, and just that kind of law, which he has had occasion to use; thus his knowledge becomes, or tends to become, a minute acquaintance with one special department … of the whole legal system. He is never educated to be a lawyer …

In Dicey's submission, the case for reforms of the kind for which the Association was calling was a strong one.[70] He turned to consider the

---

64 See text accompanying above nn. 35–37.

65 Dicey, 'Legal Education', above n. 58, 118. There is here an echo, perhaps deliberate, of the reported words of the Emperor Hadrian when asked by jurists to confer the privilege of delivering legal opinions (Digest 1.2.2.49 (Pomponius, *Enchiridion*)).

66 Dicey, 'Legal Education', above n. 58, 118.

67 ibid., 119.

68 ibid., 120.

69 ibid., 121.

70 ibid., 122.

'purely conservative' objection that the present system worked well in practice.[71] Although not dismissive of that sentiment, he pointed to recent changes in working practices at the bar (in particular, the decline of special pleading) as justifying a fresh approach.[72] To the possible objection that barristers were advocates, not lawyers, reliant on skills of rhetoric rather than legal knowledge, and that the profession should not be closed to talented orators,[73] Dicey suggested that the argument rested on a false premise, for men of talent would not have the remotest difficulty in demonstrating competence in matters of legal principle, and any who were found lacking in intelligence should justifiably be excluded from the profession in the public interest.[74]

For Dicey, the practical training which reading in chambers offered was a necessary adjunct to a system of formal legal education:[75]

> No professor on the one hand will in the long run be found worth listening to, whose instruction has not a direct bearing on the practical teaching which a student receives when he passes from the class-room to a barrister's chambers.

In his closing remarks, Dicey expressed a confidence that, if a law school were founded in London, with expert professors giving lectures, the students would be found to populate it, whether or not its classes were made compulsory.[76]

The Association's proposals were neutralised by resistance from some parts of the legal profession, and from conservative forces within the judiciary (including Sir George Jessel and Lord Cairns),[77] but the clamour for reform did not fade. Instead of a 'general school of law', the momentum carried forward both to efforts to improve professional legal education[78] and to reform of the methods and curriculum in the universities, in particular in Oxford[79] and in Cambridge.[80] Although more conservatively

71 ibid., 122–23.
72 ibid., 123.
73 ibid., 124–25.
74 ibid., 125–26.
75 ibid., 126.
76 ibid., 127.
77 *The Oxford History of the Laws of England*, vol. XI, above n. 7, pp. 1190–91.
78 ibid., pp. 1195–1201.
79 Lawson, above n. 7, ch. 2.
80 For Dicey's (inadvertent) role in the creation of the Squire Law Library in that place, see Lawson, above n. 7, pp. 96–97.

worded than his earlier pieces, Dicey's inaugural lecture carried forward some of the ideas that he had first expressed more than a decade earlier.

4. DICEY EMERITUS

In 1909, Dicey took the decision to retire from his Statutory Chair. This was not the end of his academic career, for the following year he took up the newly created Lectureship in Private International Law at All Souls, which he held until 1913.[81] Nonetheless, at the age of 74, he concluded that 'it is better the Vinerian Professorship should pass into younger hands'.[82] His reasons for taking that decision are, in light of modern debates about mandatory retirement for academics, illuminating. In a letter to his wife, he confided:[83]

> I am quite certain that, as a general rule, professors here ought not to keep their posts as late as I have already held mine. ... If any one asked me how long University professors should hold office, I should answer 'generally up to 65 as in the civil service, but often up to 70, and certainly not as a rule much longer'. Though I can do my work, I cannot do it as well as I once did.

It is, here, right to acknowledge that Dicey was writing at a time when standards of health care, and life expectancy, differed greatly from those attained today. In the following passage, he referred to impediments to hearing, memory, and energy. Nonetheless, Dicey was again driven by a desire not to impair his own reputation, and the reputation of the Chair that he occupied:[84]

> I have seen too many professors who have damaged their own reputation and done harm to the University by holding their posts too long. Perhaps I may have made an error in not resigning a year or two ago.

---

81 See Dicey, 'The Extension of Law Teaching at Oxford', above n. 21. On his retirement from the Vinerian Chair, Dicey had declared that 'I should like to see if I can force on the study of the Conflict of Laws': Rait, above n. 5, p. 203. For Dicey's role in opening up the Law School in Oxford to overseas graduates, see Cosgrove, above n. 5, pp. 57–58. Dicey was succeeded in this position by Maurice (later Sir Maurice) L. Gwyer: Lawson, above n. 7, p. 120. Gwyer was, in turn, succeeded by Geoffrey Cheshire, himself elected to the Vinerian Chair in 1944: Hanbury, above n. 18, p. 241.

82 Cosgrove, above n. 5, p. 60.

83 Rait, above n. 5, p. 200.

84 ibid., p. 201.

Tellingly, he added that '[t]his conduct, if it were a mistake, was excused by me by my still feeling more internal vigour than I do now, and by the desire to add something to the income on which I retired'.[85]

More poignantly, after delivering his valedictory address,[86] Dicey accounted for the dilemma that he faced, and which others in his position will continue to face:[87]

> The occasion was to me full of sadness. I heartily wished that some law fixed one's period of retirement. It is an unpleasant thing to have to decide when to cut one's own throat.

He once more emphasised considerations of personal and institutional reputation, as overriding countervailing forces:[88]

> For my own fame, I doubt not my resignation is a wise step, and I doubt not too that it is in the long run best for the chair. But the end of a career of which I was fond, and the occasional feeling that perhaps one might have kept a pleasant employment and an income, both of which I like, longer, causes me some pangs.

5. LEGACY

It is all too easy for an academic lawyer today to be critical of Dicey, a man bound up in the events, mores, and preconceptions of his own time, conscious of his own limitations and apparently fixated on matters of reputation and status. Yet, in his writing, we see the words and motivations of an individual who thought and cared deeply about the vocation to which he had been drawn, and to the betterment of legal education and of the higher education institutions with which he was associated. The following tribute, by his biographer Richard A. Cosgrove, is worth reciting here:[89]

> Dicey set a new standard of excellence for academic lawyers and helped make that profession a worthy calling. He rescued academic law from indifference, transformed it into a field attractive to the best undergraduate minds, and opened up new areas of influence … He carried out to the best of his ability a

---

85 ibid. The University provided no pension for its professors: ibid., p. 201.
86 See above n. 19.
87 Rait, above n. 5, p. 202, in a letter to the editor of that work.
88 ibid., pp. 202–03.
89 Cosgrove, above n. 5, p. 64.

> major function of an Oxford professor: publication of significant works in his area of competence. ... And finally, he raised the Oxford Law School to a higher level of professionalism and established a tradition that still endures. For all these services, Dicey merited the accolades that posterity has bestowed.

The academic landscape that Dicey describes is, in so many ways, different from our own, but it is not too distant for us to recognise the challenges faced by its occupiers. For the students, the pressures and shortcomings of academic curricula designed around assessment windows. For academics, disquiet about rates of pay, casualisation, pension arrangements, and retirement norms, and debates as to the optimal balance between teaching and research for postholders. More specifically, in legal academic circles, changes in the models for professional qualification in the solicitors' profession (with the abandonment of the concept of the 'qualifying law degree') mean that we must ourselves now address fundamental questions about the role of the universities in legal education.

As the centenary of his death passes by, we all have much to thank Dicey for, and he has left us much to think on.

DICEY AND ANALYTICAL JURISPRUDENCE

Timothy ENDICOTT*

Albert Venn Dicey blazed a trail in expounding the principles, laws, and conventions of the British constitution. Those three types of norm are crucial elements in any constitution. In offering fragments of an account of their nature, Dicey was making a significant contribution to analytical jurisprudence, by which I mean the work of clarifying the basic concepts to be used in the general theory of law. Yet he maintained a curiously detached attitude to an academic industry that already went by the name 'analytical jurisprudence', which Jeremy Bentham and John Austin had instigated by provoking others to respond to their dramatic utilitarian, empiricist theory of law.

My purpose here is to consider what Dicey said, suggested, and took for granted about the nature of principles, of laws, and of conventions. And I will ask what might best be said about those things for his purpose of explaining the British constitution. Dicey thought that many norms of the United Kingdom constitution are not legal norms, and I will defend this idea and try to explain its import. Non-legal norms are critically important to the constitution: they institute our form of executive government and

* Author's acknowledgment: I benefited from comments from Wolfgang Ernst, Alistair Mills, Sophie Ryan and Mark D. Walters, and from participants in the *Dicey + 100* colloquium on 3 October 2022.

do much to regulate it. But Dicey quite deliberately focused on law, and sidelined the non-legal. He wrote that 'the law, not the morality of the constitution [by which he meant, not constitutional conventions], forms the proper subject of legal study'.[1]

That framing of his famous book distorted his picture of the structure of the constitution. I think that it was a mistake for Dicey to think that the proper study of law professors and law students is restricted to law! Why shouldn't a law professor expound the constitution? The whole constitution is a proper object of study for a constitutional lawyer, and the law of the constitution is best understood in its true perspective as part (or as a complex array of parts) of the constitution (understood as the scheme of governance in a political community) as a whole. As John Allison has shown,[2] the reasons for Dicey's title, *Lectures Introductory to the Study of the Law of the Constitution* (and then, from the third edition in 1889, *Introduction to the Study of the Law of the Constitution*), had to do with Dicey's approach to legal education, and to his own role. He particularly wanted to establish *the law* in this field as something worthy of study. And, of course, at that he succeeded very dramatically. But I wish that he had called his book '*Introduction to the Study of the Constitution*'.[3] Then the conventions of the constitution would have been at the centre of

---

1 A.V. Dicey, *Introduction to the Study of the Law of the Constitution*, 8th ed., Macmillan & Co., London 1915, p. 413 ('*Introduction to the Study of the Law of the Constitution*'). cf. Dicey's statement in the first edition and the final edition of his book that the duty of a law professor 'is to state what are the laws which form part of the constitution, to arrange them in their order, to explain their meaning, and to exhibit where possible their logical connection': ibid., p. 31; A.V. Dicey, *Lectures Introductory to the Study of the Law of the Constitution*, Macmillan & Co., London 1885, p. 24; A.V. Dicey, *Introduction to the Study of the Law of the Constitution*, Macmillan & Co., London 1889, p. 31. Subsequent references are to the eighth edition, unless otherwise stated.

2 J.W.F. Allison, 'Preface to *The Oxford Edition of Dicey*' in A.V. Dicey, *Lectures Introductory to the Study of the Law of the Constitution*, J.W.F. Allison (ed.), Oxford University Press, Oxford 2013, pp. xxiv–xxx. Julia Stapleton gives an account of Dicey's fascination with 'the ascendancy of law in English national consciousness' – and its relation to legal education – in 'Dicey and his Legacy' (1995) 16 *History of Political Thought* 234.

3 Dicey's friend and colleague, William Anson, solved this problem by calling his book *The Law and Custom of the Constitution*, Clarendon Press, Oxford 1886–92. I do not think that there is any difference, for our purposes, between Anson's term 'custom' and Dicey's term 'convention': Dicey wrote that conventions consist of 'customs, practices, maxims, or precepts which are not enforced or recognised by the Courts': Dicey, *Introduction to the Study of the Law of the Constitution*, above n. 1, p. 413. Walter Bagehot and William Hearn, whose work Dicey admired, dealt with it by calling their books respectively: *The English Constitution*, Chapman & Hall, 1867; and *The Government of England: Its Structure, and its Development*, George Robertson, 1867. None of them shared Dicey's impulse to treat law as the subject matter.

his topic; in focusing on them, he would have been focusing on something that constitutional lawyers need to understand.

But because he made *the law* his topic, his scheme pushed aside one of the most important principles of the constitution. The principle of responsible executive government ought to have taken centre stage. It is the principle that those who exercise the executive power of the state must not be free to use it arbitrarily for their own interests and purposes, but must be constrained (at least, to some considerable extent) to respond to the wishes of others, and to act for the public good. The rule of law is an essential element in that constraint, and yet the law is only a fragment of the full explanation of our constitution's surprising degree of success (in Dicey's time and today) in securing responsible executive governance. The techniques by which the constitution does so are visible in Dicey's excellent, yet sidelong, look at conventions in Chapters 14 and 15 of his book. He came close to identifying the significance of the principle of responsible government when he argued that the primary purpose of conventions is to ensure that 'the Cabinet … shall in the long run give effect to the will of … the majority of the electors or (to use popular though not quite accurate language) the nation'.[4] And in the fourth through eighth editions, he discussed the distinctive British form of executive governance in Note III of the Appendix, 'Distinction between a Parliamentary Executive and a non-Parliamentary Executive'. But because he presented his topic as *law*, his book dealt with the constitutive framework of executive government through an unhelpful rhetorical downgrading of conventions, as something outside his topic.

Through all the successive editions of his book, Dicey articulated two 'principles' as the gist of the constitution: the sovereignty of Parliament, and the rule of law. In the last sentence of his last chapter, he wrote that the constitution's 'peculiar characteristics may be summed up in the combination of Parliamentary Sovereignty with the Rule of Law'.[5] In that summation, the UK constitution's *most* distinctive, most 'peculiar' characteristic went missing. The non-legal rules that establish and control the institutions of the executive branch of government are as important as the legal rules that determine the legal effect of judicial decisions and acts of Parliament, and are no less characteristic or distinctive of the UK constitution. And there is no good ground for Dicey's claim that the force

---

4 Dicey, *Introduction to the Study of the Law of the Constitution*, above n. 1, p. 424.

5 ibid., p. 468. cf. p. 465 ('The law of the constitution … is in all its branches the result of two guiding principles …').

of those non-legal rules results from legal difficulties that will be incurred by political actors who violate them.

That is the central message of this contribution: the non-legal elements of the constitution are crucial because they establish and regulate the executive. Their non-legal status is essential to their constitutional function, and they do not gain their normative force from the law. I will aim to convey this message through an analytical introduction to: (1) principles; (2) laws; and (3) conventions of the constitution. Then I will comment on differences between conventions and law, and on connections between them.

1. PRINCIPLES

In the first and more general sense of the word, principles are the fundamental explanatory elements – the building blocks – of an object of study. When the object of study is a normative structure such as a constitution, the fundamental explanatory elements are themselves abstract norms – which gives us the second sense of the word 'principle'. I will use the word, as Dicey generally did, in this second sense: a principle is an abstract norm of the constitution that provides a starting point for reasoning as to what is to be done in the configuration and empowerment of the institutions of the state, and in the regulation of their operations.

In a constitution, the relation between principles and practice is a relation between how things ought to be done, and how they *are* done. The underlying general principles of how a polity ought to be governed do not depend one whit on what the British do; they are all specifications of the universal principle that law and politics in any polity ought to promote and to secure the good of the community (which includes the good of public respect and protection for certain rights of individuals and of groups).

But for a principle to be a principle *of the British constitution*, it must actually guide our constitutional practice to some extent – in fact, to an extent sufficient to give it an explanatory role. It is a principle *of our law* only if it underlies and explains the doctrines of the law and the actual operations of the legal system; it is a principle *of our constitution* only if political action adheres to it, to some extent. Freedom of speech, for example, can be a principle of our constitution even if it is not always respected – indeed, that must be the case, or it would be logically impossible to describe any failure of respect for freedom of speech as a departure from *our constitutional principle*. But to some extent, respect for freedom of speech must be characteristic of our constitution if we are to be able to say that freedom of speech is a principle of our constitution.

At the same time, to call something a 'principle' of our constitution is to suggest that it is a good thing – something that, to some extent at least, makes our practice principled rather than unprincipled. Constitutional norms may be good or bad, but identifying such a norm as a *principle* implies that, to some extent, it secures the purposes of constitutionalism. We don't call the anti-constitutionalist tendencies in a country's constitutional practices its 'constitutional principles'.

So, the principles of our constitution are abstract norms that guide our actual practice (to some extent), and that promote (in some way, to some extent) the constitutional aspects of the public good.

Consider the first constitutional principle that Dicey mentioned in his book: that the King may not exercise judicial authority personally, but only through delegation to the judges. Dicey called it 'the principle enforced by the obstinacy and the fallacies of the great Chief-Justice [i.e. Sir Edward Coke]'.[6] With candour and with his fine sense of irony, Dicey said that 'no achievement of sound argument, or stroke of enlightened statesmanship, ever established a rule more essential to the very existence of the constitution'.[7] I think that he could and should have said the same of the broader principle that the executive branch of the state must operate responsibly: no rule is more essential to the very existence of the constitution. And this principle of our constitution is seen at work primarily through non-legal constitutional rules. Indeed, the laws of the constitution (such as the legal rule that the King cannot adjudicate in person) tend to limit executive power; as we will see, it is conventions that determine who holds that power and conventions control its exercise.

2. LAWS

Dicey wrote that '[c]onstitutional understandings are admittedly not laws; they are not (that is to say) rules which will be enforced by the Courts'.[8]

6 ibid., p. 16.

7 ibid., p. 18. As that passage shows, Dicey seems to have thought of principles not as something different from rules, but as, roughly, abstract rules of fundamental importance. In legal theory since his time, many scholars have tried to give the terms 'rule' and 'principle' other significations, but I think that Dicey's flexible way of using those terms is at least as helpful as any such theory-laden stipulation.

8 ibid., p. 435.

It is worth noting Dicey's originality in advancing this idea that laws are enforced by courts, and that conventions are therefore significantly different from laws. I think that it is true, and important, even though it is controversial. Scholars have dismissed it by saying that courts *might* enforce conventions,[9] or that they have *actually done so*.[10] It is indeed conceivable that courts might treat a constitutional convention as if it were a law, and it is indeed true that they have done so. But it is misleading to say that if they do so, they are *enforcing* the convention. They may be giving it a new, legal force that it gains not from its nature as a convention, but from the action of the court itself. And if they adopt a clear, open, prospective legal doctrine that constitutional conventions have legal force, even that would not undermine Dicey's distinction: constitutional conventions are not laws just because they are the customary rules of constitutional actors and institutions. Legal rules depend for their legal force on institutional decisions (including decisions of courts) that the law itself treats as sources of law.

Farrah Ahmed, Richard Albert, and Adam Perry have argued that the Supreme Court of India enforces conventions. It is an attractive idea, because Justice Kuldip Singh of the Supreme Court of India, in the famous *Second Judges' Case*, said so:

> [O]nce it is established in the court of law that a particular convention exists and the constitutional functionaries are following the same as a binding precedent then there is no justification to deny such a convention the status of law ...[11]

Was the Court 'enforcing' the convention by giving it the legal effect that it already had? Or was the Court 'enforcing' it by making a new legal rule requiring the conduct that, the Court reckoned, was required by the practice? We should be wary of this potential equivocation in the notion of 'enforcing' a convention: when the justices of the Supreme Court of India said that there was a constitutional convention requiring judicial

---

9 Nick Barber wrote that Dicey's distinction 'will fail if it is conceivable that there are some conventions which are enforced by the courts': N.W. Barber, 'Laws and constitutional conventions' (2009) 125 *Law Quarterly Review* 294, 294.

10 F. Ahmed, R. Albert and A. Perry, 'Judging Constitutional Conventions' (2019) 17 *International Journal of Constitutional Law* 787, 787; the authors aim to 'overturn' the assumption 'that conventions are always distinguishable from rules of law'. Geoffrey Marshall defended Dicey's distinction with care and intelligence: G. Marshall, *Constitutional Theory*, Clarendon Press, Oxford 1980, ch. 1.

11 *Supreme Court Advocates-on-Record Association v Union of India* (1993) 4 SCC 441, [449]. See Ahmed, Albert, and Perry, above n. 10, 801.

primacy in the appointment of judges, and that it had the status of law, they presented themselves, and evidently saw themselves, as 'enforcing' a convention in the first sense. But the analytical question is whether they were, instead, making new law, changing their country's constitution, and conferring a new legal power on judges. On this analytical question, judges have no authority.

Dicey's distinction between laws and conventions might be expressed by saying that judges change the constitution if they treat a rule as having legal force merely on the ground that it is the practice of the 'constitutional functionaries'.[12] If the judges establish a doctrine that such customary rules have legal force, then they establish for themselves a legal power to decide what the customs of politicians require, and to give a legal remedy against a breach of those requirements. The effect of the *Second Judges' Case* was not only to reallocate to judges a power of judicial appointment that the 1950 Constitution of India had conferred on the President.[13] Its effect was also to allocate to judges the power to regulate and to enforce constitutional conventions. The remarkable episode is, in my view, a dramatic illustration of the *difference* between conventions and laws: by treating a supposed convention as imposing a legal duty, the Supreme Court took control over the appointment of judges.

So Dicey's distinction is a sound and important idea. Sir Ivor Jennings thought that conventions are 'rules whose nature does not differ fundamentally from that of the positive law of England'.[14] With respect, I think that was a very significant mistake, for the courts have inherent jurisdiction to determine the positive law of England, and no institution has inherent jurisdiction to determine the requirements of conventions.

---

12 And in fact, I do not think that Ahmed, Albert and Perry disagree: 'Initially, what courts enforced were non-legal rules, that is, conventions. Eventually, that practice of enforcement, coupled with a change in judicial attitudes, brought about a shift in the rule of recognition, making what were once non-legal rules into legal rules.': AHMED, ALBERT, and PERRY, above n. 10, 805. They can square the idea that conventions are sometimes 'enforced' with the idea that the court was making 'non-legal rules into legal rules' because they take a very liberal approach to the question of what counts as 'enforcement'.

13 Constitution of India 1950: Supreme Court judges (Article 124(2)) and High Court judges (Article 217(1)) 'shall be appointed by the President', after consultation ('with such of the Judges of the Supreme Court and of the High Courts in the States as the President may deem necessary' for appointment of Supreme Court judges, and 'with the Chief Justice of India, the Governor of the State, and … the Chief Justice of the High Court' for appointment of High Court judges).

14 I. JENNINGS, *The Law and the Constitution*, 5th ed., University of London Press, London 1959, p. 74.

Dicey ought to have pointed out that the fact that courts give effect to the law is only the reverse side of the coin; the obverse is the fact that it is their legal duty to do so! It is characteristic of laws that they are enforced by courts, but conversely, they are enforced by courts because they are laws. We cannot give an account of the nature of law merely by saying that it consists of the rules to which courts give effect (even though that is true), because 'courts' is a legal term, and when we explain what courts are, we will have to explain their legal authority (their jurisdiction) and their legal *duty* to give effect to the law in their exercise of that authority.

This systematic, reflexive aspect of law is crucial to the constitution of any country. Understanding it is crucial to Dicey's educative and explanatory purposes. The law regulates itself by establishing and empowering institutions that have a duty to adhere to the law, and it authorises some of them to resolve legal disputes in a way that involves determining what the law is. The law also depends for its existence, its continuity and its development on the actual practice, in identifying the law and adhering to it, of those institutions to which it gives authority. The law authorises them to determine its requirements in particular cases, and it inevitably gives them the opportunity, and sometimes the authority, to depart from the law in particular cases, and to change its general rules. The law of the constitution is not merely more formal than the conventions of the constitution; the law of the constitution empowers courts to determine its requirements. The conventions of the constitution place power elsewhere in the machinery of governance.

This important element of a general theory of law underlies Dicey's distinction between laws and conventions: the systematic character of law is crucial not only to general jurisprudence, but also to an understanding of the law of the constitution.

3. CONVENTIONS

The rule of law secures some aspects of responsible executive government by restricting the power of the executive: *habeas corpus* and the prohibition on raising taxes without grant of Parliament in the Bill of Rights 1689 are constitutionally salient instances. But we can describe responsible executive government more broadly as a principle of the UK constitution because of the constitutional conventions that serve as techniques for securing it. They are crucial: it is not *nearly* enough that the constitution should prohibit the executive from carrying out functions that it cannot responsibly discharge (deciding judicial disputes, levying taxes …). Legal restrictions on executive power are indeed essential, but because there is so much that we need the executive branch to do in the public interest, we need something else: we need it to be configured so that, in carrying out its legitimate, lawful functions, it must respond to the interests of the community and the interests of justice.

By 1885, responsible executive government in that sense was promoted by a variety of customary norms of political practice: the government's dependence on the confidence of the House of Commons; restrictions on the powers of the monarch and of the peers; and a variety of norms of political accountability (accountability of ministers to the Prime Minister, and to each other within the Cabinet, their accountability to their party, their duty to answer questions from members of the House of Commons, and the critically important privileging of the Official Opposition, etc., all against the backdrop of the government's need for the confidence of the House, and of the requirement of periodic general elections). Those norms were supported by a variety of forms of distribution of power and of accountability *within* the executive.

The constitutional 'guardrails' (as people call them these days) against arbitrary or merely suboptimal executive action were, in 1885, and are, today, not just laws, but also the customary rules imposed by our constitution at the macropolitical level, e.g. the non-legal practices that facilitated the ousting of Boris Johnson and of Liz Truss in 2022. By 'facilitated the ousting', I mean that those Prime Ministers had to resign because they lost support from those on whom, by mere custom, the Prime Minister must depend for his or her tenure in office. The convulsions in the governance of the UK in July and October 2022 were not brought about by the law; they were the working out of political forces that ran in the channels established by the conventional constitutional need of the government for the support of a majority of the House of Commons. Those conventional arrangements are the primary ways in which our constitution lives up to its principle of responsible executive government.

At the outset of his discussion of conventions, in Chapter XIV on 'Nature of Conventions of Constitution', Dicey reiterated his claim that they do not form the proper object of study for a law professor or a law student; they are, instead, 'constitutional understandings which necessarily engross the attention of historians or of statesmen'.[15] That rather unfortunately

---

15 Dicey, *Introduction to the Study of the Law of the Constitution*, above n. 1, pp. 413–14.

suggests that the proper interests of lawyers exclude any interest that is proper to non-lawyers. Perhaps it was through an urge to justify talking about conventions in a book on *law* that he reached the surprising and unsupportable conclusion (restated in eight editions from 1885–1915) that the law is 'the true source whence constitutional understandings, which are not laws, derive their binding power'.[16] Having subordinated the role of conventions in our constitution by sidelining them from his scheme of principle, Dicey exaggerated the role of law in the constitution by claiming that the normative force of conventions depends on legal consequences.[17]

In Chapter XV, 'The Sanction by which the Conventions of the Constitution are Enforced', he set himself the question 'What is the sanction by which obedience to the conventions of the constitution is at bottom enforced?',[18] and his answer was 'it is nothing else than the force of the law':[19]

> the breach of these principles and of these conventions will almost immediately bring the offender into conflict with the Courts and the law of the land ... they cannot be broken without a breach of law.[20]

One initial flaw in the proposition that conventions cannot be broken without a breach of the law is that it is not true. Legal difficulty may or may not result from breach of conventions. Dicey himself pointed out that some breaches of convention have no such effect.[21] But the real, analytical drawback in Dicey's sanction theory of conventions lies in two related facts. The first is that the legal difficulties that Dicey identified (when they do arise) *are not sanctions*. Dicey pointed out that if a Prime Minister refused to ask the King for a dissolution after a vote of no confidence, it would eventually (presumably) become difficult to raise and to spend the funds needed to run the government.[22] But that legal difficulty would not

---

16 ibid., p. vii.

17 ibid., p. 465: 'This law of the constitution ... gives in truth even to the conventional element of constitutional law such force as it really possesses'. Here I think that 'the conventional element of constitutional law' was a mere slip for 'the conventional element of the constitution'.

18 ibid., p. 435.

19 ibid., p. 441.

20 ibid., pp. 442, 447.

21 ibid., p. 26, fn. 1 ('Some of these rules ... might be violated without any other consequence than that of exposing the Minister or other person by whom they were broken to blame or unpopularity ...').

22 ibid., p. 446.

be a sanction; it would be a predicament arising out of a disability (the Prime Minister's lack of lawful power to raise revenue without grant of Parliament). Even dire consequences are not sanctions, unless they are designed and imposed in advance by the 'superior', in Austin's terms, to secure compliance with the rule.[23]

But there is a second analytical drawback in a sanction theory of conventions: *sanctions are not essential* to customary rules. We are all subject to customary rules that are never enforced with sanctions. Even if our social group is collectively hostile to failures to comply with its customs, that is not a sanction. It is just about possible to imagine a sanction for a customary rule; it would be the intentional implementation by the community of a rule-governed, prospective threat of an evil designed by the community to induce those who are subject to a custom not to breach it. Austin's theory arbitrarily committed him to denying that we are bound by a rule if the superior who imposed the rule has not threatened a sanction. Because of his Benthamite idea of duty as liability to an evil, Austin was wilfully blind to the normative force of customs that are not backed by sanctions (and I think that more or less all customs are in that category). I cannot see any reason for Dicey to have sought to explain conventions by identifying a sanction; it seems that he was influenced by Austin's unjustifiable theoretical preoccupation.

Dicey's sanction theory of conventions was an unpersuasive solution to a puzzle: 'The puzzle is to see what is the force which habitually compels obedience to rules which have not behind them the coercive power of the Courts'.[24] Sanctions have no general role in explaining obedience to rules (general, peremptory norms) of custom in general, or of the constitution in particular. And in any case, you cannot explain the nature of rules (customary or otherwise) by pointing to the factors that compel obedience to them. The question of why people obey rules can be a fascinating question of social psychology, but to ask the question is to presuppose an understanding of what it is that they are supposed to obey.

For a new start in explaining the nature of constitutional conventions, we might start with Ivor Jennings' refreshingly sanction-free explanation, which has been the most prominent alternative to Dicey's account. To identify a convention, Jennings said that we should ask 'first, what are the precedents; secondly, did the actors in the precedents believe that

---

23 J. Austin, *The Province of Jurisprudence Determined*, John Murray, London 1832, pp. 138–39.

24 Dicey, *Introduction to the Study of the Law of the Constitution*, above n. 1, p. 436.

they were bound by a rule; and thirdly, is there a reason for the rule?'[25] This famous set of questions implies that a convention must be practised and accepted *as* a rule by the participants in the practice, *and must be a reasonable rule*. I do think that this approach has an attraction: in a sense, customary rules can only be explained by reference to the reasons for having them. *And yet* (and this tension in the explanation of social rules runs through analytical jurisprudence), an explanation of customary rules must allow for the possibility that a customary rule might be a bad one for a community to have, and a good one for an individual to violate. Some customs are vicious. And in identifying the genuine value of a *good* customary rule (such as the rule that the King must appoint as Prime Minister the leader of the party with a majority of seats in the House of Commons, if there is such a person), we need to be able to say *this is our rule, and a good one too*. It is not its *value* that makes it true to say that it is our rule.

At least Bentham and Austin kept this point at the front of their minds; indeed, their incoherent[26] sanction theory of duty-imposing rules was their attempt to explain how such a rule could be good *or* bad. H. L. A. Hart shared their insistence on explaining the nature of rules without regard to their merits. His theory suggested that we do not need Jennings' third question, and in fact – as a matter of identifying what counts as a convention – that we *must not* ask it. Hart explained a customary rule as a combination of a regular pattern of conduct in accordance with the rule, plus a 'reflective critical attitude' toward that conduct.[27] He insisted that this critical attitude did not entail any *judgment* by the participants that a rule ought to be followed. Unlike Jennings, Hart didn't even want to talk about beliefs on the part of the participants as to what is to be done. He only pointed out ways in which they behave.

There is a striking irony in the fact that Hart thought he could elucidate the *normativity* of customary rules by pointing out *facts*. In a demolition of Hart's practice theory of rules, in *Practical Reason and Norms*, Joseph Raz pointed it out: the practice theory 'deprives rules of their normative character'.[28] I do not think that Raz ever gave any straightforward articulation of a better theory of customary rules. But we can work out its

---

25 Jennings, above n. 14, p. 136.

26 For an explanation of its incoherence, see H.L.A. Hart, *The Concept of Law*, 3rd ed., Oxford University Press, Oxford 2012, pp. 82–87.

27 ibid., p. 57.

28 J. Raz, *Practical Reason and Norms*, Hutchinson, London 1975, p. 53.

elements from his theory of authority.[29] He said that a person or agency claims authority if it claims to give reasons for action that are also reasons not to act on some other considerations. For example, with a wave of a hand, a traffic officer who directs you to stop your car is purporting to give you a reason to pull over and is also, implicitly, claiming that that reason is 'protected' by an exclusionary reason not to act on other considerations (such as the fact that you could get your shopping done sooner if you hit the accelerator). If you can better respond to the reasons for action that apply to you by treating the traffic officer's gesture as a reason to pull over regardless of some other considerations, then the traffic officer really has authority.

The normative force of custom can be explained in a similar way: to comply with a customary rule is to treat the regular pattern of conduct (the practice) as a protected reason for action. If the community does so (rightly or wrongly), then the community has a customary rule. Insofar as the members of the community treat their community's customary practice as establishing a rule, they are treating the practice as a protected reason. Stating the rule in the normative language that Hart considered so important is indeed a way of displaying an attitude; such a normative statement also entails that the rule's requirements are valid. And they *are* valid, if the rule *is* a protected reason for action.

So, we might say that Jennings was right, in a sense, that there must be 'a reason for the rule', so long as we remember that this is a statement from what Hart called the internal point of view. The conventions of the UK constitution *are rules* because the participants in UK constitutional practice treat them as protected reasons for action: e.g., a reason for Queen Elizabeth II to appoint Boris Johnson as Prime Minister if he is the leader of a party that gains a majority in the House of Commons, regardless of other considerations (the wisdom of his plans, as it may be, or his fitness for the job …).

What would it take for there to be good reason to go along with the done thing in constitutional matters, to the exclusion of other considerations? The principles of the constitution could give such reason, if following the customary rule is a better way of giving effect to those principles than acting on the principles directly. You do not need custom to tell you to act on principle. And in fact, acting on principles is, in a sense, excluded

29 For further discussion of how to do this, see T. Endicott, 'What Use has Approved' (2020) 33 *Ratio* 220.

when you act on a customary rule. Democracy is a fundamental principle of the constitution. But when Queen Elizabeth II had to decide whom to appoint as Prime Minister after the general election of December 2019, the last thing the British polity needed was for her to ask herself what would best promote democracy. By treating it as a rule that she had to appoint the leader of the party that had secured a majority of seats in the House of Commons (as the practice required her to do), the Queen could more successfully do what she had reason to do, than she could have done by acting directly on the abstract principle of democracy. There are many ways in which the principle of democracy might be promoted and respected. Queen Elizabeth was not free to choose the best way of promoting democracy; she was bound by a conventional rule to appoint Boris Johnson as Prime Minister. It was her duty to do so, regardless of his fitness for the job, because that rule is indeed a protected reason for action by the monarch. The conventions of the constitution get their normative force chiefly from the value of customary practices in requiring ways of acting that promote the principles of the constitution. That co-ordinating function, absolutely essential for the public good, makes constitutional conventions into binding, protected reasons: a matter of duty. And their resulting normativity owes merely nothing to the law.

4. THE DIFFERENCES AND THE CONNECTIONS BETWEEN CONVENTIONS AND LAW

The distinction between the *conventions* and the *law* of the constitution is that conventional constitutional practices or 'understandings', as Dicey aptly called them, operate without the array of systematising rules of recognition, change, and adjudication that Hart identified as characteristic of a legal system. There are no rule-governed techniques for determining whether a convention exists and what it requires; change in conventions is unregulated; no agency is authorised to resolve disputes over their content and application or to decide what is to be done if they are breached.

So Dicey was right that conventions and laws are significantly different, and he pointed to the significant difference (though he did not fully explain it) in his reference to 'enforcement' of law by courts. The distinction is fundamental and consequential for the ordering of the state; conventions confer no power on a court to determine either: (1) their existence; (2) their requirements; (3) the grounds (if any) for making an exception to the rule; or (4) what is to be done, if anything, in the event of a breach.

To illustrate the importance of the difference, consider two conventions that Dicey mentioned, which have been replaced by laws since his time. First: Dicey mentioned the constitutional convention in the United States that a president should only serve two terms (the 22nd Amendment in 1951 made that into a legal rule of the Constitution, after Roosevelt had been elected four times). Secondly: Dicey mentioned the British constitutional convention that Parliament should meet as frequently as required by the nation's affairs:[30]

> Suppose that Parliament were for more than a year not summoned for the despatch of business. This would be a course of proceeding of the most unconstitutional character. Yet there is no Court in the land before which one could go with the complaint that Parliament had not been assembled.

On 24 September 2019, the United Kingdom Supreme Court changed the constitution in Gina Miller's second case, assuming unprecedented authority to regulate the timetable of Parliament, after Boris Johnson advised the Queen to prorogue for a period when the judges thought that Parliament ought to be in session.[31] The Court held that Mrs Miller could go before the High Court with her complaint that Parliament ought to be in session. In their reasons for the Court, Lady Hale and Lord Reed did not mention Dicey's opinion, which was flatly contrary to the Court's unanimous decision. Dicey had presented the non-justiciability of prorogations as something so obvious that it provided a useful illustration of the fact that (as the Supreme Court held in *Miller No. 1*)[32] courts do not enforce constitutional conventions. The Court created a legal rule in *Miller No. 2* to regulate a form of governmental decision that, until 24 September 2019, had been regulated by 'a constitutional practice or understanding'.

If you change the constitution by making a constitutional convention (such as a custom that American presidents should not serve more than two terms, or an 'understanding' that Parliament at Westminster ought to be in session when it needs to meet) into a legal requirement (such as the 22nd Amendment, or the rule in *Miller No. 2*), you make it impossible

---

30 Dicey, *Introduction to the Study of the Law of the Constitution*, above n. 1, p. 436, cf. p. 442.

31 *R. (Miller No. 2) v Prime Minister, Cherry v Advocate General for Scotland* [2019] UKSC 41. See T. Endicott, 'Making Constitutional Principles into Laws' (2020) 136 *Law Quarterly Review* 175.

32 *R. (Miller) v Secretary of State for Exiting the European Union* [2017] UKSC 5, [141]–[151].

for the persons subject to the rule to act on their own determination of what the rule requires, or to make an exception to it. This can be a very significant reallocation of constitutional power. I wonder if Roosevelt's third and fourth elections were good exceptions to the rule. Today, US law deprives candidates, parties, and voters of the opportunity to judge. The 22nd Amendment to the US Constitution is a good rule just if it is better for those actors not to be able to do so.

And making a convention into a law creates a judicial jurisdiction to determine the requirements of the rule. By the constitutional change brought about in *Miller No. 2*, the judges took upon themselves authority to decide when Parliament needs to meet do its job.

5. CONCLUSION

Dicey's contemporaries came to think of him as an Austinian, and the idea has been popular ever since. And yet, as Mark D. Walters has very helpfully shown, there was a deep difference of outlook between Dicey and Austin.[33] Dicey, according to Walters, 'did not regard himself as a philosopher of law and he never published a sustained account of his own approach to jurisprudence'.[34] In this contribution, I have been imagining how Dicey might have developed that approach if he had benefited not only from his innate good sense, but also from the twentieth century accomplishments in analytical jurisprudence of Hart and Raz.

Dicey showed good taste and a reliable sensibility in his opposition to the work of John Austin,[35] without articulating the actual deep-running *analytical* drawbacks in Austin's jurisprudence. And although he described himself as a Benthamite,[36] he was too good-tempered to share the intellectual rage that drove the command theory of law.[37] Yet Dicey's misplaced urge to find the sanction that enforces conventions reflects Austin's influence. It would take H. L. A. Hart to refute Bentham and Austin's sanction theories of legal and conventional duty. William Anson,[38] Dicey, and others pointed

---

33 M.D. Walters, *A. V. Dicey and the Common Law Constitutional Tradition: A Legal Turn of Mind*, Cambridge University Press, Cambridge 2020, pp. 142, 158–59, 334–39.

34 ibid., p. 339.

35 See 'The Study of Jurisprudence' (1879–80) 5 *Law Magazine & Review* 382, 386.

36 Walters, above n. 33, p. 361.

37 As Mark D. Walters puts it, 'Dicey disliked theoretical extremes': ibid., p. 339.

38 Anson said that Austin made an 'arbitrary and unhistorical assumption that the sovereign was at all times, and for all purposes, omnipotent': W.R. Anson, *The Law and Custom of the Constitution*, 3rd ed., Clarendon Press, Oxford 1897, p. 6.

out that Austin's scheme oversimplified and distorted the facts of sovereign power, but Hart disclosed the theory's fatal analytical drawbacks, and Raz provided the basis for a truer analytical account of the normativity of constitutional conventions.

I have argued that the normative force of customary rules in general cannot be explained by reference to sanctions for non-compliance, and that constitutional conventions do not derive their normative force from the law. Customary rules are fundamental not only to the UK constitution, but to the constitution of any state, including states with written constitutions, for the rule that such a constitution has legal effect is a customary rule. Conventions do not depend on law; the law depends on customary rules for determining what counts as law. Just as constitutional lawyers do not stray from their proper subject when they study conventions, analytical legal philosophers do not stray from their proper subject when they ask what makes a customary rule a rule.

The arbitrariness of that assumption reflects the more basic arbitrariness of Austin's idea that a duty is, by definition, a liability to a sanction willed by a superior. Austin's theory seems unhistorical, since it gives an unpersuasive account of the allocation of legal power in, e.g., the British state in the nineteenth century, but the problem is not that it is unhistorical, since the theory would not be able to give a sound account of the normativity of law in any state in any era.

PART II

DICEY AND THE CONSTITUTION

DICEY'S FORGOTTEN CONSTITUTION

Alison L. Young

If you ask anyone who has studied UK constitutional law to name two key fundamental principles of the UK constitution, it is likely that both parliamentary sovereignty and the rule of law will feature in their reply. If pressed for more information, they are equally likely to talk to you about Dicey's account of both of these principles. These accounts continue to shape UK scholarship. Our analysis of events is through the lens of their impact on parliamentary sovereignty and the rule of law. Constitutional change is assessed in terms of whether it is strengthening or weakening the relative importance of these principles.

This contribution is not designed to argue that these two principles are unimportant. Rather, it focuses on other aspects of Dicey's work that have not had the same impact – either because we have forgotten them, or because it appears at first glance that Dicey forgot to discuss them. The first is Dicey's criticism of the development of the party system and how, without check, this may lead to governments instituting and implementing constitutional change made by Parliament that is contrary to the wishes of the electorate. The second is the separation of powers, barely mentioned by Dicey and only latent in his work.

I will argue that failing to take account of these forgotten elements not only undermines the accuracy of our assessment of the UK constitution, but may also threaten the delicate balance of powers needed to provide a normative justification for the UK's predominantly political constitution.

1. DICEY, EXECUTIVE DOMINANCE, AND THE RISE OF PARTY POLITICS

The clearest and most accessible source of Dicey's account of his frustrations with party politics and its impact on representative democracy are found in his introduction to the eighth edition of *The Law of the Constitution*.[1] These concerns are expressed through Dicey's observation of changes in constitutional conventions, or, more accurately, the rules of the procedures of the House of Commons which he classified as conventions, given that these provisions are not suitable for enforcement by the courts. He was concerned by the extent to which conventions increased the power of the executive in relation to the power of the legislature. They curtail debate, thereby 'checking obstruction' to Bills by 'lessening the means possessed by a minority for delaying debates in the commons'.[2]

Dicey also accepted the analysis of political theorists at the time who pointed out the continual rise of party politics in England over the end of the Victorian and into the Edwardian era.[3] Dicey concluded that: 'Party warfare in England is, in short, conducted by leading parliamentarians who constitute the actual Cabinet or the expected Cabinet'.[4] The role of both the legislature and the electorate had been diminished. Fewer MPs delivered speeches in the House of Commons than had been the case in the past. There were few checks on the powers of the Cabinet that could command a steadfast majority in the Commons. There was little, if any, ability of an opposition member to successfully initiate and carry a Private Member's Bill through Parliament. The role of the electorate was reduced to voting every five years to keep the same Cabinet or replace it with the expected Cabinet.

These criticisms sound all too familiar. The only difference is whether 'Cabinet' would be replaced by 'Government' or 'Prime Minister' in today's analysis. What may be less known is that they were expressed by Dicey in 1915. Even less well-known will be that Dicey's thoughts on the problems faced by the party system had been expressed prior to his introduction to

---

1 A.V. Dicey, *Introduction to the Study of the Law of the Constitution*, 8th ed., Macmillan & Co., London 1915, p. li. See also A.V. Dicey, *Lectures Introductory to the Study of the Law of the Constitution*, J.W.F. Allison (ed.), Oxford University Press, Oxford 2013, pp. 442–50, 474–84 ('*The Law of the Constitution*').

2 Dicey, *The Law of the Constitution*, above n. 1, p. 444.

3 See, e.g., A.V. Dicey, 'Will the Form of Parliamentary Democracy be Permanent?' (1899–1900) XIII *Harvard Law Review* 70.

4 Dicey, *The Law of the Constitution*, above n. 1, p. 448.

the eighth edition, in a lecture on 'representative government',[5] as well as in work looking at referendums.[6] What is becoming more well-known is Dicey's response to these problems.

Dicey did not advocate a change in the electoral system to weaken the power of the executive. He understood the necessity of ensuring that there is a strong government to deal with the ordinary day-to-day business of running the country. His concern was when a strong government could push through legislation that changed the constitution that had the backing of the Parliament but which did not have the backing of the people. It is in this context that he advocated the use of referendums, as a form of people's veto over constitutional change that could be enacted by a strong government without the approval of, or even contrary to the wishes of, a majority of the electorate.

We are perhaps all too familiar with this assessment of the UK's constitution in the post-Brexit era. First past the post delivers governments with large majorities which, when combined with the internal rules within Parliament, provides a means by which governments can steer legislation through Parliament. If anything, this ability has grown. Standing Order No. 14, for example, prioritises government business within Parliament. Whilst the kangaroo and guillotine, noted by Dicey as means of curtailing debate, may no longer be present, they have been replaced by programme motions and business motions. Programme motions set the timetable for legislative scrutiny. As we saw in 2019, this can be used to push all stages of legislation through the House of Commons in one day. Whilst the events of 2019 also illustrate that backbench and opposition MPs can play a greater role in scrutinising and even initiating legislation which contradicts preferred governmental policies, this was due to an unusual combination of circumstances – a minority government and an important constitutional issue that cut within as well as across party lines.[7] It is also

---

5 A.V. Dicey, 'Representative Government' in A.V. Dicey, *Comparative Constitutionalism*, J.W.F. Allison (ed.), Oxford University Press, Oxford 2013.

6 See A.V. Dicey, 'The Referendum and its Critics' (1910) 212 *Quarterly Review* 551, and 'Ought the Referendum to be Introduced into England?' (1890) LVII *Contemporary Review* 506. For a detailed discussion of this work, see M. Qvortrup, 'A.V. Dicey: The Referendum as the People's Veto' (1999) XX *History of Political Thought* 531; R. Weil, 'Dicey was not Diceyan' (2003) 62 *Cambridge Law Journal* 474; L. Trueblood, *Referendums as Representative Democracy*, Hart, Oxford 2022; M. Qvortrup and L. Trueblood, 'Schmitt, Dicey, and the power and limits of referendums in the United Kingdom' (2022) 42 *Legal Studies* 396.

7 See M. Russell, 'Brexit and Parliament: The Anatomy of a Perfect Storm' (2021) 74 *Parliamentary Affairs* 443.

important to note the extent to which the Speaker plays a role through interpreting the standing orders of the House of Commons, as well as making rulings which then become part of established practice.[8]

In addition to empowering the executive to push through legislation it wishes, other 'conventions' – i.e. non-legally enforceable rules that Dicey would categorise as conventions – have developed which have the effect of minimising the extent to which Parliament can hold the government to account for its actions. The Ministerial Code, for example, is not able to be legally enforced per se, although aspects of the Code may be justiciable in the sense that courts may provide an advisory judgment setting out the interpretation of its provisions.[9] Whilst its provisions reflect established practices and background legal rules, its creation, interpretation, and enforcement are in the hands of the executive. Ministers are 'personally responsible for deciding how to act and conduct themselves in the light of the Code and for justifying their actions and conduct to Parliament and the public'.[10] The Prime Minister determines whether alleged breaches of the Ministerial Code are investigated, including determining whether investigations initiated by the Independent Adviser should be investigated further.[11] The Prime Minister also has the final say over whether a breach has been committed and, if so, the consequences of that breach. It is the Prime Minister who reissues the Ministerial Code, normally towards the beginning of their term of office, and who publishes any further revisions to the Code.

The setting down of these provisions in published codes may help to facilitate accountability. It provides the electorate with the ability to focus on whether Ministers are adhering to these standards. When alleged breaches become widely reported by the media, then this can place more pressure to ensure that standards are upheld, and Ministers are called to account for their actions. However, whether a Minister is required to resign may well depend more on the character of a particular Prime Minister than on the relative defects in their conduct.

What the events of 2022 also illustrate is the extent to which party members, particularly backbench MPs, can play a role in holding

---

8 See M. Hutton and others (eds.), *Erskine May's Treatise on the Law, Privileges, Proceedings and Usage of Parliament*, 25th ed., LexisNexis Butterworths, London 2019, para. 4.25.

9 *R. (FDA) v Prime Minister* [2021] EWHC 3279 (Admin).

10 Cabinet Office, 'Ministerial Code', December 2022, para. 1.6 <https://www.gov.uk/government/publications/ministerial-code>.

11 ibid., para. 1.4.

Ministers and Prime Ministers to account. The role of backbench MPs in legislation is well-documented.[12] Backbench MPs who are members of the same political party as the government can co-ordinate to threaten to vote against a government Bill unless some of its provisions are amended. They can also provide a channel through which members of the House of Lords can express their concerns, providing further backing for potential amendments. Backbench MPs and Ministers can also play a role in holding Prime Ministers to account for their actions. The en masse resignations of Ministers in Boris Johnson's government were able to place the Prime Minister in a position where he had no choice but to resign. In a similar manner, a few months later, members of her political party forced the resignation of Liz Truss as Prime Minister, in response to her failed economic policies and her lack of leadership over whether a vote on fracking was, or was not, a matter of confidence.

Political parties play a larger role in the constitution than in Dicey's time. It is still possible for a strong majority government to make constitutional changes of which the electorate either would not approve, or of which it is likely to be unaware – for example through the enactment of the Dissolution and Calling of Parliament Act 2022. Constitutional change may also occur through acts of the executive alone, modifying the Ministerial Code or changing the manner in which its provisions are interpreted or enforced. Political parties may also provide the main means through which Ministers and Prime Ministers are held to account for their actions. Should we have paid more attention to this lesser-known aspect of Dicey's work, focusing on the root of the problem rather than his suggested solution of a people's veto over constitutional change?

2. DICEY AND THE SEPARATION OF POWERS

Dicey's writings do not have an account of the separation of powers in the traditional sense. There is no discussion of the distinct powers of the executive, the legislature, and the judiciary, nor of the relationship between them. However, this does not mean that issues relating to the separation of powers are not relevant to Dicey's work. His distinction between law and convention provides an example of a different focus – the separation between law and politics. Conventions were distinct from law because they

---

12 See M. Russell and D. Gover, *Legislation at Westminster: Parliamentary Actors and Influence in the Making of British Law*, Oxford University Press, Oxford 2017.

were not enforced by the courts. They were concerned with political issues, matters of policy that were not suited for legal resolution.[13]

As Mark D. Walters recognises in his excellent work, the distinction between law and convention appears arbitrary.[14] However, this assessment misunderstands Dicey's account. Dicey was not merely setting out a descriptive account of whether a rule or principle of the constitution was found in a constitutional convention or in the law. Rather, he was setting out areas of the constitution that did not have the quality of being suited for court enforcement. Most of the conventions discussed by Dicey were those relating to the Crown – for example the conventions that require the Monarch to exercise their powers of consent to legislation, the dissolution and prorogation of Parliament, and the appointment of Ministers in line with the views of their Ministers. Dicey did not regard these as suitable for enforcement by the courts. This is because they concerned matters of political discretion, determined either through an exercise of power or party politics.[15]

This separation of powers between the legal and the political can be understood in terms of Dicey's account of the law. Dicey's focus was on the common law. The common law evolves through a specific form of legal reasoning. Judges look to previous decisions not just to find precedents, but also to discover principles that run through these cases, providing a distinct legal narrative. This relies on reasoning from specific principles. It does not focus on how these principles are tempered by issues of power or party politics.[16] This reliance on background principles was relevant not just to how courts developed the common law, but also to how they interpreted legislation.[17]

Dicey did not, however, think that conventions were purely matters of power. Conventions are also meant to ensure that power and party politics are balanced with constitutional principles. Ministers internalised

---

13 See, I. Stewart, 'Men of Class: Aristotle, Montesquieu and Dicey on "Separation of Powers" and "the Rule of Law"' (2004) 4 *Macquarie Law Journal* 187; B. Foley, 'Diceyan Ghosts: Deference, Rights, Policy and Spatial Distinctions' (2006) 28 *Dublin University Law Journal* 77; D. Dyzenhaus, 'Formalism's Hollow Victory' (2002) IV *New Zealand Law Review* 525.

14 M.D. Walters, *A. V. Dicey and the Common Law Constitutional Tradition: A Legal Turn of Mind*, Cambridge University Press, Cambridge 2020, pp. 144–48.

15 ibid., pp. 342–46.

16 ibid., pp. 355–57.

17 See T.R. Hickman, 'Constitutional Dialogue, Constitutional Theories and the Human Rights Act 1998' (2005) *Public Law* 306.

the principles underpinning constitutional government. They form the internal limits on the power of Parliament.[18] With regard to the conventions determining the exercise of the monarch's prerogative powers, at the time of Dicey's evaluation, the Privy Council played a more direct role in advising the monarch. Members of the Privy Council provided a further means of ensuring that the monarch exercised their powers in line with constitutional principles, balanced against the influence of power and party politics that would influence the advice of the monarch's ministers.

This distinction between laws, which are enforceable by the courts, and conventions, which are not, still plays an important role in the UK constitution. It was most recently reiterated by a majority of judges in the Supreme Court in *Miller v Secretary of State for Exiting the European Union*, with regard to the Sewel convention. The Sewel convention stems from a statement by Lord Sewel, the Minister of State for Scotland, during the progress of the Scotland Bill, which became the Scotland Act 1998, through Parliament. Section 28 of the Act preserves the ability of the UK Parliament to legislate in areas that have been devolved to Scotland. Lord Sewel stated that he would expect that a convention would be established that Westminster would not normally use this power without the consent of the Scottish Parliament. This convention was later expressed in a Memorandum of Understanding between the UK government and the devolved governments.[19]

The issue arose as to whether the convention could be legally enforced, specifically in the context of its recognition in the Scotland Act 2016. Before looking at this specific issue, the majority of the Supreme Court examined the relationship between law and convention, confirming the Diceyan view that conventions are not enforced by courts: 'Judges … are neither the parents nor the guardians of political conventions; they are merely observers'.[20] Whilst conventions may be relevant to the law, they are neither created by the courts through developing the common law, nor are they enforced by the courts.

18 P.P. Craig, *Public Law and Democracy in the United Kingdom and the United States of America*, Oxford University Press, Oxford 1991, ch. 2.

19 Cabinet Office, 'Devolution: Memorandum of Understanding and Supplementary Agreements, Between the United Kingdom Government, the Scottish Ministers, the Welsh Ministers, and the Northern Ireland Executive Committee', October 2012, para. 14 <https://www.gov.uk/government/publications/devolution-memorandum-of-understanding-and-supplementary-agreement>.

20 *R. (Miller) v Secretary of State for Exiting the European Union* [2017] UKSC 5, [2018] AC 61, [146].

Although some question whether this strict delineation remains following the decision of the Supreme Court in *Miller v Prime Minister, Cherry v Advocate General for Scotland*,[21] a closer examination of the reasoning demonstrates that the delineation has actually been maintained.[22] The Court referred to parliamentary accountability when determining the scope of the prerogative power of prorogation. Parliamentary accountability, however, is not just a convention. It is also a constitutional principle that can be used to justify the development of conventions and of the common law.[23] The convention of individual ministerial accountability, for example, provides a means through which a constitutional convention upholds parliamentary accountability. The legal doctrine that prerogatives cannot modify or frustrate statutory provisions is also justified, at least in part, by parliamentary accountability.[24]

The acceptance of the separation between law and politics is also illustrated by the Court's approach to issues of justiciability when courts determine whether an issue is said to be inherently unsuitable for judicial determination because of its subject matter. There are two main categories: constitutional limits and cases which do not engage private rights, or which are not reviewable as a matter of public law.[25] The former category reflects Dicey's distinction between law and politics. If the appointment and

---

21 *R. (Miller No.2) v Prime Minister, Cherry v Advocate General for Scotland* [2019] UKSC 41, [2020] AC 373. See also the discussion of this case by Timothy Endicott in his excellent contribution to this volume.

22 See, e.g., J. Finnis, 'The Law of the Constitution before the Court: Supplementary Notes on The Unconstitutionality of the Supreme Court's prorogation judgment', Policy Exchange, 2019 <https://policyexchange.org.uk/wp-content/uploads/The-Law-of-the-Constitution-before-the-Court.pdf>; M. Loughlin, 'The Case of Prorogation: The UK Constitutional Council's ruling on the appeal from the judgment of the Supreme Court', Policy Exchange, 2019 <https://policyexchange.org.uk/wp-content/uploads/2019/10/The-Case-of-Prorogation.pdf>; M. Loughlin, 'A Note on Craig on *Miller; Cherry*' [2020] *Public Law* 278.

23 P. Craig, 'The Supreme Court, Prorogation and Constitutional Principle' [2020] *Public Law* 248, 'Response to Loughlin's Note on Miller; Cherry' [2020] *Public Law* 282, and 'Constitutionality, Convention and Prorogation' in D. Clarry (ed.), *The UK Supreme Court Yearbook, Volume 10: 2018–2019 Legal Year*, Appellate Press, London 2021; M. Elliott, 'A new Approach to Constitutional Adjudication? Miller II in the Supreme Court', Public Law For Everyone, 24 September 2019 <https://publiclawforeveryone.com/2019/09/24/the-supreme-courts-judgment-in-cherry-miller-no-2-a-new-approach-to-constitutional-adjudication/>; A.L. Young, 'The Prorogation Case: Re-inventing the Constitution or Re-imagining Constitutional Scholarship?' in D. Clarry (ed.), *The UK Supreme Court Yearbook, Volume 10: 2018–19 Legal Year*, Appellate Press, London 2021, p. 357.

24 *Case of Proclamations* (1610) 12 Co Rep. 74; *R. (Miller) v Secretary of State for Exiting the European Union*, above n. 20.

25 *Khaira v Shergill* [2014] UKSC 33, [2015] AC 359.

removal of ministers is non-justiciable, this is because the UK constitution recognises that these decisions are made by the Prime Minister and involve an evaluation of party politics and the ability of the Prime Minister's government to continue to hold political power through commanding the confidence of the House of Commons. The decision of the Prime Minister may also be influenced by the Ministerial Code, which reflects principles of good constitutional government. However, the Ministerial Code can be interpreted by the courts when this concerns issues that are suited for resolution by the courts or which involve individual rights, for example determining the meaning of bullying or harassment.[26] Such a question is not purely a matter of power or party politics. These issues also influence whether prerogative powers are justiciable, in the sense that courts may assess their exercise and not merely their existence or extent.[27]

3. FORGOTTEN LESSONS

The most obvious lesson we appear to have forgotten is that, even though 'law' and 'politics' are different realms, they are connected. The most obvious conclusion would appear to be that, by focusing so much on Dicey's account of parliamentary sovereignty and the rule of law, we have forgotten to check whether the UK's system really does provide sovereignty for Parliament, or sovereignty for the executive. Dicey's concern was that our focus on the legal sovereign – Parliament – meant that we lost sight of the political sovereign – the people. His suggested people's veto referendum was designed to ensure that the necessary strong government could not achieve constitutional change that was contrary to the wishes of the people.

This forgotten lesson is all the more pertinent in the post-Brexit constitution. The constitutional change of Brexit was not one initiated by a strong government against the wishes of the people. It was one initiated by the people which has, in turn, strengthened government in a different manner, enabling a government to use populist tactics to rely on the will of the people to push through constitutional change. Yet the result may be the same. Constitutional change may be pushed through in the name of the will of the people, yet this will of the people may not fully reflect the will of the majority of the electorate.

---

26 *R. (FDA) v Prime Minister*, above n. 9.

27 *Council of Civil Service Unions (CCSU) v Minister for Civil Service* [1985] AC 374 (HL); *R. (Miller) v Prime Minister* [2019] EWHC 2381 (QB), [2019] 4 All ER 299.

This is not to argue that the UK is populist, in the sense of adopting a populist ideology. Rather, it is to recognise how referring to the will of the people is used as a tactic of government. The will of the people is not understood in the sense that it would have been understood by Dicey's people's veto: an amalgamation of the wishes of the electorate, voting on a specific issue in a referendum following a fully informed debate in Parliament in favour of a specific constitutional change. Rather, when used as part of populism, the 'will of the people' is an artificial construct. The government determines that one homogenised view is the true will of the people. This will of the people must prevail over the views of experts. There is no need for deliberation or scrutiny over the government's plans to implement the will of the people. The will of the people must prevail.

We have forgotten another lesson underpinning the divide between law and politics. Both rely on upholding good principles of constitutional government. Those suited to enforcement by the courts are upheld through the law. Those which rely, instead, on power and party politics are not enforced by the courts. However, what happens when these political mechanisms do not uphold principles of constitutionalism?

In the post-Brexit constitution, we have seen two Bills which included provisions designed to enable the UK to act contrary to its international law obligations under the Northern Ireland Protocol.[28] Neither became law. The first saw these provisions removed by the acceptance of amendments from the House of Lords combined with reaching an agreement with the European Union. The second, originally argued to be a breach justified by the doctrine of necessity in international law, was put on hold following the Windsor Framework. The Illegal Migration Act 2023 contains provisions that are likely to breach the UK's obligations under the European Convention on Human Rights, as well as the Refugee Convention.[29] Whilst it is true that, assessed from the sole perspective of domestic law, Parliament can enact legislation which breaches its international law obligations, it is hard to imagine that Dicey would have seen these Bills as fully justified by parliamentary sovereignty. He may have been more likely to call for a people's veto over this proposed legislation which sought to undermine the rule of law in such a radical way.

---

28 The Bill which became the United Kingdom Internal Market Act 2020, and the Northern Ireland Protocol Bill 2022–23.

29 See the Equality and Human Rights Commission, 'Illegal Migration Bill, House of Commons – Report Stage' and 'Illegal Migration Bill, House of Lords – Second Stage', 2023 <https://www.equalityhumanrights.com/en/legal-responses/parliamentary-briefings>.

There have also been examples in which the divide between law and politics has become blurred in the opposite direction. For example, the Prime Minister obtained legal advice regarding the approach of the Privileges Committee in its investigation of whether the Prime Minister misled the House with regard to statements made about Partygate.[30] Following legal advice from its own advisor, and the Clerk of the Journals, the Privileges Committee concluded that 'the focus of the House's jurisdiction is on whether or not an action or omission obstructs or impedes or has a tendency to obstruct or impede the functioning of the House' and that accordingly, 'in broad terms, intention is not necessary for a contempt to be committed'.[31] The Prime Minister's legal advice contradicted this conclusion, stating that intention was necessary. The advice also questioned whether the procedures adopted by the Privileges Committee were fair, raising, inter alia, concerns as to whether Boris Johnson's legal counsel would be able to speak on behalf of his client, or to cross-examine witnesses. In rejecting these claims, the Privileges Committee drew attention to the need to distinguish a report of the Committee from legal proceedings: parliamentary process is not the same as criminal law.[32] It is just as important to recognise that political inquiries are conducted differently from legal cases, which may explain why they are unsuited to resolution by the courts. To blur the line may prevent Parliament from upholding principles of political accountability, as well as potentially requiring courts to take decisions that are not within their constitutional expertise.[33]

---

30 Joint Opinion of Lord Pannick QC and Jason Pobjoy, 1 September 2022 <https://assets.publishing.service.gov.uk/government/uploads/system/uploads/attachment_data/file/1102126/Joint_Opinion_of_Lord_Pannick_QC_and_Jason_Pobjoy_1.9.2022_-_Committee_of_Privileges_-_Boris_Johnson__Matter_referred_on_21_April_2022_.pdf>. It is not clear whether the legal opinion was commissioned by Boris Johnson in his personal capacity or by HM Government. The Privileges Committee understood that this was commissioned by HM Government, but this has not been confirmed. House of Commons, Committee of Privileges, 'Matter referred on 21 April 2022: comments on joint opinion of Lord Pannick QC and Jason Pobjoy', 3rd Report of Session 2022–23, HC 713, 26 September 2022, para. 3.

31 House of Commons, Committee of Privileges, 'Matter referred on 21 April 2022: proposed conduct of inquiry', 2nd Report of Session 2022–23, HC 632, 21 July 2022, para. 6.

32 House of Commons, Committee of Privileges, 'Matter referred on 21 April 2022: comments on joint opinion of Lord Pannick QC and Jason Pobjoy', 3rd Report of Session 2022–23, HC 713, 26 September 2022.

33 *R. (SC) v Secretary of State for Work and Pensions* [2021] UKSC 26, [2022] AC 223, [180]–[185] (Lord Reed).

I would argue that there are two clear lessons we should learn from re-examining Dicey. First, we need to rethink the extent to which we regulate political parties. This is not to advocate that political parties should be extensively controlled. There is also a fundamental need to ensure freedom of association to uphold a healthy democracy, where political parties can be formed which represent a wide spectrum of political opinion. However, it is to recognise the extent to which the way in which a party organises its internal structure can have an impact on the constitution.

We have seen this most starkly in 2022, where problems arose when the internal procedures for electing a new leader of the Conservative Party meant that Liz Truss was chosen as the new leader given the strength of support from members of the party, even when this was not reflected in her receiving a majority of votes from Conservative MPs. Did the lack of support from a majority of her backbench MPs make it harder for the then Prime Minister to demonstrate that her government had the confidence of the House of Commons and did this contribute to her eventual resignation?

Problems may arise not merely from the way in which leaders are chosen. Great emphasis is placed on manifesto promises. The Salisbury-Addison convention, for example, prevents the House of Lords from voting against, or proposing wrecking amendments to, legislation found in the government's manifesto. However, there may be little, if any, input into a manifesto from grass roots party members. Manifesto promises may also be vague, rather than providing a clear detailed account of a policy that the government wishes to achieve. Does this really provide an ability for the electorate to choose between competing policies? If not, this may give rise to similar problems of the potential to change the constitution in a manner that does not have the support of a majority of the electorate, particularly as it will be harder for backbench MPs to challenge manifesto commitments, and more justifiable for the Prime Minister to make this a matter of confidence to ensure backbench support.

Second, it requires a re-examination of Dicey's justification of parliamentary sovereignty and its relationship with the rule of law. It often appears as if Dicey advocates parliamentary sovereignty purely descriptively. There were, at the time, no examples of legislation that had not been able to impliedly repeal earlier legislation, demonstrating that Parliament was sovereign. Dicey's theory can also be regarded as providing a normative justification for parliamentary sovereignty, based on a need to respect the electorate as the political sovereign, combined with the need to ensure efficient government. There would be no need for stronger legal checks over Acts of Parliament given the internal constraints of Members of

Parliament and the ability of the courts interpreting legislation in a manner that upheld the rule of law. However, if there is evidence of a failure of these internal restraints, or a recognition that these restraints stem mostly from the political party which may have a greater motivation to preserve power than to uphold constitutional principles, does this mean that we should no longer prize Dicey's conception of parliamentary sovereignty as the key principle of the UK constitution?

I would argue that, rather than modifying or replacing Dicey's conception of parliamentary sovereignty or continuing to see parliamentary sovereignty as in tension with the rule of law, we should, instead, focus on Dicey's latent theory of the separation of powers. To understand how this may work, we need to examine the distinction between the power to make laws, and the power to make or modify the constitution. Dicey's conception of parliamentary sovereignty appears to vest both of these powers in Parliament. Those who advocate, instead, that the rule of law should be the key principle of the UK constitution regard courts as having both of these powers. As parliamentary sovereignty is itself a principle of the common law, it can be modified by the courts. It is the courts, through developing the common law, who identify and uphold the rule of law.[34]

My account of the separation of powers, however, argues that both the courts and Parliament are required to successfully change fundamental aspects of the UK constitution.[35] It draws on Dicey's distinction between law and politics, recognising that the institutional and constitutional features of Parliament and the courts make them more suited to determining different issues. This recognition can help these institutions to work together to make better constitutional provisions. My theory also argues that the indeterminate nature of the relative constitutional roles of Parliament and the courts may create tension, but may also provide a means through which each may defend, and refine, their relative role in changing circumstances.

It is only possible for Parliament and the courts to work together in this manner when the UK constitution recognises one aspect of Dicey's parliamentary sovereignty – continuing parliamentary legislative supremacy. Dicey advocated that Parliament cannot bind its successors.

---

34 A.L. Young, *Democratic Dialogue and the Constitution*, Oxford University Press, Oxford 2017.

35 A.L. Young, 'The Relationship between Parliament, the Executive and the Judiciary' in J. Jowell and C. O'Cinnéide (eds.), *The Changing Constitution*, 9th ed., Oxford University Press, Oxford 2019, p. 325.

Any future Parliament could overturn legislation enacted by a previous Parliament, thus ensuring that each incarnation of Parliament had legally unlimited law-making powers. This aspect of Dicey's conception of parliamentary sovereignty prevents Parliament from modifying fundamental constitutional rules without input from the courts. If Parliament were able to bind its successors, then this would enable any one Parliament to not only enact, but also to entrench fundamental constitutional change. Continuing parliamentary legislative supremacy also prevents courts from modifying the rule of law to make fundamental constitutional change without input from Parliament. Any change made by the courts can be overturned by legislation.

This also requires us to accept that parliamentary sovereignty is itself a customary rule and a principle.[36] It must be accepted by a sufficient number of officials in the legislature, the executive, and the judiciary to ensure its maintenance. It is accepted to the extent that it is recognised as a normatively valid constitutional principle. Parliamentary sovereignty is justifiable, in part, due to it upholding the electorate as the political sovereign. This requires vigilance to ensure that Parliament acts in a manner that does not undermine this principle. It is also justified when this ensures that political checks and balances are able to uphold good principles of constitutional governance. Continuing parliamentary legislative supremacy is justified as it facilitates a process of constitutional change which balances this need to respect the political sovereignty of the people and the need to uphold good principles of constitutional government. Problems arise when the will of the people is not balanced against the need for constitutionalism, upheld through political as well as legal accountability over the government.

[36] See the contribution of Endicott to this volume for an account of principles.

DICEY ON LEGALITY AND EQUALITY

Mark D. Walters

In his famous book, *The Law of the Constitution*, Albert Venn Dicey asserted that the 'rule of law' embraces the idea of 'equality before the law'.[1] The connection that Dicey drew between legality and equality has inspired both praise and criticism in the century after his death. By placing a conception of equality at the heart of the rule of law, Dicey opened up promising but contested lines of inquiry into the nature of constitutionalism within the common law tradition. Where those lines lead depends, in part, on what Dicey meant by legal equality.

In many jurisdictions today, equality is understood to be a fundamental human right – a right to be free from discrimination based on race, ethnicity, religion, sex, and other grounds, a right that furthers a vision of society in which everyone's equal moral worth is affirmed. The emergence of equality in this sense is usually understood to be part of the social changes that defined the latter half of the twentieth century. Could Dicey, a self-described 'mid-Victorian',[2] have had anything so modern in mind by 'equality before the law'? Surely not.

Yet this answer is only partly correct. An exploration of Dicey's work beyond *The Law of the Constitution* may suggest different perspectives for understanding the connection that he made between legality and equality

1 A.V. Dicey, *Introduction to the Study of the Law of the Constitution*, 8th ed., Macmillan & Co., London 1915, p. 189 ('*The Law of the Constitution*').

2 A.V. Dicey to James Bryce, 4 August 1911, James Bryce Papers, Bodleian Library, Oxford University, MSS Bryce 3: 100–08 ('*Bryce Papers*').

in his book. On one reading of his work, we may see the ingredients for the argument that the equal moral worth of everyone is embedded within the very idea of what law is within a regime governed by the rule of law. Even if this claim proves unconvincing, however, exploring Dicey's attitudes about equality will at least complicate our understanding of the history of ideas relating to law and legality, perhaps in ways that will help us in meeting the challenge that the promise of equality still presents for the ideal of legality today.

1. DICEY'S RULE OF EQUAL LAW

The idea of 'equality before the law' introduced by Dicey in *The Law of the Constitution* is both rich in normative potential and thin in stated substance. It will be recalled that in his book, Dicey sought to explain the British constitution from a legal perspective, organising his account around two principles: parliamentary sovereignty and the rule of law. He explained the rule of law by reference to three points.

First, no one can be deprived of liberty or property except for a breach of law established in the 'ordinary' legal manner, and so public authorities may not exercise 'wide, arbitrary, or discretionary powers'.[3] Second, 'no man is above the law' but rather 'every official, from the Prime Minister down to a constable' is subject to 'the ordinary law', and this 'equality before the law' means there can be nothing in England corresponding to the separate public law of France.[4] And, third, 'general principles of the constitution', including 'the right to personal liberty', are drawn from judicial decisions of common law courts rather than legislated codes of the kind found in 'foreign' constitutions.[5]

Although equality is implicit within Dicey's first and third points, it was in making his second point that he introduced the phrase 'equality before the law'. But what kind of equality is this? Paul Craig argues that Dicey's equality is formal rather than substantive in character. Craig, following Geoffrey Marshall, states that while equality before the law may mean 'the equal subjection of all classes to a common rule', it does not convey 'any qualitative view about the sort of law to which all are subject', and the

3 Dicey, *The Law of the Constitution*, above n. 1, pp. 183–84.
4 ibid., pp. 189, 198.
5 ibid., pp. 191, 192–93, 199.

legislature may make laws that make 'unequal provision for some as against others'.[6] Marshall said that, for example, 'abominable' laws in South Africa authorising racial discrimination would satisfy Diceyan requirements for the rule of law.[7] Craig goes on to say that, aside from the point about public officials and private persons, Dicey offered no principles governing the analysis of other forms of differential treatment between people, and articulated no general theory that might animate a substantive conception of equality.[8] This reading of Dicey has not gone unchallenged. Trevor Allan has argued that the 'formal equality between citizen and official' at the heart of Dicey's rule of law means that official power must always be interpreted by judges in the ordinary common law way, and through this distinctive style of interpretation it is 'thereby transmuted into a substantive equality' or a principle of 'constitutional equality' that secures to everyone equal concern and respect.[9]

Whichever reading of Dicey is accepted, it is fair to say that Dicey left the idea of equality before the law under-developed in his book. Dicey did say that 'legal equality' means the 'equal subjection' to the law of everyone, no matter their 'rank', 'condition', or 'class',[10] and so he seemed to have in mind a broader principle than just equality between officials and citizens. Indeed, in a footnote, he claimed that legislation granting immunities to trade unions exposed 'the rule of equal law' to 'peril',[11] suggesting that the rule of law is not simply the rule of what the legislature decrees as law but is rather a standard against which differential treatment of people by legislation may be read, assessed, and criticised.

But what theory of equality explains why certain kinds of differential treatment violate the rule of law and others do not? Could that theory encompass the idea of non-discrimination on grounds of race, religion, sex, etc., that we now associate with the modern human right to equality? Although Dicey failed to offer a theory of equality like this in *The Law of the Constitution*, there is a hint of such a theory. In a footnote in the introduction to the 1915 edition, Dicey gave a short explanation of 'the

---

6 P. Craig, 'Formal and Substantive Conceptions of the Rule of Law: An Analytical Framework' [1997] *Public Law* 467, 472–73, quoting G. Marshall, *Constitutional Theory*, Clarendon Press, Oxford 1971, pp 138–39.

7 Marshall, ibid., p. 138.

8 Craig, above n. 6, 472–73.

9 T.R.S. Allan, *Constitutional Justice: A Liberal Theory of the Rule of Law*, Oxford University Press, Oxford 2001, pp 19–20.

10 Dicey, *The Law of the Constitution*, above n. 1, pp. 189, 198.

11 ibid., p. 200, fn. 1.

sort of equality' that exists in the United Kingdom, observing that a British subject may live, work, vote, and even be a cabinet or prime minister no matter 'the race to which he belongs' or 'the religion which he professes'.[12] Dicey made this point in the course of lamenting the fact that this sort of equality was not secured throughout the British Empire. When discussing colonial legislatures in Chapter 2, he gave the example of a Transvaal statute that restricted immigration into the colony of subjects of 'Asiatic origin'.[13] Writing privately, Dicey stated that this law 'puts natives of India in a position which I do not think ought to be imposed on any British subject', and that the imperial government had 'gone too far' in allowing this colonial law to stand.[14]

So, perhaps Dicey did have a substantive view of equality after all. Still, it must be conceded that in *The Law of the Constitution* his statements about that sort of equality are fleeting, and his failure to connect them with his statements about 'equality before the law' and the 'rule of law' is perplexing.

2. EQUALITY BEYOND LEGALITY

Looking beyond *The Law of the Constitution*, Dicey had a lot to say about equality, some of it commendable and some of it offensive. In this discussion, I focus on Dicey's views about race and racial equality. Dicey was (as he said) a mid-Victorian, but ideas about race were contested within Victorian society. The debate about race between Thomas Carlyle and John Stuart Mill in 1849, for example, took place against changing views about science, empire, and diverse cultures, and while Carlyle clearly represented a vicious conservative racism, it is debated whether Mill was also racist, if only in a polite liberal way.[15] The Carlyle-Mill debate was reignited in the

---

12 ibid., p. xxxvii, fn. 1.

13 ibid., pp. 115–16, fn. 2.

14 A.V. Dicey to Arthur Berriedale Keith, 1 May 1908, in R.F. Shinn and R.A. Cosgrove (eds.), *Constitutional Reflections: The Correspondence of Albert Venn Dicey and Arthur Berriedale Keith*, University Press of America Inc., Lanham 1996, pp. 25–26 ('*Dicey-Keith Correspondence*').

15 D.T. Goldberg, 'Liberalism's Limits: Carlyle and Mill on "The Negro Question"' (2000) 22 *Nineteenth Century Contexts* 203, 204; B. Schultz, 'Mill and Sidgwick, Imperialism and Racism' (2007) 19 *Utilitas* 104; G. Varouxakis, '"Negrophilist" Crusader: John Stuart Mill on the American Civil War and Reconstruction' (2013) 39 *History of European Ideas* 729.

mid-1860s during the Eyre controversy.[16] Mill led efforts by the Jamaica Committee to bring to justice the Governor of Jamaica, Edward Eyre, for his brutal treatment of Blacks after the Morant Bay uprising, and Carlyle rallied Eyre's defence. The contest reaffirmed the fractured nature of Victorian attitudes about race.[17] Popular opinion in Britain favoured Eyre, and indeed favoured the slave-owning southern states in the American civil war that had just ended.

There was, however, no question where Dicey stood on these issues. 'We were once credited with an ardent love for freedom, for justice, and for truth', he wrote in 1873, yet '[w]e have shown our love for freedom by applauding and aiding a body of slaveowners' and '[w]e have shown our love of justice by refusing even to try a colonial governor accused of oppression and murder'.[18] Dicey played a small role in the Eyre controversy, joining his cousins James Fitzjames Stephen and Leslie Stephen on the Jamaica Committee. One could say the Dicey-Stephen clan was carrying on a family tradition, for Dicey's grandfather, James Stephen, was part of the 'Clapham Sect' that campaigned against slavery in the British West Indies. Dicey's family had a powerful influence on his intellectual development and may have left him predisposed towards a certain commitment to equality.[19]

Even so, Dicey's approach to equality was frustratingly inconsistent. He supported votes for women, but then became an opponent. His book, *Letters to a Friend on Votes for Women*, reveals much about his approach to sex and equality, but it also provides an entry point into his views on race and equality. In *Letters to a Friend*, Dicey distinguished between 'civil or private rights' that everyone must enjoy equally and 'public or political rights' that might be distributed unequally for the good of the nation.[20] He then suggested that it might be unwise to extend political rights to those not practically able to wield political power, giving as an example the failure of the 'noble' experiment of extending the franchise to former slaves

---

16 See in general R.W. Kostal, *A Jurisprudence of Power: Victorian Empire and the Rule of Law*, Oxford University Press, Oxford 2005.

17 H.W. Fulweiler, 'The Strange Case of Governor Eyre: Race and the "Victorian Frame of Mind"' (2000) 29 *CLIO: Journal of Literature, History, and the Philosophy of History* 119.

18 A.V. Dicey, 'Louis Napoleon: 1851 and 1873' (1873) 13 *Fortnightly Review* 197, 203.

19 M.D. Walters, *A. V. Dicey and the Common Law Constitutional Tradition: A Legal Turn of Mind*, Cambridge University Press, Cambridge 2020, pp. 14–30 (on Dicey's family), 53–57 (on the Jamaica Committee).

20 A.V. Dicey, *Letters to a Friend on Votes for Women*, John Murray, London 1909, pp 31–32 ('*Letters to a Friend*').

after the American civil war.[21] The right of Blacks to vote in the United States had, he said, been reduced to a 'sham and a fraud'.[22]

Indeed, during the Jim Crow era, southern American states imposed measures that effectively eliminated African-Americans from the electoral rolls.[23] But did it follow that Blacks should not have been given the right to vote? On this point, Dicey relied upon the views of prominent African American leaders at the time. Even 'the most sagacious of the men of colour', he said, advocated securing 'civil' rights for former slaves before securing 'political' rights.[24] Worried that the comparison might offend his readers, however, Dicey then stated that he did not mean to suggest that 'English women' occupied 'anything like the position of ignorant and scarcely civilized negroes'.[25]

It is important to ask how this offensive language fits within Dicey's views about race, ethnicity, and culture. Returning to the 1915 footnote in *The Law of the Constitution*, in which he said that one could become a cabinet or prime minister no matter one's race or religion, Dicey went on to say that although it was 'true' that it was 'extremely improbable' that persons not 'in reality Englishmen by race' might ascend to high office, 'it is not wholly true'. Dicey welcomed the fact that members of racial minorities were elected to office. Dicey was critical of Lord Salisbury when, 'in an ill-fated moment', he referred to someone running for Parliament as a 'black gentleman'; '[h]e might have been black, yellow, or any other colour,' said Dicey, 'but, having been born within our dominions, [he] was a British subject'.[26] Dicey valued 'the sort of equality' (to use his expression from the 1915 footnote) that existed in Britain. As we shall see, he viewed with satisfaction the fact that subjects from India had been elected to Parliament.

But Dicey the mid-Victorian sometimes spoke in terms not easily understood today. In essays published in 1897 and 1898, he argued for the adoption of an 'isopolity', or dual citizenship for citizens of the United Kingdom and the United States, in order to advance the interests of the

---

21 ibid., p. 72.
22 ibid.
23 X. Wang, *The Trial of Democracy: Black Suffrage & Northern Republicans, 1860–1910*, University of Georgia Press, Athens 1997.
24 Dicey, *Letters to a Friend*, above n. 20, p. 73.
25 ibid.
26 A.V. Dicey, 'The Rights of English Citizens. I. – British Nationality' (1899) 6 *Working Men's College Journal* 144.

Anglo-Saxon race.[27] Common Anglo-American citizenship made sense, Dicey said, because 'the English-speaking peoples are destined in a century or two to become the dominant power through the civilized world', an ascendency due to the fact that both 'Englishmen and Americans' are 'profoundly influenced by the spirit of legalism' and are thus better prepared 'than Frenchmen or Germans to acquiesce in the judgment of a properly constituted tribunal: this, indeed, is the main point on which the Anglo-Saxon race has reached a stage of civilization to which other nations have hardly attained'.[28]

It has been argued that Dicey's essays on isopolity, taken together with private comments he made about the 'White Australia' immigration policy, betray sinister racist intentions, that Dicey dreamed of a white 'Angloworld'.[29] But there are reasons to doubt this reading. Dicey's contrast of the Anglo-Saxon race with the French and Germans suggests that by 'race' in this context he meant 'nation'. Furthermore, the Anglo-American isopolity he envisaged would have been a multi-racial one. Indeed, Dicey's isopolitan dream seems to have had a rather cosmopolitan character. He wrote:[30]

> The common citizenship which already prevails throughout the British Empire has brought, and has most rightly brought, into Parliament men who by race, language, and religion are far less closely connected with us than are the citizens of Massachusetts or of Illinois, and Englishmen may see not only with calmness but with satisfaction, natives of India take their seats at Westminster; but they surely may see with just as much calmness, and just as much satisfaction, a citizen of Vermont or Connecticut seated side by side with a Parsee or a Hindoo.

The problem for Dicey was that by the early twentieth century, the ideal of equality seemed to be slipping away in the Colonies. It was, he said, increasingly difficult 'to establish throughout the Empire that equal citizenship of all British subjects which exists in the United Kingdom and which Englishmen in the middle of the nineteenth century' – that is, mid-Victorians like him – 'hoped to see established through the length and

27 A.V. Dicey, 'A Common Citizenship for the English Race' (1897) 71 *Contemporary Review* 457 ('Common Citizenship'); A.V. Dicey, 'England and America' (1898) 82 *Atlantic Monthly* 441 ('England and America').

28 Dicey, 'England and America', above n. 27, 442, 444.

29 D. Bell, *Dreamworlds of Race: Empire and the Utopian Destiny of Anglo-America*, Princeton University Press, Princeton 2020, pp 261–72.

30 Dicey, 'Common Citizenship', above n. 27, 462.

breadth of the Empire'.[31] With racist South African laws in mind, Dicey observed that Britain was destined to become 'more and more responsible for injustice or hard treatment in respect of the natives of the Dominions which she has not really the power to forbid'.[32] For Dicey, imperialism was morally justified because it extended to the world the blessings of (English) legalism.[33] The seeming impossibility of securing legal equality between diverse peoples in the Colonies was thus a point of deep personal regret for him: 'the satisfaction in the maintenance of the Empire', he said, '[is] lessened by the fact that we cannot ensure throughout its length & breadth the equal citizenship of all British subjects';[34] the failure of equal citizenship 'damps my enthusiasm as an Imperialist'.[35] Far from pushing for a white Angloworld, Dicey's private expression of understanding for the racial restrictions on immigration adopted by Australia in 1901 was given, he said, '[g]reatly against my will & what one may call one's natural prejudices'.[36] A few years later, Dicey rediscovered his natural prejudice toward equality and, as we have seen, criticised the Transvaal law restricting immigration of Asian subjects.

Dicey did not think the Anglo-Saxon race was superior to other races, but he clearly thought that its culture or civilisation was. Like most Victorians, he distiguished between civilised and uncivilised peoples. A civilised society, he wrote, has 'passed beyond the stage of progress during which men are occupied wholly or principally in what may strictly be called the struggle for existence' and has developed arts, sciences, literature, and politics.[37] His derogatory reference to the 'Cherokee Indian' in *The Law of the Constitution* reflects attitudes about culture that were, sadly, on full display in the case law of the time.[38] But Dicey also thought that imperial

---

31 Dicey, *The Law of the Constitution*, above n. 1, p. xxxvii.

32 Dicey to Keith, 6 July 1914, *Dicey-Keith Correspondence*, above n. 14, pp. 133–34.

33 D. Lino, 'The Rule of Law and the Rule of Empire: A.V. Dicey in Imperial Context' (2018) 81 *Modern Law Review* 739; K. Sharma, 'The Rule of Law and Racial Difference in the British Empire' in S. Wheatle and E. O'Loughlin (eds.), *Diverse Voices in Public Law*, Bristol University Press, Bristol 2023, pp. 15–34.

34 Dicey to Keith, 16 June 1914, *Dicey-Keith Correspondence*, above n. 14, pp. 124–25.

35 Dicey to Keith, 3 June 1914, *Dicey-Keith Correspondence*, above n. 14, pp. 116–17.

36 Dicey to Bryce, 16 May 1902, *Bryce Papers* 3, above n. 2, pp. 13–16.

37 A.V. Dicey, 'Ancient Constitutionalism and Modern Constitutionalism' in J.W.F. Allison (ed.), *The Oxford Edition of Dicey*, vol. 2, Oxford University Press, Oxford 2013, pp. 196–97.

38 Dicey, *The Law of the Constitution*, above n. 1, p. 17. cf. *R. v St. Catharines Milling and Lumber Company* (1885) 10 OR 196 (HC), (1886) 13 OAR 148 (CA), (1887) 13 SCR 577, (1888) 14 App Cas 46 (JCPC) on the rights of Indigenous peoples in Canada.

authorities needed to intervene within colonies to act as 'protector of the rights of natives of Eastern and of more or less uncivilised countries' from settlers and their local governments.[39] His offensive reference to 'scarcely civilized' Blacks in the American South found in *Letters to a Friend* may be seen as a product of this mixing of cultural arrogance and paternalistic concern. For Dicey, civilisation meant respecting diversity. The persecution of Jews in certain European countries was, he said, a form of 'barbarism',[40] an 'offence against civilisation'.[41] The enslavement of Africans was 'a disgrace to civilization'.[42] But civilisation implied a kind of superiority too. He spoke of 'the generous enthusiasm for raising backward races of the world, such as the negroes of America, to a position of freedom and equality', a 'public virtue' that he feared was in decline.[43]

Dicey connected the decline in public virtue with the rise of white supremacist sentiment in the United States. An article in the journal *Nineteenth Century* in 1899 that advocated racial segregation and claimed Blacks were 'inferior' and subject to the 'rule of the white man', was, Dicey said, 'as wicked a thing as I ever read'.[44] An article in *The Spectator* in 1901, criticising President Theodore Roosevelt for inviting Booker T. Washington to dine at the White House on the grounds that '[t]he white men should be acknowledged by the black men as the superior caste', prompted Dicey to ask the editor if he could publish a response, for the article:

> lays down a doctrine which if true is as applicable to the Cape [that is, South Africa] as to S. Carolina & which if once accepted, will bring to the ground the strongest of the moral justifications for the destruction of the Boer Republic.[45]

---

39 Dicey to Keith, 27 June 1914, *Dicey-Keith Correspondence*, above n. 14, pp. 131–32.

40 A.V. Dicey, 'Introduction' in L. Wolf (ed.), *The Legal Sufferings of the Jews in Russia: A Survey of Their Present Situation and a Summary of Laws*, T. Fisher Unwin, London 1912, p. i.

41 A.V. Dicey, 'Russian Intolerance, and the Duty of Liberals' (1882) 2796 *The Spectator* 11.

42 A.V. Dicey, *Lectures on the Relation Between Law and Public Opinion in England During the Nineteenth Century*, 2nd ed., Macmillan & Co., London 1914, p. 461, fn. 2 ('*Law and Public Opinion*').

43 ibid., pp. lvii–lviii.

44 E.L. Banks, 'The American Negro and His Place' (1899) 46 *The Nineteenth Century* 459, 461–62; A.V. Dicey to Charles E. Norton, 3 September 1899, Charles Eliot Norton Papers, Houghton Library, Harvard University, MS. Am. 1088.14, no. 1745.

45 Anon., 'The Negro Problem in America' (1901) 87 *The Spectator* 595; A.V. Dicey to John St. Loe Strachey, 31 October 1901, John St. Loe Strachey Papers, UK Parliamentary Archives, STR 5/5/9 ('*Strachey Papers*').

Booker T. Washington was a leading African American spokesperson of the day and his visit to the White House sparked outrage in the South.[46] Dicey had met Theodore Roosevelt a few years earlier and was not impressed – Roosevelt had acted like 'an overgrown schoolboy'.[47] But Dicey's opinion of Roosevelt changed due to his 'admirable' decision to invite Washington to the White House.[48] Said Dicey, inviting 'a gentleman of colour to dinner' would not 'make up for [the] outrages in the South', but it signalled an intention to protect the rights of Blacks.[49] Dicey's reference, in *Letters to a Friend*, to the 'most sagacious of the men of colour' who advised against pressing for Black political rights before civil rights were secured was likely a reference to Booker T. Washington, for Washington had advocated this strategy.[50]

Dicey's views about race were developed in an essay, published in the American periodical *The Nation*, in which he criticised his friend James Bryce for advocating for racial segregation and against interracial marriage in order to protect the purity of the blood of civilised or advanced peoples.[51] Dicey rejected Bryce's claim about the link between racial purity and civilisation, and he rejected racial segregation imposed by law. While the law could not compel friendly relations between races, nor should it mandate their separation. Dicey acknowledged that '[t]he line between social and legal equality is in truth hard to draw' and he conceded that '[t]he formal recognition of equal legal rights when the real enjoyment thereof is denied, increases instead of lessen[s] the irritation of the race which suffers from its denial'.[52] However, the denial of legal equality through legislating racial segregation would be far worse. Wrote Dicey, '[r]igid separation fosters that very pride of race and that contempt for men who, on the ground of color, are counted as inferiors, which statesmanship and humanity alike wish to remove'.[53] 'The dogma of human equality, in

---

46 D. Davis, *Guest of Honor: Booker T. Washington, Theodore Roosevelt, and the White House Dinner That Shocked a Nation*, Atria, New York 2012.

47 A.V. Dicey to James Bryce, 29 December 1899, *Bryce Papers* 2, above n. 2, pp. 276–82.

48 A.V. Dicey to Charles Eliot, 27 December 1901, Charles W. Eliot Papers, Harvard University Archives, UAI 5.150, Box 36.

49 A.V. Dicey to John St. Loe Strachey, 4 November 1901, *Strachey Papers*, above n. 45, STR 5/5/9.

50 R.J. Norrell, *Up from History: The Life of Booker T. Washington*, Belknap Press of Harvard University Press, Cambridge 2009, p 124.

51 A.V. Dicey, 'Mr. Bryce on the Relation Between Whites and Blacks' (10 Jul. 1902) 75 *Nation* 26.

52 ibid., 26.

53 ibid., 28.

the only sense in which it can be entertained at all by any reasonable man, is the cornerstone of democratic government', Dicey continued, and:

> every supporter of democratic institutions does believe and feel that, from a political point of view, the characteristics which men have in common are of far more importance than the features, marked though they may be, in which they differ from one another.[54]

Although these observations on democracy and equality suggest a broader political theory of equality, Dicey never really developed that theory fully in his writing. On the one hand, he applauded Jeremy Bentham for rejecting talk of 'natural rights' or broad declarations that 'men are born and remain free and equal' associated with French 'revolutionary dogmatism'.[55] On the other hand, he acknowledged that Bentham's utilitarianism had its own 'rigid dogmas' and that many of Bentham's ideas came to dominate political discourse only in a 'loose' and 'common sense' way 'under the name of liberalism'.[56] Dicey concluded that the resulting 'individualistic liberalism' that emerged in the first half of the nineteenth century helped society to focus on the shared humanity of different races; although the abolition of slavery was required 'by the principle of utility' and 'by the conscience of mankind', the cause of abolition was 'strengthened by an unswerving faith in the essential similarity and equality of all human beings whether blacks or whites'.[57] Whatever its full theoretical justification, this liberal theory of equality aimed at securing equal legal, civil, and ultimately political rights, though Dicey appreciated that over time, democracy might lead to increased calls for social equality, or the view '[that] equality of rights also conferred equality of social advantages' – or 'socialism' as opposed to 'liberalism'.[58] Of course, Dicey himself would always stick closely to liberalism and a liberal theory of equality.

3. LEGALITY AND EQUALITY REVISITED

This analysis shows clearly that Dicey recognised a substantive conception of equality that firmly embraced a conception of racial equality. Although

54 ibid., 28.
55 Dicey, *Law and Public Opinion*, above n. 42, pp. 171–72.
56 ibid., pp. 169–70, 171.
57 ibid., p. 461.
58 A.V. Dicey, 'England in 1848' (1920) 234 *Quarterly Review* 221, 232.

he held views now considered morally offensive, he also asserted ideas that are recognisable as forming the core of today's conception of equality as a human right. We return, then, to the question of whether he saw a connection between this kind of equality and the 'equality before the law' that forms an integral part of his account of the 'rule of law'.

The answer suggested by the materials already examined is that when Dicey spoke of 'legal equality' between races he had in mind the 'legal equality' contemplated by the rule of law. Sometimes he made this connection clear. Returning to the Eyre controversy, for example, the Jamaica Committee did score one important legal victory – the denunciation of Eyre's conduct by the Lord Chief Justice, Sir Alexander Cockburn, in a charge to a grand jury in one of the unsuccessful prosecutions of Eyre.[59] In a tribute to Cockburn written after his death, Dicey stated that '[n]o impartial man can now doubt' that Eyre's actions against Blacks in the Colony 'ought to have been investigated by a criminal court', and '[n]o impartial man can doubt that the reason why no such investigation took place was that English juries were not prepared to administer the law equally between whites and blacks'; it was thus the 'great duty' of the judge to 'exert all his influence to insure that law should be respected throughout the length and breadth of the British dominions', and this duty Cockburn had performed by exhibiting 'the leanings and salutary prejudices, so to speak, of an English judge … in favour of individual freedom, and an unconquerable suspicion of every form of legalized lawlessness'.[60] Even if the terms were not used, this is a striking statement about 'equality before the law' and 'the rule of law' and their relationship to racial equality.

Dicey made these connections even more explicitly in his reaction to the so-called Ilbert Bill controversy in 1883. The Ilbert Bill, a bill drafted by Sir Courtenay Peregrine Ilbert for the Legislative Council for India, would have given Indian magistrates criminal jurisdiction over Europeans, and this provoked outrage in India and Britain.[61] Dicey wrote:[62]

> The whole agitation against Mr. Ilbert's bill is as worth attention as anything which has taken place in England for the last twenty years. It is not a mere

---

59 F. Cockburn (ed.), *Charge of the Lord Chief Justice of England to the Grand Jury at the Central Criminal Court in the Case of the Queen Against Nelson and Brand*, William Ridgway, London 1867.

60 A.V. Dicey, 'Sir Alexander Cockburn' (1881) 10 *International Review* 397, 410.

61 E. Hirschmann, *"White Mutiny": The Ilbert Bill Crisis in India and the Genesis of the Indian National Congress*, South Asia Books, Columbia 1980.

62 A.V. Dicey, 'The Prevalence of Lawlessness in England' (2 Aug. 1883) 37 *Nation* 95.

> protest against the details of a given piece of legislation; it is admittedly a protest against the idea that all classes of British subjects ought so far as possible to be insured equal rights before the law. It is impossible not to see that something far more is at stake than the question whether one or two native magistrates shall have jurisdiction over Europeans. The true point at issue is, whether our government of India shall or shall not be carried on upon the principle that a native of Bengal is as truly a British subject as a native of Middlesex, and that the aim of our English rule should be ultimately to place all subjects of the Queen in a position of legal equality. Whenever this is accomplished the rule of law will prevail throughout the whole British Empire. Meanwhile, the Conservatives of to-day boldly assert not only that our rule in India does rest, but that it ought avowedly to be made to rest, upon force, upon privilege, upon that kind of permanent inequality of classes which is absolutely opposed to the true supremacy of legality, which is but another name for systematic justice.

This is a powerful, unequivocal statement on the connection between equality before the law, the rule of law, and equality of members of racial (and ethnic and religious) communities. If we read Dicey's passages on the rule of law written only a few years later in *The Law of the Constitution* through the lens of this statement, the claim that we considered at the outset of this contribution – that Dicey's equality before the law was formalistic or empty – must be reconsidered.

It may still be said in response that even if the rule of law protects substantive human rights to equality, it remains formal or thin in the sense that, on Dicey's account of the constitution, Parliament may exercise its legislative sovereignty to enact unequal laws which courts are bound to enforce. This response shifts our attention from the question about what the rule of law is to the question about how it relates to the principle of parliamentary sovereignty. It is important to understand, however, that there is a profound difference of constitutional principle between saying, on the one hand, that a statute which discriminates on the basis of race does not violate the rule of law because 'equality before the law' refers to a formal, as opposed to a substantive, conception of equality, and saying, on the other hand, that such a statute does violate the rule of law because 'equality before the law' refers to a substantive conception of equality, though given the doctrine of parliamentary sovereignty, the statute is still legally valid.

Once it is established that Dicey's *The Law of the Constitution* is properly read as adopting this second, more robust, understanding of the rule of law, then all of the powerful interpretive imperatives that Dicey himself associates with the 'spirit of legality' or 'the general spirit of the common law' that mandate reading laws and the powers they confer consistently with the rule of law come into play to protect the fundamental human right to equality.[63] In this contribution, I have focused on Dicey's second rule-of-law point about equality before the law. Although beyond the scope of this contribution, one would, at this point, wish to bring back into the analysis Dicey's first point about non-arbitrariness and his third point about the importance of ordinary common law method, and then to consider the possibility of a more holistic understanding of his rule of law and equality.

I will close by connecting two unlikely allies to Dicey's cause as a way of illustrating what this holistic account might entail.[64] The seventeenth-century judge, John Doderidge, stated that common law reasoning is a sort of interpretive oscillation between law 'in *concreto*' and law 'in *abstracto*', and the 'unwritten law' identified through this interpretive ascent and descent secures 'equality of reason'.[65] In an early iteration of the idea of 'reflective equilibrium' at the centre of his theory of justice, the twentieth-century philosopher John Rawls argued that through moral reasoning aimed at refining the articulation of specific and general to ensure consistency, everyone is treated as a moral equal, just as 'in the parallel case at law' it is said that 'all men shall be equal before the law'.[66] Threading substantive conceptions of equality through an interpretive process dedicated to an equality of reason, the kind of moral reasoning found in common law reasoning, the full normative potential for Dicey's idea of 'equality before the law' begins to take shape, and it can be seen how the equal concern for the moral worth of everyone, no matter their differences, animates a spirit of legality that brings the rule of law to life.

---

63 Dicey, *The Law of the Constitution*, above n. 1, p. 409.

64 For a more detailed account, see Walters, above n. 19, pp. 259–98, 358–77. For another account with similar results, see Allan, above n. 9, pp. 19–20.

65 J. Doderidge, *The English Lawyer, Describing A Method for the managing of the Lawes of this Land*, I More, London 1631, pp. 190, 210, 237, 241, 268, 270.

66 J. Rawls, 'Outline of a Decision Procedure for Ethics' (1951) 60 *Philosophical Review* 177, 178, 182, 184, 186, 192. In general, see J. Rawls, *A Theory of Justice*, Belknap Press of Harvard University Press, Cambridge 1971.

DICEY, PARLIAMENTARY SOVEREIGNTY, AND THE PRINCIPLE OF LEGALITY

Hasan DINDJER*

1. INTRODUCTION

Dicey's account of parliamentary sovereignty is not exactly a neglected aspect of his work. Nevertheless, it bears revisiting. To see why, it will be instructive to bring Dicey's account into contact with two recent developments in UK constitutional law.

The first development is a cluster of cases decided by the Supreme Court that endorse, or appear to endorse, a revisionary understanding of parliamentary sovereignty. According to this understanding, Parliament's sovereignty is encroached on where Parliament is subject to certain kinds of practical pressure in legislating, and where courts interpret statutes by reference to considerations other than the intentions of Parliament.

The second development is the growing role played by the interpretive approach known as the 'principle of legality'.[1] The principle holds that

---

* For discussion of the issues in this contribution I thank Tom Adams, Joshua Getzler, Jeffrey Goldsworthy, Fred Wilmot-Smith, Robert Stevens, Mark D. Walters, Alison Young, attendees at the Dicey + 100 conference, and the editors of this volume.

1 See e.g., *R. v Secretary of State for the Home Department, ex parte Simms* [2000] 2 AC 115 (HL).

statutes are to be interpreted so as to be compatible with certain basic constitutional norms, unless they contain especially clear words to the contrary. Judicial reasoning in this vein is hardly new,[2] but the principle has been deployed to particularly striking effect in several recent cases,[3] and has emerged as among the most potent and distinctive judicial techniques in contemporary public law.

These two developments stand in tension. The principle of legality is not well characterised as being limited to divining legislative intentions, and it inevitably exerts pressure on Parliament to legislate compatibly with fundamental constitutional principles. If the Supreme Court's recent, revisionary approach to parliamentary sovereignty is sound, the principle of legality rests on unstable foundations.

That implication can be resisted, and the tension dissolved, by rejecting the revisionary approach to parliamentary sovereignty. That is the route I will take. Parliamentary sovereignty is not a doctrine that requires Parliament to be unencumbered by practical pressures, nor one that mandates a particular, controversial theory of statutory interpretation. In its recent pronouncements, the Supreme Court has, in short, deviated from the Diceyan conception of parliamentary sovereignty it claims to embrace.[4]

2. DICEY'S CONCEPTION OF PARLIAMENTARY SOVEREIGNTY

As is well known, Dicey said that parliamentary sovereignty 'means neither more nor less' than that Parliament has 'the right to make or unmake any law whatever' and that 'no person or body is recognised by the law of England as having a right to override or set aside the legislation of Parliament'.[5] The first limb, which Dicey called the positive aspect, and

---

2 See e.g., *Dr Bonham's Case* (1608) 8 Co Rep 107a, 77 ER 638; (1609) 8 Co Rep 113b, 77 ER 646.

3 *R. (Evans) v Attorney General* [2015] UKSC 21, [2015] AC 1787; *R. (Privacy International) v Investigatory Powers Tribunal* [2019] UKSC 22, [2020] AC 491; *R. (Miller) v Prime Minister* [2019] UKSC 41, [2020] AC 373, 2 ('*Miller No. 2*').

4 In pursuing this argument, I do not treat Dicey as any kind of authority, but as a theorist whose views on parliamentary sovereignty are in some respects attractive, and which continue to represent the law. For some indication of the (many) unattractive features of Dicey's thought, see e.g., D. Lino, 'The Rule of Law and the Rule of Empire: A.V. Dicey in Imperial Context' (2018) 81 *Modern Law Review* 739.

5 A.V. Dicey, *Lectures Introductory to the Study of the Law of the Constitution*, J.W.F. Allison (ed.), Oxford University Press, Oxford 2013, p. 28 ('*The Law of the Constitution*').

which we might also call the *plenary authority* principle, concerns the scope of Parliament's power. The second, which Dicey called the negative aspect, we might also call the *legal supremacy* principle: it concerns the legal effects of Parliament's exercise of legislative authority.

Dicey's account is now the official position of the Supreme Court. In *Miller No. 1*, the majority cited Dicey's formulation in holding that parliamentary sovereignty was a 'fundamental principle' of the UK constitution that was 'conclusively established'.[6] Lord Reed's dissent in *Privacy International* again cited Dicey's account, noting that it had been common ground between the majority and minority in *Miller No. 1*.[7]

The question is how this understanding of the principle has fared in practice more recently. I shall not consider *Miller No. 2*, whose approach to parliamentary sovereignty I have previously argued is not only justified, but follows naturally from Diceyan premises.[8] Instead, I shall focus on two recent cases decided unanimously by the Supreme Court, both of whose sole judgments were delivered by Lord Reed.

3. THE SUPREME COURT'S REVISIONARY VIEW OF PARLIAMENTARY SOVEREIGNTY

In *Elan-Cane*, the question was whether Article 8 of the ECHR (right to a private life), taken alone or together with Article 14 (right against discrimination), required the Home Secretary to issue 'X' passports to those, like the claimant, who identified as having no gender.[9] The claimant's appeal was unanimously dismissed. Central to the Court's reasoning was the proposition that since the Strasbourg court would treat the government's

6 *R. (Miller) v Secretary of State for Exiting the European Union* [2017] UKSC 5, [2018] AC 61, [43] ('*Miller No. 1*').

7 *Privacy International*, above n. 3, [209].

8 See H. Dindjer, 'Prorogation as a Breach of Parliamentary Sovereignty', *UK Constitutional Law Blog* (16 September 2019) <https://ukconstitutionallaw.org/2019/09/16/hasan-dindjer-prorogation-as-a-breach-of-parliamentary-sovereignty/>. The Court here repeated a similar formulation of parliamentary sovereignty to that endorsed in *Miller No. 1*, above n. 6. See *Miller No. 2*, above n. 3, [41]–[42]. It omitted explicit mention of the plenary authority principle, but it must have had it in mind in concluding at [42] that parliamentary sovereignty would be undermined if the executive could 'prevent Parliament from exercising its legislative authority for as long as it pleased'.

9 *R. (Elan-Cane) v Secretary of State for the Home Department* [2021] UKSC 56, [2022] 2 WLR 133.

policy as within the UK's margin of appreciation under the Convention, it followed that the policy complied with the Human Rights Act.

The inference is not inevitable. In the earlier case of *Re G*, which held that the ban on unmarried couples adopting in Northern Ireland was contrary to Articles 8 and 14, the House of Lords had rejected just this logic.[10] It insisted instead on conceptual space between Convention rights as a matter of international law and the meaning of the corresponding rights protected as a matter of domestic law under the HRA, which a domestic court had to elaborate according to 'what it considers to be a principled and rational interpretation'.[11] In *Elan-Cane*, Lord Reed characterised this view in *Re G* as merely obiter.[12] More strikingly for our purposes, he argued that the view expressed in *Re G*, if adopted, would represent a 'significant encroachment on the principle of Parliamentary sovereignty'.[13]

This was, he thought, because of its combined effect with section 3 of the HRA, which requires legislation to be read compatibly with the Convention rights 'so far as it is possible to do so', and which has been understood to require interpretations which Parliament may not have intended. Thus, non-intentionalist interpretation is called for by section 3 quite apart from the *Re G* approach. But Lord Reed thought non-intentionalist interpretation to ensure compatibility *with domestic courts' own interpretation of Convention rights* 'would go considerably further' than non-intentionalist interpretation *to ensure compatibility with international law* (i.e. Strasbourg's authoritative interpretation).[14]

10 *In re G (Adoption: Unmarried Couple)* [2008] UKHL 38, [2009] 1 AC 173.

11 ibid., [38] (Lord Hoffmann).

12 This seems more doubtful than Lord Reed suggests. Lord Hoffmann's conclusion in the text referred to his own assessment, reached prior to considering the Strasbourg jurisprudence directly on point, that the ban lacked a rational basis: [20]. Although he considered it 'not at all unlikely' that the Strasbourg court would agree with his assessment (at [27]), he went on to hold, after substantial discussion of the point, that it 'should make no difference' (at [30]) whether his favoured interpretation went further than Strasbourg would go. Baroness Hale, after a review of the authorities, said she was 'unsure' whether Strasbourg would regard the position in Northern Ireland as within the UK's margin of appreciation (at [115]), but that 'if the matter is within the margin of appreciation which Strasbourg would allow to us, then we have to form our own judgment' (at [120]). Lord Mance agreed both with (what he saw as) Lord Hoffmann's assessment that the ban would likely be held incompatible by Strasbourg and his view that even if it would not, it should be held incompatible by the House of Lords: [125]–[126]. He then proceeded to develop the point that '[t]he meaning of the new domestic rights scheduled to the 1998 Act is a matter of domestic law' (at [129]). Lord Hope, the remaining member of the majority, placed less emphasis on the domestic courts' own assessment, but also said he agreed with Lord Hoffmann: [56].

13 *Elan-Cane*, above n. 9, [90].

14 ibid.

Is this conclusion sound? It is difficult to understand why this distinction should have the significance Lord Reed attributes to it. From the perspective of parliamentary sovereignty, it can surely make no difference whether legislation is being interpreted in accordance with international law as determined by an international court, or in accordance with a national court's own elaboration of rights protected in international law and given effect in domestic law. Parliamentary sovereignty has no special connection with international law. Moreover, as a matter of Diceyan principle, the *Re G* approach does not offend plenary authority (since it leaves Parliament free to legislate as it wishes) or legal supremacy (since Parliament is free to abolish or disapply the interpretive approach). We return to these points later.

Lord Reed's fundamental concern may have been to do with non-intentionalist interpretation more generally. That impression is supported by the next case, *UNCRC*.[15] It concerned two Bills passed by the Scottish Parliament which sought to incorporate, respectively, the UN Convention on the Rights of the Child and the European Charter on Local Self-Government. The issue was whether these Bills were within the powers granted to the Scottish Parliament by the Scotland Act 1998. This depended, inter alia, on whether they would have modified the 'power of the Parliament of the United Kingdom to make laws for Scotland' as guaranteed in section 28(7) of the Scotland Act. The Supreme Court held that certain provisions of the two Bills would modify Westminster's law-making power and were, therefore, outside the competence of the Scottish Parliament. Two types of provision which were held to fall foul of that constraint are important for our purposes.

First, the Bills would have imposed requirements to read certain legislation affecting Scotland, including legislation passed by the UK Parliament, compatibly with the treaties. These were analogous provisions to section 3 of the HRA and were meant to require interpretations that might not accord with Parliament's intended meaning. According to Lord Reed, because the provisions would produce results Parliament did not intend, they would require the courts to 'modify the meaning and effect of Acts of Parliament' and so 'plainly impose a qualification on [Parliament's] legislative power'.[16] The tacit premise is that a statute's legal effect is limited to what Parliament intended.

---

15 *In re United Nations Convention on the Rights of the Child (Incorporation) (Scotland) Bill* [2021] UKSC 42, [2021] 1 WLR 5106.

16 ibid., [28].

Second, the Bills would have allowed courts to declare certain future legislation affecting Scotland, including legislation passed by the UK Parliament, to be incompatible with the international treaties. As under section 4 of the HRA, such declarations did not purport to affect the validity or bindingness of the statutes declared incompatible.[17] The Supreme Court objected to these provisions on several grounds. Most important for present purposes was the argument that, 'since [they] would impose pressure on Parliament to avoid the opprobrium which such a finding would entail', they 'plainly affect[ed] Parliament's power to make laws for Scotland'.[18]

Although Lord Reed's analysis on both points is, strictly speaking, addressed to the question of whether the provisions modify the 'power' of Parliament 'to make laws for Scotland', the context of Lord Reed's discussion strongly suggests he also took the provisions to be incompatible with parliamentary sovereignty. For example, in the context of discussing the declarative provisions, he claimed that section 4 of the HRA itself constituted a qualification of parliamentary sovereignty, albeit one imposed by Parliament.[19] Two propositions, therefore, emerge from these cases. First, parliamentary sovereignty is held to require that the legal effect of statutes is all and only what Parliament intended. Second, the Court maintains that imposing pressure on Parliament to avoid opprobrium encroaches on parliamentary sovereignty.

4. THE PRINCIPLE OF LEGALITY

I want to put some pressure on these propositions and to consider what they might imply or portend for the principle of legality. That principle holds that Parliament is only taken to abrogate, or authorise the abrogation of, certain fundamental constitutional norms if it uses especially clear statutory language to do so. It has been used to protect common law rights,[20] access to the courts,[21] and the rule of law more widely.[22] I shall therefore refer to 'norms' rather than only 'rights'.[23]

---

17 The Court also held that the Bills' backward-looking declarative provisions, which were much stronger than s. 4 of the HRA, exceeded the Scottish Parliament's competence: see ibid., [37]–[46].

18 ibid., [52].

19 ibid., [50]. See also [29] where the link to parliamentary sovereignty is made.

20 See e.g., *Simms*, above n. 1; *R. v Secretary of State for the Home Department, ex p Daly* [2001] 2 AC 532 (HL).

21 See e.g., *R. (UNISON) v Lord Chancellor* [2017] UKSC 51, [2020] AC 869; *Privacy International*, above n. 3.

The principle is threatened by the recent account of parliamentary sovereignty. In the first place, the principle's operation often seems strained if viewed as a narrow exercise in discerning Parliament's intentions. *Privacy International* offers the most vivid example.[24] Section 67(8) of the Regulation of Investigatory Powers Act 2000 provided in relevant part that 'determinations, awards, orders and other decisions of the [Investigatory Powers] Tribunal (including decisions as to whether they have jurisdiction) shall not be subject to appeal or be liable to be questioned in any court'. By a majority, the Supreme Court held that this did not oust the jurisdiction of the High Court, because Parliament failed to use sufficiently clear words. The majority held that, in light of the courts' hostility to ouster clauses expressed in *Anisminic*[25] and subsequently, if Parliament had sought to oust the High Court it should have excluded review of, for example, 'purported' determinations.[26] Notably, Lord Carnwath's judgment (with which Lady Hale and Lord Kerr agreed) suggests that the legal effect of a statute does not depend on whether it comports with a 'likely interpretation of Parliament's intentions' if Parliament 'has failed to make its intention sufficiently clear'.[27] This is difficult to reconcile with the suggestion that parliamentary sovereignty necessitates the implementation of Parliament's intentions.

It might be said in response that Parliament's intention is an 'objective' matter, equivalent to what Parliament is reasonably taken to have intended, or else the meaning that results from correctly applying relevant interpretive doctrines to its words. It might, therefore, be said that even an approach such as Lord Carnwath's will pick out Parliament's intentions, properly understood. This would, of course, be to employ 'intention' in a stipulative, fictional sense. What someone intends is not identical to what others (reasonably or otherwise) take them to intend, any more than what someone believes or desires is identical to what others take them to believe or desire. In any event, objectifying 'intention' reframes but does not resolve the original tension. For now there is a conflict between what Parliament

22 See e.g., *Evans*, above n. 3.

23 I do not mean thereby to claim that every principle or value underlying the constitution is, or ought to be, protected by the principle of legality.

24 *Privacy International*, above n. 3.

25 *Anisminic v Foreign Compensation Commission* [1969] 2 AC 147 (HL).

26 *Privacy International*, above n. 3, [111], [164].

27 ibid., [111] (here referring to a materially similar predecessor statute). Lord Lloyd-Jones's concurring judgment, which agreed with the plurality's conclusion on the effect of s. 67(8), is more ambiguous on the question of legislative intent: see [164]–[166].

'subjectively' (actually) intends and what it 'objectively' (fictively) intends or is taken to intend. That such a tension is possible is presupposed by the Supreme Court's suggestion that interpretive rules, such as section 3 of the HRA, depart from Parliament's intentions. And just the same kind of conflict is at issue where the principle of legality results in a statute having a legal effect even if that effect is not a 'likely interpretation of Parliament's intentions'.

A second way in which the new view of parliamentary sovereignty poses a problem for the principle of legality is that the principle undoubtedly exerts practical pressure on Parliament. For if Parliament wishes to abrogate fundamental rights or constitutional norms, it can only do so explicitly, and must therefore, as Lord Hoffmann put it in *Simms*, 'squarely confront what it is doing and accept the political cost'.[28] Parliament as a whole may bear this cost, and there is also the cost, or risk, borne by the government seeking to steer a Bill through Parliament. In *Privacy International*, Lord Carnwath speculated that a more explicit ouster clause 'might not have been expected to survive Parliamentary scrutiny'.[29]

5. DISSOLVING THE TENSION

The tension, then, between the revisionary view of parliamentary sovereignty and the principle of legality, is real. But we should, I propose, reject the revisionary view of sovereignty that gives rise to it. It is a mistake to think that parliamentary sovereignty requires a Parliament free of practical pressures on the way it exercises its legislative power.[30] There is nothing in the Diceyan view of sovereignty elsewhere endorsed by the courts which suggests this. Neither plenary authority nor legal supremacy has anything to say about it. Parliamentary sovereignty is not a doctrine about the practical ease of legislating or the pressure to legislate. If it were, it would imply that Parliament becomes less sovereign as Bills become less popular, or as newspapers urge legal reform. Courts' judgments, too, can have implications for political life: they can affect parties' reputations, inspire political opposition, uncover lacunae in the law, bring media

---

28 *Simms*, above n. 1, 131E–F.

29 *Privacy International*, above n. 3, [111].

30 It does not follow that it is permissible to deny Parliament meaningful opportunities to exercise that power at all, as I have argued previously: see Dindjer, above n. 8. Long prorogations threaten the plenary authority principle; ordinary political or pragmatic pressures on what law Parliament makes do not.

attention to an issue, and so on. Courts are, in these ways, inevitably political as well as strictly legal actors, in effect if not by design. But such effects do not change the legal reality of Parliament's sovereignty, any more than do protests outside Westminster or the critical words of a UN special rapporteur. This is not to deny that we can intelligibly speak of 'sovereignty' in some political sense that is wider than its legal sense. Dicey noted that there were many 'obviously unwise or tyrannical' enactments that Parliament 'never would and (to speak plainly) never could pass',[31] but that did not touch the question of its legal sovereignty.[32]

Moreover, it is a mistake to view parliamentary sovereignty as requiring that the legal effect of a statute be all and only what Parliament intended. Once again, there is nothing in the plenary authority or legal supremacy principles, elsewhere endorsed by the courts, that would require such an inference. Indeed, it is clearly possible to affirm the doctrine of parliamentary sovereignty but to be a sceptic about the very idea of legislative intention. Before his appointment to the Supreme Court, Andrew Burrows argued that talk of legislative intention was 'an unhelpful fiction or mask that should be avoided altogether'; he did not thereby become a sceptic about parliamentary sovereignty.[33] Parliamentary sovereignty is consistent with a range of views about statutory interpretation: the textualist is not therefore a denier of parliamentary sovereignty; nor is the pluralist, who says that legislative intentions, but not only legislative intentions, matter in determining the legal effect of statutes. Parliamentary sovereignty gives Acts of Parliament the highest position in the legal hierarchy, but it does not settle how marks on a page – the words used in statutes – contribute to the content of the law.[34]

These points open up space to construe the principle of legality robustly. While the principle can often be fairly understood as a heuristic by which courts discern Parliament's intentions, I shall suggest it is also justified in part by non-intentionalist arguments, so that it can be justifiably deployed even if the result diverges from the meaning Parliament was most likely to have intended. Where might such a non-intentionalist justification lie?

---

31 Dicey, *The Law of the Constitution*, above n. 5, p. 42.

32 ibid., p. 191.

33 A.S. Burrows, *Thinking about Statutes: Interpretation, Interaction, Improvement*, Cambridge University Press, Cambridge 2018, pp. 17–18.

34 On which there are a range of possible views: see M. Greenberg, 'Legislation as Communication? Legal Interpretation and the Study of Linguistic Communication' in A. Marmor and S. Soames (eds.), *Philosophical Foundations of Language in the Law*, Oxford University Press, Oxford 2011.

Let us return to *Simms* and consider Lord Hoffmann's dictum more fully. He said:[35]

> The principle of legality means that Parliament must squarely confront what it is doing and accept the political cost. Fundamental rights cannot be overridden by general or ambiguous words. This is because there is too great a risk that the full implications of their unqualified meaning may have passed unnoticed in the democratic process.

This passage gives two quite different justifications for the principle of legality. The second, that the implications of a statute might be missed without explicit words, is ultimately rooted in legislative intent, at least of the counterfactual kind. The suggestion appears to be that the principle of legality prevents statutes unwittingly having an effect that Parliament would have opposed had it understood the statute's implications. It can be understood as a way of responding to 'legislative blind spots'.[36]

Yet Lord Hoffmann's first point, that Parliament must be open about its decisions and accept their political costs, is not intentionalist. It might be developed in several ways. According to the first, *reasoned justification*, argument, the government, and Members of Parliament generally, ought to offer reasoned public justifications for their actions, especially where fundamental rights or other constitutional norms are at stake. This is essentially a requirement of public justification. According to the second, *accountability*, argument, the government, and Members of Parliament generally, ought to bear any political costs, such as a loss of parliamentary or electoral support, associated with supporting Bills that stand to breach fundamental constitutional norms. The idea here is that *political* constitutionalism cannot function effectively if political actors (including voters) are denied information they need in order to hold the government and MPs to account. In both cases, a requirement of explicit language helps ensure that potential breaches of constitutional norms are acknowledged and addressed. But the two arguments are distinct: the government and MPs might openly justify their actions without bearing a political cost, or might conversely bear a political cost even if they offer a reasoned justification. Both arguments, however, see the principle of legality playing an essentially democracy-reinforcing role.

---

35 *Simms*, above n. 1, 131E–F.

36 On which see R. Dixon, *Responsive Judicial Review: Democracy and Dysfunction in the Modern Age*, Oxford University Press, Oxford 2023.

A third, *directly norm-protecting*, argument goes further. It enlists the principle of legality to 'protect rights for their own sake', as Jeffrey Goldsworthy has put it.[37] This is not the occasion to develop the argument fully, but let me sketch its outlines, as I see them. The essential idea is that the courts should, on the one hand, strive to protect the integrity of basic constitutional norms while, on the other, respecting the sovereignty of Parliament. They can do so by requiring especially clear language in order for a statute to effect the abrogation of a fundamental constitutional norm. This both discourages Parliament from passing such norm-breaching legislation, by raising the costs of doing so, and ensures that generally or abstractly worded statutes do not have norm-breaching effects. At the same time, the principle so understood respects parliamentary sovereignty since Parliament retains the power to abrogate (or amend) fundamental constitutional norms. All that is required is for it to use sufficiently clear language.

If this seems radical, it should not. It goes no further than Lord Hoffmann's own oft-cited approach in *Simms*, in which he suggested that UK courts, 'though acknowledging the sovereignty of Parliament, apply principles of constitutionality little different from those which exist in countries where the power of the legislature is expressly limited by a constitutional document'.[38] Nor does it go further than Lord Neuberger, who, in *Evans*, characterised the principle of legality as operating to limit the extension of a statutory test so as 'not to undermine the fundamental [common law] principle, or at least to minimise any encroachment onto it'.[39] Lord Bingham, meanwhile, observed that the requirement to clearly state an intention to introduce a provision that would 'strike ordinary people as unfair or disproportionate or immoral' must 'operate as a discouragement, not least because of the increased risk of media criticism and parliamentary and popular resistance'.[40] These judges all supposed the principle of legality was justified in part as a way of protecting constitutional norms directly for their own sake, not simply as an exercise in discerning actual legislative intentions.

How much of this picture would Dicey himself have endorsed? It seems tolerably clear that Dicey did not build an exclusively intentionalist

---

37 J. Goldsworthy, 'The Principle of Legality and Legislative Intention' in D. Meagher and M. Groves (eds.), *The Principle of Legality in Australia and New Zealand*, Federation Press, Annandale 2017.

38 *Simms*, above n. 1, 131G.

39 *Evans*, above n. 3, [115].

40 Lord Bingham, 'Dicey Revisited' [2002] *Public Law* 39, 48.

interpretive methodology into his theory of parliamentary sovereignty. He had ample opportunity to add such a condition and did not. Moreover, he embraced what we would now see as robust principle-of-legality reasoning. He denied the natural law view that statutes could be void merely in virtue of offending against morality or international law, but he sought to explain cases which might seem to lend support to such an approach on the footing that:

> the judges, when attempting to ascertain what is the meaning to be affixed to an Act of Parliament, will presume that Parliament did not intend to violate the ordinary rules of morality, or violate the principles of international law, and will therefore, wherever possible, give such an interpretation to a statutory enactment as may be consistent with the doctrines both of private and of international morality.[41]

It is true that Dicey refers here to a presumption about what Parliament intends, but he does not say whether he means actual or constructive intentions. He would certainly have been right to observe that courts tend to couch their conclusions in 'intention'-speak. But Dicey does not say that interpretation is legitimate only to the extent that it discerns Parliament's actual intentions. Quite to the contrary. When discussing the relationship between parliamentary sovereignty and the rule of law in the context of executive power, Dicey says:[42]

> Parliament is supreme legislator, but from the moment Parliament has uttered its will as lawgiver, that will becomes subject to the interpretation put upon it by the judges of the land, and the judges, who are influenced by the feelings of magistrates no less than by the general spirit of the common law, are disposed to construe statutory exceptions to common law principles in a mode which would not commend itself either to a body of officials or to the Houses of Parliament, if the Houses were called upon to interpret their own enactments.

Judicial interpretation for Dicey is thus a process by which the courts give effect in part to the 'general spirit of the common law', and do so proactively and creatively: statutory interpretation will, Dicey says, 'always exercise the ingenuity of our judges'; there is always room for 'what is in truth judicial legislation'.[43] In this process, statutes will be interpreted in a way that would

41 Dicey, *The Law of the Constitution*, above n. 5, pp. 38–39.
42 ibid., pp. 183–84.
43 A.V. Dicey, *Lectures on the Relation between Law and Public Opinion in England During the Nineteenth Century*, Liberty Fund, Indianapolis 2008, p. 352.

'not commend itself' to Parliament if it were itself to interpret its own enactments. This striking claim is tantamount to saying that legislation will be interpreted in a way that Parliament did not intend. If anything, Dicey's claim is too strong: the point is surely instead that legislation *may* be interpreted in a way that Parliament did not intend. Dicey elsewhere criticises English courts for hewing too closely to the wording of statutes, instead of feeling more 'at liberty' to interpret them, especially by reference to their 'spirit'.[44] But this is presumably not all that Dicey has in mind in this passage of *The Law of the Constitution*, since he immediately contrasts the 'spirit of the common law' with 'notions derived from the traditions of a despotic monarchy' that he believed prevailed abroad.[45] The approach of the common law, however, 'leads to [parliamentary sovereignty] being exercised in a spirit of legality'.[46]

All of this reflects Dicey's theoretical commitment that the content of the law brought about by the passage of a statute is some function of both parliamentary action and any judicial interpretation. Thus, powers conferred by a statute 'are never really unlimited' since they are 'confined', not only 'by the words of the Act itself' but 'what is more, by the interpretation put upon the statute by the judges'.[47] In a different context, Dicey wrote that, although statutes are 'manifestly the work of Parliament', they 'often receive more than half their meaning from judicial decisions'.[48]

Overall, there is a strong case for concluding that Dicey did not hold that intentionalism was the only interpretive method compatible with parliamentary sovereignty, or the only legitimate interpretive method *tout court*. Indeed, although he did not expand much on the point, he seems to have actively countenanced non-intentionalist interpretation as a guarantor of the rule of law. But Dicey did not, so far as I am aware, consider interpretive presumptions as ways of directly seeking to discourage certain kinds of legislation in the way I have suggested.

Be that as it may, my primary interest is normative rather than exegetical, so let me return to the argument that the principle of legality

---

44 ibid., p. 351. Dicey does not define the 'spirit' of an Act, but since the common law in general can have a 'spirit', according to Dicey, the spirit of something cannot be straightforwardly equivalent to the intention of its framer.

45 Dicey, *The Law of the Constitution*, above n. 5, p. 184.

46 ibid. As Mark D. Walters makes plain, this was not a casual remark by Dicey but a carefully crafted piece of prose. See M.D. Walters, *A. V. Dicey and the Common Law Constitutional Tradition: A Legal Turn of Mind*, Cambridge University Press, Cambridge 2020, pp. 281–82.

47 Dicey, *The Law of the Constitution*, above n. 5, p. 183.

48 Dicey, above n. 43, p. 349.

ought to be used in part to directly protect constitutional norms, where doing so is consistent with parliamentary sovereignty. This argument no doubt involves a delicate balancing act. There is always a risk of upsetting the separation of powers. The principle of legality must therefore be subject to constraints. Two particularly important constraints, not necessarily the only ones, stand out. First, it must be possible for Parliament to have drafted a clause that would achieve its intended effect. If there were no conceivable form of words which the court would be prepared to credit to achieve the relevant end – if the presumption were irrebuttable – the principle of legality would be a strike-down power in disguise.[49] Second, the principle of legality must be paired with a defensible conception of which constitutional rights and other norms merit the special protection the principle affords. That is, of course, no trivial requirement.

It is sometimes said that if statutory interpretation is not confined exclusively to discerning Parliament's intentions, it is unmoored from principle and so no longer subject to any clear limit beyond the values favoured by judges.[50] The objection might well be thought to prove too much: unless one takes all of public law to be an elaboration of the ultra vires principle, it inevitably consists in principles and doctrines whose content and justification turn on judgments of constitutional value – on the courts' elaborating ideas such as the rule of law, equality, rights, and so on, in relation to a continually shifting range of circumstances. As a general matter, this calls not for judicial abstention but for an institutionally sensitive, incremental approach to the elaboration of public law doctrine. Jason Varuhas notes, with respect to the principle of legality's protection of private law rights, that those rights' 'status within the normative order of the common law is well-established: fundamental rights in person and property are a signal feature of the English constitutional tradition'.[51] Of course, the constitutional inheritance of the present is always the constitutional innovation of the past. For the common law to protect any rights at all is for it to reflect and embed contestable judgments of moral and political value, even if those judgments were first made long ago. Public law cannot sensibly be stripped of all of this.

---

49 I bracket in this contribution the merits of such strong-form judicial review and assume for present purposes that courts should not engage in it. It would, of course, not be compatible with parliamentary sovereignty and would have to be defended on separate grounds.

50 See e.g., P. Sales, 'Legislative Intention, Interpretation, and the Principle of Legality' (2019) 40 *Statute Law Review* 53, 61; J. Varuhas, 'The Principle of Legality' (2020) 39 *Cambridge Law Journal* 578, 602.

51 Varuhas, above n. 50, 580.

The sceptical argument is perhaps better understood not as a critique of all normative judgment in public law adjudication, but as the concern that it is unclear how constitutional principle can be coherently brought to bear *in interpreting legislation*. The objection can be taken in two ways. It might, first, be a conceptual objection. Interpretation, the argument may go, is the discernment of something like speaker-meaning, that is, intended meaning. Any attempt to protect constitutional norms for their own sake is therefore not interpretation. Yet for present purposes there is no need to enter into debates on the proper scope of 'interpretation'. If one favours a narrow view of it, we can speak instead of some broader notion such as 'construction' or 'determining the legal effect of a statute'. This removes any conceptual difficulty.

The objection may, second, have a decision-procedural character. It might be wondered how, in practice, constitutional norms can operate on a text so as to explain any particular interpretive (or 'constructional') outcome. Yet that seems precisely the question to which the principle of legality supplies the answer. The principle gives a framework according to which, when a protected constitutional norm is engaged, a statute is held not to abrogate that norm unless the statute uses especially clear words to that effect. This seems as close to an action-guiding principle of interpretation as one could hope for at this level of generality. Of course, it leaves many finer points to be worked out, for example, concerning which norms ought to function as 'triggers' for the principle, and whether some norms merit more robust protection than others.[52] There is already an accumulating body of law on these points; further refinement would be welcome and can be expected as the doctrine matures. That we do not already have it should not lead us to abandon the developing doctrine. Indeed, even if the principle of legality is understood only as a tool for ascertaining legislative intention, the task of specifying a coherent set of triggers remains but would have to proceed solely on the basis of speculation about Parliament's probable intentions.

There remains the concern that the principle of legality used other than as an intentionalist device involves the courts 'modify[ing] the meaning and effect of legislation'.[53] The thought may be that Parliament intended to enact p, but the principle of legality directs the court to give the statute some other effect, q. The point might be taken further: if the courts give

52 See Varuhas, above n. 50 for a thorough discussion of these and other complications.

53 *UNCRC*, above n. 15, [28], there speaking of a provision analogous to s. 3 of the HRA. Critiques in a similar vein have been expressed in the context of the principle of legality as a directly norm-protecting doctrine. See e.g., J. Goldsworthy, *Parliamentary Sovereignty: Contemporary Debates*, Cambridge University Press, Cambridge 2010, pp. 309–11.

effect to *q* rather than *p*, they have in effect refused to apply *p*. Yet this apparently attractive argument goes through only if the legal effect of a statute is nothing more than Parliament's intention in passing it. That is immediately problematic on its own terms, since Parliament can have multiple, potentially conflicting, intentions: to pass a given text with certain syntactic and semantic features; to make some specific change to the law; to make some more general change to the law; to bring about some social or political change; and so on.[54] Given this, even intentionalism must reckon with the possibility that for some *p* intended by Parliament, the courts must give effect to *not-p*. More broadly, I have already suggested that there is a conceptual gap between what Parliament intends, or for that matter the text of a statute it has passed, and a statute's legal effect. The legal effect of a statute is determined in part, too, by common law rules, which include not only background substantive doctrines of public and private law but also interpretive rules determining how certain types of statutory text will take effect in law. The 'statute' in the relevant sense – or if one prefers its 'contribution to the content of the law'[55] – is, I am suggesting, the output rather than the input of these processes, so to speak of interpretive principles amending a statute is, in a certain sense, premature.

These considerations lead quickly into the dense thickets of debates on statutory interpretation, and this is not the occasion to enter them further. So let me return, in concluding, to my more modest claim that the principle of legality understood to directly protect constitutional norms is compatible with parliamentary sovereignty. Grant that the principle of legality allows the courts to treat some texts intended to mean *p* as having the effect *q*. What this formulation leaves out is that Parliament can itself, through explicit words, amend, abolish, or disapply any common law doctrine that would license the holding of *q*. For any given proposition *p* Parliament wishes to enact, it retains the power to ensure that the legal result is *p*.[56] That is consistent with the plenary authority principle, since, for any *p*, Parliament may bring it about that *p* is law, and it is consistent with the legal supremacy principle, since if Parliament exercises this power, no court or other actor may treat *p* as not law. As I have tried to suggest, this, rather than the Supreme Court's more recent revisionary understanding, is the essence of parliamentary sovereignty.

---

54 See Greenberg, above n. 34.

55 ibid., p. 218.

56 Here I bracket the question whether – for logical, semantic, or similar reasons – there may be propositions, or combinations of propositions, which it is impossible for Parliament to enact as law.

The Old Mortality Society (c 1860) (© National Portrait Gallery, London, and reproduced with permission.)

Back row: Joseph Frank Payne, John Warneford Hoole, Thomas Hill Green, James Bryce, Aeneas James George Mackay.
Front row: George Rankine Luke, Algernon Charles Swinburne, John Nichol, Albert Venn Dicey, Thomas Erskine Holland.

Albert Venn Dicey (1895) (© Oxfordshire County Council – Oxfordshire History Centre, and reproduced with permission.)

Commemoration Plaque, All Souls College (© All Souls College. Used with permission of the Warden and Fellows of All Souls College, Oxford.)

St Sepulchre's Cemetery (© Wolfgang Ernst) (see inscription, preceding the Editors' Preface in the preliminary pages of this book)

PART III

DICEY AND THE CONFLICT OF LAWS

DICEY'S *CONFLICT OF LAWS* THEN AND NOW

Lord COLLINS of Mapesbury

1. INTRODUCTION

The 1923 review of the third edition (1922, with Arthur Berriedale Keith) of Dicey's *Conflict of Laws* in the *Harvard Law Review*, by the great American scholar of the conflict of laws and author of the First Restatement, Professor Joseph Beale, contains a touching tribute:[1]

> The last time I saw Professor Dicey was just two years ago, at his home in Oxford. He looked gray, old and broken, feeble and deaf, but he was mentally alert and vigorous. He was engaged with Dr. Keith in this new edition of his Conflict of Laws, and discussed with interest and understanding the changes which the war had wrought in the subject. We talked, too, of the first time I had met him, … and of his visit to my class, and his envy of my fifty students; he never could get together more than half a dozen students for the Conflict of Laws in Oxford. I left him sadly, for I knew that I should look upon his face no more. He lived to finish this edition with Dr. Keith's sympathetic help.
>
> …

---

1 J.H. BEALE, 'A Digest of the Law of England with Reference to the Conflict of Laws (Book)' (1923) 36 *Harvard Law Review* 766, 766–67.

In saying that Dicey on the Conflict of Laws is one of the foremost English legal treatises written in the last century one does only the barest justice; but one must also point out two defects which an English treatise must have, when compared with the outstanding American works of the same sort. In the first place the 'welter of decisions' from which we suffer has at least this merit: that it gives the legal author rich store of authority on which to draw. He sees the rules which he is formulating in operation in so many ways that he can wisely limit and qualify them, and his final statement of law has an authority which can come only from wide maturity of experience. Compared with that of the American lawyer, the juridical apparatus of his English brother is limited and narrow. In the second place the English author is awed by his material; he dare not criticize the lightest word, the most ill-considered dictum of a judge. Dicey is a true scholar; yet he could say, in his preface to this edition, that the editors 'have treated the conflict of laws solely from the point of view of the law of England as it at present stands. … They have not attempted to defend the English rules as to the conflict of laws as being always in accordance with the dictates of logic or of expediency, and they have borne in mind that the commentator or expositor of a law has no need to play the part of an apologist or reformer.' It is almost pathetic to think of the aged scholar following the infelicitous dicta of a Kekewich or a Lord Coleridge, sinking his own knowledge of his chosen subject out of reverence for official utterance. We have this one great good, at least, from our superfluity of courts of law: that a decision, like the work of a scholar, must win its authority by its own merit.[2] If Dicey could have spoken his own mind, if he could have considered the American and Colonial decisions which he knew and studied, this work would be more than one of the best of its kind; it would stand among the works, the very few, which are at the head of legal literature in any country. A kind man, a gentle scholar, a learned lawyer, full of honors and truly lamented, Dicey has left in this work a noble monument to his learning.

2. COMITY AND ACQUIRED RIGHTS

In his article 'On Private International Law as a Branch of the Law of England' in 1890[3] (much of which he incorporated in Chapter 1 of the first

---

2 A similar criticism was made by E. Rabel, *The Conflict of Laws: A Comparative Study*, vol. 1, 2nd ed., University of Michigan Press, Ann Arbor 1958, p. 12, who said that the English writers refrained from criticism of the courts and left the law in the incoherent state represented in the cases: 'The often re-edited treatise of Dicey (1896) illustrates this descriptive method with its finest and its less desirable characteristics.' The present editors do not hesitate to criticise decisions which they consider to be wrong.

3 A.V. Dicey, 'On Private International Law as a Branch of the Law of England' (1890) 6 *Law Quarterly Review* 1. Dicey did not like the expression private international

edition), Dicey rejected the view that the enforcement of foreign law was a matter of 'comity'.[4] He considered that the controversy over the application of comity was 'little better than examples of logomachy', i.e. purely verbal. If it meant that foreign law could have no effect beyond the territory of the sovereign by which it was imposed, it stated a real and important fact, but if it meant that foreign law was applied out of courtesy, e.g. to the French Republic, 'then the term comity is used to cover a view which, if really held by any serious thinker, affords a singular specimen of confusion of thought produced by laxity of language'.

When this view was reproduced in the first edition of Dicey's *Conflict of Laws* in 1896,[5] Professor Sir Frederick Pollock wrote to Dicey to say that: '... I rejoice in your summary abolition of that confusing term comity'.[6] But there are now very many modern English decisions in the conflict of laws which employ the concept of comity. The more recent editions of Dicey, building on research which the present author did several years ago for a collection in honour of Sir Peter North (editor of successive editions of Cheshire's *Private International Law*, and later Cheshire and North),[7] endeavour to show that the concept of comity is increasingly used in common law countries, not as an explanation for the system of the conflict of laws, but as a tool for applying or reshaping the rules of the conflict of laws. In particular, it is used in a sense which owes much to the rules of public international law, namely respect for the territorial jurisdiction of other states.

But Dicey's view that comity is not the basis of the conflict of laws still stands, although the 'acquired rights' or 'vested rights' theory which he espoused has not found favour. Dicey's first general principle[8] was that: 'Any

---

law, which he described in his book on Domicile as 'an unfortunate misnomer' (A.V. Dicey, *The Law of Domicil as a Branch of the Law of England: Stated in the Form of Rules*, Stevens & Sons, London 1879, p. iii). He followed the positivist view that public international law was not really law because 'they are not commands proceedings from any sovereign' (A.V. Dicey, *A Digest of the Law of England with Reference to the Conflict of Laws*, Stevens & Sons, London 1896, p. 14 ('*Conflict of Laws*, 1st ed.')). But although the rules of private international law were 'laws' in that sense, they were not international because they related to private rights (ibid.).

4 Dicey (1890), above n. 3, 9–10.

5 Dicey, *Conflict of Laws*, 1st ed., above n. 3, p. 10.

6 R.A. Cosgrove, *The Rule of Law: Albert Venn Dicey, Victorian Jurist*, University of North Carolina Press, Chapel Hill 1980, p. 168.

7 L. Collins, 'Comity in Modern Private International Law' in J. Fawcett (ed.), *Reform and Development of Private International Law: Essays in Honour of Sir Peter North*, Oxford University Press, Oxford 2002, p. 89.

8 Until the seventh edition in 1958, 'General Principles' were set out in Chapter 1. Even as late as that edition, the expression 'civilised country' was retained, although it

right which has been duly acquired under the law of any civilised[9] country is recognised, and, in general, enforced by English Courts, and no right which has not been duly acquired is enforced or, in general, recognised by English Courts'. What was 'duly acquired' or had 'not been acquired' of course begged the question, and in the sixth edition in 1949 the phrases were supplemented by, respectively, 'which is applicable according to the English rules of the conflict of laws' and 'in virtue of an English rule of the conflict of laws'. In this form, Falconbridge considered that the acquired rights theory was stated 'in a fairly innocuous form'.[10]

As Rheinstein said:[11]

> But how can an English court know whether or not a right has at all been acquired under the law of a foreign country, unless it is directed to look to the law of that particular country by some rule of law. This rule of law must, of necessity, be one either of a legal system superior to English law or English law. Dr. Lipstein has modified Dicey's old formulation by clearly indicating that the right to be enforced or recognized by the English court must have been acquired under that foreign law 'which is applicable according to the English rules of the conflict of laws.' As soon as this insertion is made, there arises the theoretical question of whether the right to be enforced or recognized by the English court can still properly be described as one acquired under foreign law or whether, in jurisprudential analysis, it would not be more correct to speak of a right created by English law upon the pattern of the foreign law referred to by the English choice of law rule; and if that is done, why not drop altogether the talk about enforcement of rights and simply speak of the application of some law, English or foreign, as directed by the English choice of law rule?

---

was said: '... the distinction between "civilised" and "uncivilised" countries does not appear to have any practical importance for purposes of English rules of the conflict of laws' (J.H.C. Morris (ed.), *Conflict of Laws*, 7th ed., Stevens & Sons, London 1958, pp. 10–11).

9 The first to the fifth editions contained an appendix note dealing with conflict of laws issues relating to uncivilised countries ('Law governing acts done in uncivilised countries'). Thus it was said: 'A domiciled Englishman who settles in China, and *a fortiori* in a strictly barbarous country, retains his English domicil' (Dicey, *Conflict of Laws*, 1st ed., above n. 3, p. 723).

10 J.D. Falconbridge, 'Dicey's Conflict of Laws' in R.E. Megarry (ed.), 'Reviews and Notices' (1950) 66 *Law Quarterly Review* 104. On the vested rights theory see also D.F. Cavers, 'Dicey's Conflict of Laws by J. H. C. Morris' (1950) 63(7) *Harvard Law Review* 1278, 1279–80.

11 M. Rheinstein, 'Dicey's Conflict of Laws' (1950) 25 *New York University Law Review* 180, 181–82.

3. THE EVOLUTION OF DICEY'S RULES

Dicey's first book, published in 1870, was entitled *A Treatise on the Rules for the Selection of the Parties to an Action*. Dicey wrote this book while devilling for Sir John Coleridge, then the Solicitor General and later Attorney General and Lord Chief Justice. As quoted in Cosgrove, he described it to one of his oldest friends, Viscount Bryce,[12] in 1917 as 'the best book I ever wrote'.[13] He said in the preface:

> The aim of this treatise is to reduce … the law of parties into a series of rules, each of which is illustrated by appropriate cases and examples and confirmed, wherever this is possible, by quotations from judgments or from the pages of writers of acknowledged reputation. The practical advantage of the arrangement … is that it enables the reader to see at a glance what the rule of law is.[14]

The book does not deal with the conflict of laws, apart from a short section on causes of action arising beyond the jurisdiction, including treatment of a few cases still of practical or historical interest today.[15]

In 1879, Dicey published his second book, *The Law of Domicil as a Branch of the Law of England: Stated in the Form of Rules*. Oliver Wendell Holmes wrote in the same year to Bryce to say that the work was 'most admirably done'.[16] Dicey, preferring the conflict of laws terminology of, especially, Huber and Story said: 'The law of domicil is often looked at as a branch of the subject called by the unfortunate misnomer Private International Law'.[17] But, he said, in this work the law of domicile was considered solely as a part of English law, and no attempt was to be made

---

12 A contemporary of Dicey at Oxford, later Regius Professor of Civil Law, cabinet member, and ambassador to the United States.

13 Cosgrove, above n. 6, p. 33.

14 An anonymous reviewer in 'Dicey's Parties to an Action' (1871) 31 *Law Magazine and Law Review; or, Quarterly Journal of Jurisprudence*, 101–11 said: 'The arrangement, or rather the division of the book into rules, which are numbered, and run through the entire volume without discrimination as to the subjects thus catalogued, is worse than useless; it is distracting. It aggravates the difficulties of obtaining, if it does not altogether frustrate the attempt to gain, a general view of the subject, with a due subordination of the parts. There is a natural order in every structure, and this should by all means be preserved'.

15 *The Halley* (1867–68) LR 3 Ch App 479; *Emperor of Austria v Day and Kossuth* (1861) 3 De GF & J 217; *Scott v Seymour* (1862) 1 Hurl & Colt 219.

16 Cosgrove, above n. 6, p. 43.

17 Dicey (1879), above n. 3, p. iii.

to determine whether the rules which made up the law of domicile, as administered by English courts, were or were not the same as the rules administered by foreign tribunals, and forming, therefore, part of foreign legal systems. In discussing the use of rules, he says: 'I have, in short, applied to the law of domicile the method of stating the law which nine years ago I employed in my treatise on Parties to an Action'.[18]

In 1949 Mr John Morris (not yet Dr Morris) wrote in the preface to the sixth edition of Dicey's *Conflict of Laws* that:[19]

> The technique of Rule, Comment and Illustrations is not one which all of us would have adopted if we had been writing our own book on the Conflict of Laws. The method has the disadvantage that it is sometimes apt to produce a false sense of certainty when authority is scant or conflicting. Provided this disadvantage is borne in mind, and the tentative character of some of the Rules is fully appreciated, the method undoubtedly possesses advantages for the practising lawyer; and we are satisfied that to have abandoned it would have been to go beyond our province as editors.

As Westlake pointed out in his review[20] of the first edition, the technique of Rules, Comment and Illustration were to be expected from the author of *Domicil*, and 'countenanced by the form adopted in some of the Indian codes'. The Indian Penal Code of 1860 contained illustrations, as did the Indian Contract Act 1872.[21] But Westlake suggested that the method was better suited to legislation than to exposition, especially 'where the matter does not possess the certainty which is not only the business of a legislator, but also within his power, to introduce into a subject even where he does not find it there'.[22]

---

18 ibid., p. v.

19 J.H.C. Morris (ed.), *Conflict of Laws*, 6th ed., Stevens & Sons, London 1949, p. xiv. cf. G.W. Bartholomew, 'Dicey and the Development of English Private International Law' (1959) 1 *Tasmanian Law Review* 240, 260, said: 'This is surely an extraordinary attitude. It is to make the bottle more important than the wine'.

20 J. Westlake, 'A Digest of the Law of England with reference to the Conflict of Laws' (1896) 12 *Law Quarterly Review* 397.

21 See Bartholomew, above n. 19, 261, who says that Dicey's method stems from Macaulay's suggestion that illustrations might be appended to the Indian Codes and that this model was adopted by writers who had served as draftsmen for the Indian codes: J.F. Stephen, *A Digest of the Law of Evidence*, Macmillan & Co., London 1876; F. Pollock, *A Digest of the Law of Partnership*, Stevens & Sons, London 1877. The use of illustrations dates from drafts of the Indian Codes in the early 1860s. Sir James Fitzjames Stephen was Dicey's cousin.

22 Westlake, above n. 20, 397–98.

Falconbridge recognised in his review of the sixth edition (1949) that this feature of the work contributed to its extraordinary 'popularity'.[23] But the other side of the coin, as Falconbridge said elsewhere, was that:[24]

> [T]here is a regrettable tendency on the part of judges to treat Dicey's propositions as a final statement, perfect in form and merely subject to be checked and modified here and there. This excessive judicial respect for the form of Dicey's 'rules' tends to discourage any new investigation of the underlying principles of the conflict of laws and any consequent revision of the language of the rules in the light of new investigation.

It must be accepted, of course, that the Rules feature works best as a distillation of judicial decisions, and that it does not work so well for statutory material (especially legislation derived from EU law, or EU law itself). That feature, however, is not only a reason for the work's popularity but almost certainly also for its great influence. The Rules themselves (quite apart from the text itself) have been cited in over 400 available judgments in the last 10 years and have no doubt been deployed in argument in many others. It may, for example, be noted that what is now Rule 20 states that 'English courts have no jurisdiction to entertain an action: (1) for the enforcement, either directly or indirectly, of a penal, revenue or other public law of a foreign State; or (2) founded upon an act of state'. The Comment makes it clear that the principle is not one of jurisdiction, but a rule of substantive law, but that the Rule has been retained in this form because it has been cited with approval in many decisions.

4. UNITED STATES AUTHORITIES

Another feature of the first edition was the inclusion of United States' cases. The first edition explained that:

> [p]ains have been taken to render this treatise useful to American no less than to English readers. For the promotion of this object Professor J.B. Moore, of Columbia College,[25] New York has appended to each of the leading chapters of this Digest a statement of American law on the subject … His name is a sufficient guarantee for its accuracy …[26]

---

23 FALCONBRIDGE, above n. 10, 104.
24 For stronger language, see BARTHOLOMEW, above n. 19, 260–62.
25 An error for Columbia University.
26 DICEY, *Conflict of Laws*, 1st ed., above n. 3, p. v.

As Westlake's review said: 'Prof. J.B. Moore's notes are very full, and we need scarcely say that their learned contributor has a scientific position in his country equal to that of the principal author in England.'[27]

These were omitted from the second edition because, as the preface pointed out,[28] American cases were little used by English lawyers and it was impossible to deal with them sufficiently for American readers, and both American and English decisions could be accessed since the publication in 1896 of Professor Beale's admirable *A Selection of Cases in the Conflict of Laws*. Some American cases were restored for the fifth edition in 1932. But Dr Morris omitted American cases from the sixth edition in 1949, and said: 'The first edition contained references to many such cases, for which an American lawyer assumed sole responsibility'.[29] This reference to 'an American lawyer' is a very insular (and, it has to be said, ignorant) description of the American author, rather like Bridge LJ's reference to 'a United States text-book written by a Mr. Williston'[30] when referring to the great multi-volume work on the law of contract by Professor Williston. For the 'American lawyer' who contributed the notes to the first edition of Dicey was none other than Professor John Bassett Moore, author of Moore's *A Digest of International Law* in eight volumes and Moore's *International Arbitration* in six volumes, and the first United States judge on the Permanent Court of International Justice, from 1922–28. As indicated above, Westlake said in his review in 1896 that Professor Moore 'has a scientific position in his country equal' to that of Dicey.[31] Today there are relatively few United States cases cited in Dicey, other than (mainly US Supreme Court) cases on international conventions, largely because the United States conflicts law has diverged dramatically from English law in areas still governed by the common law.

By the time of the publication of the great work of Beale, *Conflict of Laws* (1935),[32] some United States cases were cited in footnotes to the main Dicey text, but Beale wrote:

> Dicey's book, first edition 1896, is excellent; but being based on English authorities alone its analysis is rather simple. It is the enormous bulk of our

---

27 Westlake, above n. 20, 397.

28 A.V. Dicey, *A Digest of the Law of England with Reference to the Conflict of Laws*, 2nd ed., Stevens & Sons, London 1908, pp. v–vi.

29 Morris (ed.), above n. 19, p. xvi.

30 *Cia Barca de Panama SA v George Wimpey & Co Ltd (No 1)* [1980] 1 Lloyd's Rep 598, 609 (CA).

31 Westlake, above n. 20, 397.

32 J.H. Beale, *A Treatise on the Conflict of Laws*, Baker, Voorhis & Co., New York 1935.

> case law which has enabled American scholars to analyze the Conflict of Laws and develop it in a way which is impossible to an English author who has only a few decisions and some judicial conjectures to deal with.[33]

This was somewhat unfair not only on the first edition with its notes on United States cases, but also on the then current Keith's fifth edition in 1932,[34] which cited some 4,000 English decisions.

5. RECEPTION AND DEVELOPMENT

The book was a success from the outset. It was reviewed favourably by the two leading scholars in the English-speaking world. In the *Harvard Law Review*, Professor Joseph Beale said that 'Professor Dicey has written the best book on the subject'.[35] Professor John Westlake,[36] who had written the pioneering *A Treatise on Private International Law* (1858)[37] and who was close to Dicey, concluded his long review in the *Law Quarterly Review* by describing the book as being one 'which must be before us in detail whenever leisure permits us to deal with any subject on which it treats'.[38]

After collaborating with Dicey on the third edition, which was published in 1922, Professor Arthur Berriedale Keith[39] edited the fourth and fifth editions, published in 1927 and 1932 respectively. When Dr Morris passed on the general editorship to the present author, he said that the book had gone into decline under Keith, and in the biographical note on Dr Morris, which has appeared unchanged in the editions since 1987, the reference to his low opinion of the Keith editions has been retained. It would not be a profitable exercise to go over the 1932 edition in the light of the then case law to see whether the criticism is justified, but that edition was reviewed favourably in the *Law Quarterly Review* by 'AD McN' (later Sir Arnold

33 ibid., p. xi.

34 A.B. Keith (ed.), *A Digest of the Law of England with Reference to the Conflict of Laws*, 5th ed., Stevens & Sons, London 1932.

35 'Dicey's Conflict of Laws' (1896–97) 10(3) *Harvard Law Review* 168.

36 Westlake was the Whewell Professor of International Law at the University of Cambridge.

37 J. Westlake, *A Treatise on Private International Law, or, The Conflict of Laws, with Principal Reference to its Practice in the English and Other Cognate Systems of Jurisprudence*, W. Maxwell, London 1858.

38 Westlake, above n. 20, 401.

39 Regius Professor of Sanskrit and Comparative Philology at the University of Edinburgh. His other writings were mainly in constitutional law and the British Empire.

McNair and then Lord McNair, Whewell Professor of International Law in Cambridge and subsequently judge and President of the International Court of Justice),[40] and in 1935, Professor Joseph Beale, at that time the most eminent conflicts scholar in the English-speaking world, must have been referring to the 1932 edition when he said that Dicey's book was excellent.[41]

It is not unlikely that Keith was unjustly maligned by an Oxford clique consisting of Professor Geffrey Cheshire, John Morris, Martin Wolff,[42] and John Foster. In the preface to the first edition of his *Private International Law* in 1935, Professor Cheshire paid tribute to Mr J. G. Foster, Fellow of All Souls, and All Souls Lecturer in Private International Law, who had made time in the midst of a busy life to read the proofs of the book: 'Not a few amendments are due to his acumen and insight'.[43] Foster, later Sir John Foster, a successful QC, an MP and a junior minister in Churchill's government of 1951, and an extraordinary personality, wrote in the same year about Dicey's *Conflict of Laws*:[44]

> The amazing erudition of the present editor has made it possible for this massively repellent volume to contain a prodigious amount of learning. The defect of the book lies in the fact that the outlook is often insular even where there are no English authorities to prevent the laying down of a logical system. Dicey is usually excellent where it is a question of finding all the authorities on a given point, and deplorable where the rules on any particular subject-matter are inchoate, e.g. assignments, or the effect of s.3 of Lord Kingsdown's Act. The danger of the book lies in the great respect paid to it by the courts, who are prone to take for granted the theories of Dicey on the points in question.

In the first edition of his fine work, *Private International Law* (1945), Martin Wolff referred to the fact that Dicey had received a special prominence, but noted: '[s]ee, however, J. Foster's remarks on Dicey's work' in the 1935 *British Yearbook of International Law*.[45] In his second edition in 1950, no

40 'Dicey's Conflict of Laws' (1933) 49(1) *Law Quarterly Review* 131.
41 Beale, above n. 32, p. xi.
42 This eminent scholar, a refugee from Nazi Germany, was never given an academic position in England, but from 1938 until his death in 1953, All Souls College gave him a research grant and an office in college.
43 G.C. Cheshire, *Private International Law*, Oxford University Press, Oxford 1935, p. ix.
44 J.G. Foster, 'Some Defects in the English Rules of Conflict of Laws' (1935) 16 *British Yearbook of International Law* 84, 101, 102–3.
45 M. Wolff, *Private International Law*, Oxford University Press, Oxford 1945, p. 45, para. 38, fn. 2.

doubt in deference to his colleague John Morris, Martin Wolff revised the reference to 'see, however, J. Foster's remarks on Dicey's work, before it was taken over by J.H.C. Morris'.[46]

6. DR JOHN MORRIS AND BEYOND

In 1945, John Morris was invited to undertake the editorship of Dicey's *Conflict of Laws* but (as he put it in the preface to the sixth edition) by October 1946 he felt that the task was beyond his strength and he therefore invited seven learned friends to help him. Those friends included several who were, or were to become, of special eminence. They were Zelman (later Sir Zelman) Cowen, Rupert (later Sir Rupert) Cross, Otto (later Sir Otto) Kahn-Freund, Dr (later Professor) Kurt Lipstein, Dr (later Professor) Clive Parry, Mr R. S. (Rex) Welsh, and Professor Ben Wortley.

Although the basic structure of the work was unchanged, major portions were rethought and rewritten. One of its characteristics, which the present writer (and with him, in the current 16th edition, Professor Jonathan Harris) has sought to retain, was that there was a unity of style and approach, and respect for the traditions of the work, which is not always achieved in long-standing works with several contributors.

Several challenges have had to be faced. The first challenge was the increasing application of statutory law on the subject, mainly, but not exclusively, implementing international conventions, especially the Hague Conventions,[47] and also recommendations of the Law Commission. There

46 M. Wolff, *Private International Law*, 2nd ed., Clarendon Press, Oxford 1950, p. 45, para. 3, fn. 3.

47 See especially the Hague Conventions on: the conflict of laws relating to the form of testamentary dispositions (1961) (Wills Act 1963); the service abroad of judicial and extrajudicial documents in civil or commercial matters (1965); the recognition of divorces and legal separations (1970) (Family Law Act 1986); the taking of evidence abroad in civil or commercial matters (1970) (Evidence (Proceedings in Other Jurisdictions) Act 1975); the civil aspects of international child abduction (1980) (Child Abduction and Custody Act 1985); jurisdiction, applicable law, recognition, enforcement and co-operation in respect of parental responsibility and measures for the protection of children (1996) (Civil Jurisdiction and Judgments Act 1982, as amended); choice of court agreements (2005) (Civil Jurisdiction and Judgments Act 1982, as amended); the international recovery of child support and other forms of family maintenance (2007) (Civil Jurisdiction and Judgments Act 1982, as amended). See also: Diplomatic Privileges Act 1964; Uniform Laws on International Sales Act 1967; Consular Relations Act 1968; International Organisations Act 1968; Recognition of Divorces and Legal Separations Act 1971 (now Family Law Act 1986,

are more than 600 statutes and statutory instruments referred to in the current edition, compared with a mere handful in the first edition.

The second challenge is the ever-increasing volume of case law which has to be considered, and, where necessary, noted. Two factors have contributed to the enormous increase in case law from the first edition, where the cases could be counted in hundreds, to the current edition, where there are some 9,000 cases in the table: the first is the huge increase in international litigation in London, fuelled by London's reputation as a litigation and arbitration centre, and by the impact of globalisation; and the second is the vastly increased accessibility to written judgments caused by the proliferation of specialist law reports and by instant access to judgments online.

The third challenge was that from the 11th edition in 1987, the work has had to accommodate the ever-increasing volume of law (beginning with the Brussels Convention on jurisdiction and the enforcement of judgments in civil and commercial matters[48] (and the parallel, subsequently revised, Lugano Convention)[49] and the Rome Convention on the law applicable to contractual obligations)[50] emanating from the European Economic Community and later the European Union: in particular, the recast Brussels I Regulation,[51] which (together with its predecessor, the Brussels I Regulation)[52] for most practical purposes superseded the Brussels Convention; the Brussels IIa Regulation on recognition and enforcement of judgments in matrimonial matters and matters of parental

Pt. II); Matrimonial Proceedings (Polygamous Marriages) Act 1972 (now Matrimonial Causes Act 1973, s. 47); Maintenance Orders (Reciprocal Enforcement) Act 1972, Pt. II; Domicile and Matrimonial Proceedings Act 1973; Arbitration Act 1975 (replaced by Arbitration Act 1996, ss. 9 and 100–104); State Immunity Act 1978; Civil Jurisdiction and Judgments Act 1982 (as amended); Matrimonial and Family Proceedings Act 1984, Pt. III; Foreign Limitation Periods Act 1984; and Private International Law (Implementation of Agreements) Act 2020.

48 Brussels Convention on jurisdiction and the enforcement of judgments in civil and commercial matters [1972] OJ L299/32.

49 Lugano Convention on jurisdiction and the recognition and enforcement of judgments in civil and commercial matters [2007] OJ L339/3.

50 Convention 80/934/EEC on the law applicable to contractual obligations [1998] OJ C27/34.

51 Council Regulation (EU) 1215/2012 of 12 December 2012 on jurisdiction and the recognition and enforcement of judgments in civil and commercial matters [2012] OJ L351/1.

52 Council Regulation (EC) 44/2001 of 22 December 2000 on jurisdiction and the recognition and enforcement of judgments in civil and commercial matters [2001] OJ L12/1.

responsibility;[53] the Maintenance Regulation;[54] the recast Insolvency Regulation;[55] the Service and Taking of Evidence Regulations;[56] and the Rome I and Rome II Regulations on contractual and non-contractual obligations respectively.[57]

The fourth challenge was the effect of the United Kingdom's withdrawal from the European Union. It entailed not only complex transitional arrangements to deal with judgments given before, or litigation pending at, withdrawal, but also the retention (at least for now) of important EU law, including the Rome I and Rome II Regulations, and the consumer contract and employment contract jurisdictional provisions in the recast Brussels I Regulation. In addition, for reasons which are not easily explicable, the intra-UK jurisdictional provisions in the Civil Jurisdiction and Judgments Act 1982, Schedule 4, which were based on the Brussels I Regulation, have not been substantially altered. The result is that more than 400 decisions of the European Court in Luxembourg have been cited in the current edition, and its future decisions will continue to be monitored.

This is not the place for promotion of the work, but, to conclude on a lighter note, it may be relevant to point out that when it was published in 1896, the price was 30 shillings (£1.50) for about 800 pages in large type with generous margins. That is the equivalent today of about £150. If the fact that it now consists of well over 3,000 pages with much smaller type is taken into account, proportionally the 16th edition is now somewhat cheaper than it was in 1896.

---

53 Council Regulation (EC) 2201/2003 of 27 November 2003 concerning jurisdiction and the recognition and enforcement of judgments in matrimonial matters and the matters of parental responsibility [2003] OJ L338/1.

54 Council Regulation (EC) 4/2009 of 18 December 2008 on jurisdiction, applicable law, recognition and enforcement of decisions and cooperation in matters relating to maintenance obligations [2009] OJ L7/1.

55 Council Regulation (EU) 2015/848 of 20 May 2015 on insolvency proceedings (recast) [2015] OJ L141/19.

56 Council Regulation (EC) 1393/2007 of 13 November 2007 on the service in the Member States of judicial and extrajudicial documents in civil or commercial matters (service of documents) [2007] OJ L324/79 and Council Regulation (EC) 1206/2001 of 28 May 2001 on cooperation between the courts of the Member States in the taking of evidence in civil or commercial matters [2001] OJ L174/1.

57 Council Regulation (EC) 593/2008 of 17 June 2008 on the law applicable to contractual obligations (Rome I) [2008] OJ L177/6 and Council Regulation (EC) 864/2007 of 11 July 2007 on the law applicable to non-contractual obligations (Rome II) [2007] OJ L199/40.

READING DICEY'S PRIVATE INTERNATIONAL LAW IN THE PENUMBRA

Empire and Gender

Roxana BANU

1. INTRODUCTION

Most readings of Dicey's private international law *Digest* have been fixated on providing a definitive answer to a few questions: whether Dicey was truly a positivist;[1] whether Dicey took 'the final and decisive step' in isolating English private international law scholarship from continental European thought;[2] and whether his principle of the recognition of vested rights was a helpful and

---

1 For a very interesting discussion see D. DYZENHAUS, 'Not an Isolated, Exceptional and Indeed Contradictory Branch of Jurisprudence' in R. BANU, M. GREEN and R. MICHAELS (eds.), *Philosophical Foundations of Private International Law*, Oxford University Press, forthcoming 2024.

2 G.W. BARTHOLOMEW, 'Dicey and the Development of English Private International Law' (1959) 1 *Tasmanian University Law Review* 240, 242.

coherent alternative to theories focused on comity.[3] I argue that reading Dicey's private international law work through these questions is both unhelpful and misleading. As I show in Section 2, these questions are unhelpful because they do not reveal anything of essence about Dicey's thought when asked in the abstract and they are misleading because they encourage us to read Dicey within overly narrow, unrealistic analytical categories.

Instead, in Section 3, I propose that we read Dicey's private international law thought in the penumbra, in other words, in the areas where Dicey seems most uncertain about his own propositions, their context, and their implications, namely questions of empire and gender. However, in encouraging us to look at Dicey's forays into these questions I do not mean to make the implausible claim that Dicey was either a feminist or an anti-imperialist. In other words, the value of reading Dicey in the penumbra of his thoughts on these matters does not rest in his substantive views on gender[4] and empire.[5] The value rests in appreciating that some of the analytical dilemmas that Dicey sets out in the introduction to the *Digest* take on a new meaning in the context of empire and gender questions. Following Dicey in this penumbra brings us into thus far unexplored corners of his private international law work, which in turn would prompt us to write different and overdue histories of the field.

2. THREE COMMON READINGS

In 1896 when Dicey published his *Digest* on the conflict of laws, he announced that his project was different from what had been previously written in the field. He outlined three sets of theoretical dichotomies and his position within them to frame the nature of his own project.

First, he distinguished between a 'theoretical' and a 'positive' method of discerning private international law rules.[6] Theoretical scholars, primarily continental European ones, allegedly 'passed almost imperceptibly from the question as to what are, to the different inquiry as to what ought to

---

3 R.D. Carswell, 'The Doctrine of Vested Rights in Private International Law' (1959) 8 *International and Comparative Law Quarterly* 268.

4 See A.V. Dicey, *Letters to a Friend on Votes for Women*, John Murray, London 1909. See also M. Keyes, 'Women in Private International Law' (2019) available at <https://papers.ssrn.com/sol3/papers.cfm?abstract_id=3817113>.

5 See for example D. Lino, 'The Rule of Law and the Rule of Empire: A.V. Dicey in Imperial Context' (2018) 81 *Modern Law Review* 739.

6 A.V. Dicey, *A Digest of the Law of England with Reference to the Conflict of Laws*, Stevens & Sons, London 1896, p. 15.

be, the principles of private international law'. Their goal was to discover 'fundamental principles of private international law … through study and reflection'.[7] By contrast, those following the 'positive' method to which Dicey subscribed, focused on 'the all-important doctrine that no maxim is a law unless it be part of the municipal law of some given country'.[8]

This initial dichotomy spilled uncritically into a second one, between a universalist and a particularistic perspective in private international law. Those who followed a theoretical framework allegedly allowed themselves to postulate a 'fictitious authority of a common law of Europe' in private international law.[9] By contrast, those following the positive method were unapologetic about focusing on the private international law rules of a given country, since they 'start from the fact that the rules for determining the conflict of laws are themselves "laws" in the strict sense of that term, and that they derive their authority from the support of the sovereign in whose territory they are enforced'.[10]

Finally, Dicey connected these two sets of distinctions to a third one via a muddled analytical terrain. Unlike other private international law scholars, primarily Joseph Story, he rejected the proposition that private international law is informed by comity. In Dicey's view, 'the application of foreign law is not a matter of caprice or option, it does not arise from the desire of the sovereign of England, or of any other sovereign to show courtesy to other states'.[11] To commit to a positive method, avoid the 'fictitious authority of the common law of Europe',[12] and reject comity was to admit:

> … the broad distinction between rules which are strictly laws, as being part of the municipal law of one particular country (our own), and rules prevailing in other countries, which are not laws to us at all, since they do not rest on the authority of our State: and it completely avoids the errors which have arisen from confusing the rules of so-called Private International Law, which are in strictness 'laws' but are not 'international, with the principles of international law properly so-called, which are 'international' since they regulate the conduct of nations towards each other but are not, in the strict sense of the term 'laws'.[13]

---

7 ibid., pp. 15–16.
8 ibid., p. 19.
9 ibid., p. 20.
10 ibid., p. 18.
11 ibid., p. 10.
12 ibid., p. 20.
13 A.V. Dicey, *The Law of Domicil as a Branch of the Law of England: Stated in the Form of Rules*, Stevens & Sons, London 1879, p. v. See also A.V. Dicey, 'On Private International Law as a Branch of the Law of England' (1890) 6 *Law Quarterly Review* 1 and (1891) 7 *Law Quarterly Review* 113.

In the end, Dicey tells us that 'courts do not enforce foreign laws, but rights acquired under foreign laws' and that 'the impossibility of otherwise determining whole classes of cases without gross inconvenience and injustice to litigants', rather than comity, motivates the field of private international law.[14]

Dicey's self-positioning within these dichotomies invited three different readings of his work.

2.1. 'SEDUCTIVELY INCOHERENT'

American scholar Hessel Yntema portrayed Dicey as 'seductively incoherent'.[15] Dicey, for example, tells us that comity cannot be accepted because it only expresses the motivation for applying foreign law in the first place, but it cannot indicate which law to apply in particular cases.[16] But, of course, much the same can be said about Dicey's preferred principle of the recognition of vested rights. Furthermore, Dicey portrays his principle of the recognition of vested rights as 'the enunciation of a maxim or the statement of a fact', which makes it unclear how his maxim/fact dichotomy maps onto his theoretical/positivist distinction.[17] While Dicey was clear that 'no maxim is a law unless it be part of some municipal law',[18] he concedes that the recognition of vested rights is an underlying principle, rather than a positivist rule and that existing decisions in English private international law do not reference this principle 'in so many words'.[19] Instead, the principle was a 'generalisation' taken from court decisions, judicial dicta and the theory of scholars like Story, Westlake, and Savigny, 'of acknowledged weight and authority'.[20]

If incoherence is meant to signal a failure to stick to set boundaries between philosophical schools of thought, the charge is unfairly directed to Dicey and unfair in general. Not only can the strict boundaries between the different philosophical perspectives be rethought, but private

14 Dicey, above n. 6, p. 10.
15 H. Yntema, 'Dicey: An American Commentary' (1951) 4 *International Law Quarterly* 1.
16 Dicey, above n. 6, p. 11.
17 ibid., p. 23.
18 ibid., p. 19.
19 ibid., p. 61: 'The doctrine, for example, which is embodied in General Principle No. I, of the extra-territorial recognition of duly acquired rights, is rarely, if ever, enunciated in its full breadth by an English Court.'
20 ibid.

international law was and remains an overlooked terrain where these boundaries were constantly being contested. Dicey tells us this much himself in the introduction, where he invites us to acknowledge that conflict of laws was a relatively young area of law, where the fundamental ideas on which a system of rules was based were still being defined and where the jurisprudence was chaotic and often contradictory.[21] Therefore, one may agree with Yntema that Dicey appears 'seductively incoherent' and yet 'appropriately expresses the situation of a branch of law composed of rules to guide national courts in more or less "international" cases'.[22]

2.2. UNREMARKABLE

Perhaps Dicey's theory was not so much incoherent, as it was unremarkable.

Although Dicey constructed his distinctions about different types of projects in private international law, he spent just as much time breaking them down. For example, he tells us that even the scholars that he labelled as 'theorists' focused primarily on the law of their jurisdiction and that references to the 'common law of Europe' were made only when the positive law of their jurisdiction ran out. They too, after all, distinguished between is and ought.[23] He also tells us that uniformity of decisions in private international law is a desideratum in his system as in any other, 'not by the fictitious' authority of a European common law but because of the fact that English judges, when acting in a legislative capacity, 'give weight to the opinion of eminent jurists'.[24] The common law of Europe becomes an 'allowable' fiction because 'judges must legislate, and do in fact legislate' with an eye to the principles adopted in other countries.[25] On the theoretical/positivist scale, there was, in other words, not necessarily a huge difference of substance, but rather of style. In a letter to Bryce at the time of the release of his *Digest* on conflict of laws, he writes that 'the "practical" man will prefer Foote, and the theorist Story or Savigny'.[26] He would have been somewhere in the middle.

---

21 ibid., p. 61.
22 Yntema, above n. 15, 4.
23 Dicey, above n. 6, p. 19.
24 ibid., p. 20.
25 ibid.
26 R.S. Rait (ed.), *Memorials of Albert Venn Dicey: Being Chiefly Letters and Diaries*, Macmillan & Co., London 1925, p. 140.

By far the most problematic aspect of Dicey's work, when placed in an intellectual historical context, was precisely how to judge the novelty and coherence of his central principle of the recognition of vested rights. His principle posed two problems which had been long identified and debated by continental European scholars. First, if, as Dicey argued, only those rights were respected which had been 'duly acquired in the view of English courts', one needed a prior theory of when rights are considered duly acquired. There was, in other words, as Savigny had clarified decades earlier, a helplessly vicious circle embedded in the principle. Dicey's response was perplexing: Savigny's argument that the principle of vested rights cannot answer any or all questions of private international law 'is quite consistent with maintaining that this principle does define the object in the main' of conflict of laws.[27]

The second problem with the vested rights principle relates to Dicey's ambivalence about whether the state or rights come first. Recall that, according to Dicey, courts recognise rights acquired under foreign law, not foreign law directly. But Dicey did not have in mind the recognition of pre-institutional rights (though some fundamental values underlying his public policy exception could be understood in this way)[28] so it seemed that some background understanding of the normative foundations of a state's authority to vest rights was at play, but unarticulated by Dicey. The French scholar Antoine Pillet, who had developed a theory of private international law based on a universal distribution of authority among states, found it perplexing that Dicey failed to offer an explanation of a state's authority to vest rights (whether derived from international law, as Pillet argued, or not) when continental European scholars had this clear in sight.[29] To Pillet, Dicey was attempting to reinvent the wheel in a bizarre way.[30]

These critiques were acknowledged by Dicey's subsequent editors such that, by the sixth edition, it was conceded that only those rights were recognised which were duly acquired according to English private international law rules. Writing from the University of Tasmania in 1959

---

27 Dicey, above n. 6, p. 31.

28 For an argument that the public policy exception in common law jurisdiction is informed by rule of law principles, see J. Langille, 'Frontiers of Legality: Understanding the Public Policy Exception in Choice of Law' [2022] 73(2) *University of Toronto Law Journal* 216.

29 For an overview of Pillet's theory, see R. Banu, *Nineteenth Century Perspectives on Private International Law*, Oxford University Press, Oxford 2018.

30 A. Pillet, 'Sur un Point Peu Apercu de la Doctrine de Dicey' [1923] 4 *Revue de droit international privé* 345.

and cataloguing Dicey's influence on private international law in England and throughout the British Empire, G. W. Bartholomew took stock:[31]

> The revised version of the first general principle therefore becomes simply a restatement that the English courts will recognise any right whose creation is sanctioned by the English courts – a proposition which neither dazzles us with its brilliance nor awes us with its profundity. Savigny had pointed out the circularity of Dicey's original formulation. The editors of the sixth and the seventh editions have thus avoided this fatal circularity by the brilliant expedient of replacing it with a tautology. From a *circulus in probando* to a tautology in sixty glorious years: this is real progress.

However, it seems too easy to charge Dicey with failing to innovate on the theoretical front. On the one hand, this was never Dicey's project.[32] On the other hand, despite charging Dicey for being unremarkable, Bartholomew himself conceded that Dicey's ambivalent centring of the field on the notion of vested rights exposed for the first time some of the most intricate methodological puzzles of the field, including renvoi, incidental question, and characterisation.[33]

2.3. A QUINTESSENTIAL POSITIVIST?

Frederick Pollock thought Dicey's apparent incoherence and lack of insight were explained by his 'ahistorical' perspective on law and his adherence to positivism. He was allegedly too wedded to 'the harsh and narrow so-called analytical school of English jurisprudence'.[34] But this charge is also unhelpful. Dicey relied on positivism to justify writing a book on English private international law, but he was not an anti-comparativist. Also, while he rejected the a priori theoretical model of continental European scholars, he thought the method:

> brings into prominence the consideration which English lawyers are apt to forget: that the choice of one system of law rather than of another for the

31 Bartholomew, above n. 2, 248.

32 In response to Pillet's charge that Dicey did not manage to clarify the nature of the principle of vested rights as an anchor for a theory of private international law, Sir Frederick Pollock offered this response on behalf of Dicey: 'I believe Dicey would not know his own child if he saw it paraded in the full-dress costume of a universal theory … and thereupon charged with being an impostor.' See F. Pollock, 'Professor Pillet on Dicey's Introduction' (1924) 40 *Law Quarterly Review* 271, 273.

33 Bartholomew, above n. 2, 254–58.

34 See Pollock, above n. 32, 272.

> decision of a particular case is dictated by reasons of logic, or convenience, or of justice, and is not a matter in any way of mere fancy or precedent.[35]

Furthermore, his vested rights theory is in many ways less positivistic than that of the continental European theorists he was arguing against. Dicey insists on a distinction that 'may seem verbal, but it is in truth both real and important', namely that courts 'never enforce foreign laws but rights acquired under foreign laws'.[36] Recognising foreign laws directly would allegedly go against a positivist understanding of separated legal systems,[37] but what positivist rule mandated the recognition of vested rights? Dicey's interlocutor, the French universalist scholar Antoine Pillet, similarly referred to a principle of vested rights. But for Pillet, the recognition of vested rights was ultimately a duty grounded in international law (understood as a set of customary laws recognised as valid by all 'civilized' States).[38] Since, for Pillet, rights were vested through state authority, states had a duty to recognise each other's rights to vest such rights. Some of Dicey's writings resemble Pillet's and indeed Dicey refers to Pillet's theory as an extremely instructive one.[39] But Dicey seems ultimately much more ambivalent about the foundation of the principle of vested rights and much less clear about the relationship between vested rights and state authority. This is something that both Pillet[40] and Pollock understood well.[41]

3. READING IN THE PENUMBRA

The three ways in which Dicey has been read thus far are not particularly helpful or revealing. In typical late nineteenth-century fashion, Dicey was both positivist and anti-positivist, he had both particularistic inclinations and was open to comparative analysis, and his critique of comity is

---

35 Dicey, above n. 6, p. 17.

36 ibid., p. 10.

37 For a helpful discussion of the Austinian thesis in the context of conflict of laws see R. Dworkin, 'Comments on the Unity of Law Doctrine (A Response)' in H.E. Kiefer and M.K. Munitz (eds.), *Ethics and Social Justice*, State University of New York Press, New York 1968.

38 A. Pillet, *Principes de droit international privé*, Allier Frères, Paris 1903.

39 A.V. Dicey, *A Digest of the Law of England with Reference to the Conflict of Laws*, 2nd ed., Stevens & Sons, London 1908, p. 13, fn. 1 (stating that Pillet's 'argument deserves careful study').

40 Pillet, above n. 30.

41 Pollock, above n. 32.

more polemical than deeply analytical. It seems more fruitful to take Dicey's eclecticism, and that of many other nineteenth-century private international law scholars, at face value. This eclecticism or ambivalence prompts Dicey to ask helpful questions about the extent to which private international law rules applied throughout the British Empire and the way in which gender questions were challenging some core theoretical and methodological questions in the field.

3.1. EMPIRE

I have argued thus far that Dicey was unclear about the theoretical and conceptual role the 'state' plays in his private international law system and within his principle of the recognition of vested rights. Private international law may be precisely what led Dicey to an insight that he referenced in an undated letter to Edward Freeman and that is cited by Mark D. Walters as marking, for Dicey, the main difference between the French (and continental European, generally) and the English legal system:[42]

> In France they seem to me to start from the notion of the state and let the individual take care of himself. In England as I understand the matter we start from the rights of the individual and hardly recognise the state or Crown as having any rights of its own.

If that is true, then Dicey was 'starting from the rights of the individuals' in a way that did indeed seem unfamiliar and confusing to state-centric internationalist continental European scholars of the nineteenth century who thought that private international law was about an interstate recognition of sovereign authority. Furthermore, this distinction would have had an important ramification for a core question: did private international law apply to all private law relationships set in an intra-imperial context or did it operate only among colonial powers? Many continental European scholars thought the answer (in the negative) was obvious since private international law was meant to achieve an equal distribution of authority among equal sovereigns. They understood Dicey to have fully agreed with them.[43] But because Dicey's private international

42 M.D. Walters, *A. V. Dicey and the Common Law Constitutional Tradition: A Legal Turn of Mind*, Cambridge University Press, Cambridge 2020, p. 170.

43 See Pillet, above n. 30, 354.

law theory was not directly premised on a framework of interstate accommodation of authority (qua comity) or an obligation to respect each state's legitimate authority (qua customary international law), the matter was much more puzzling to him.

Dicey was conflicted about what it meant to limit private international law to a set of civilised states. On the one hand, he recognised that 'this term is of necessity a vague one'.[44] On the other hand, he believed that at least for private international law purposes one had to make a distinction between 'foreign' and 'civilised'. Judging a community as civilised would be based on a 'similarity in principle between the legal and moral notions prevailing among different communities'.[45] But if that was true, Dicey thought the circle of civilised states would have to include not just the metropoles but 'any country colonised or governed by such European state, at least in so far as it is governed on the principles recognised by the Christian states of Europe'.[46] Different parts of the Empire – though not countries where European countries enjoyed extraterritorial privileges – were civilised if and because they are governed by a European country.[47] But if governed by Britain, were the different parts of the British Empire 'foreign'? According to Dicey, they were foreign in 'a legal sense', only because in private international law cases they were designated as such.[48] This string of propositions appeared as puzzling to Dicey as they may seem to his reader. Therefore, Dicey tells us that the proposition of private international law operating among civilised states 'is simply an affirmative and limited statement; it neither affirms not denies anything as to the recognition of rights acquired under the laws of countries which are not civilised'.[49] Nevertheless, to

> … avoid unnecessary perplexity … the rules in this Digest apply only to rights acquired under the law of a civilised country. What, however, is the law, if any,

---

44 Dicey, above n. 6, p. 29.
45 ibid., p. 29.
46 ibid.
47 ibid. ('England, France, Mexico, the United States, and British India, in so far as governed by English law, were civilized countries. Turkey and China are not civilised states within the meaning of this Rule'). Dicey was still puzzled about whether, if foreign, colonies could determine on their own the 'extraterritorial' reach of their laws. See R.F. Shinn and R.A. Cosgrove (eds.), *Constitutional Reflections: The Correspondence of Albert Venn Dicey and Arthur Berriedale Keith*, University Press of America Inc., Lanham 1996 ('*Dicey-Keith Correspondence*') pp. 4–7.
48 Dicey, above n. 6, pp. 67–69.
49 ibid., p. 30. He insists on the same 'positive' assertion in the appendix on civilised states and at p. 30, fn. 2 where he asks rhetorically whether English courts may apply

> which in the opinion of English courts governs transactions taking place in an uncivilised country, e.g. in the Soudan, or in some part of the world not under the sovereignty of any ruler recognised by European law?[50]

This, 'is in many instances a matter of absolute uncertainty'.[51]

Within the *Digest*, Dicey fails to clarify what level of 'governance' or export of English legal principles would be required for a community to be considered civilised *in virtue of* being governed by Britain. He is also puzzled about whether English law or a 'common law of Christendom' is the necessary yardstick for the legal and moral similarity required.[52] Nor does he unpack his circular reasoning that different parts of the British Empire are considered 'foreign jurisdictions' in private international law because private international law cases designate them as such.[53] But Dicey was exploring precisely these kinds of questions in a private correspondence with Arthur Berriedale Keith over two decades. Keith was a colonial officer, from 1914–44 Regius Professor of Sanskrit and Comparative Philology and Lecturer on the Constitution of the British Empire at the University of Edinburgh, as well as Dicey's editor for three editions.[54] Their correspondence shows both Dicey's remarkable ignorance of the basic political and legal structure of the British Empire, but also his desire to connect questions of imperial constitutional law to conflict of laws questions.[55] Dicey was asking what kind and what level of control Britain exercised over the different parts of the Empire,[56] how the public policy exception could be conceptualised in relationship to the different parts of the Empire or when a local legislation could be considered *ultra vires* such that rights emanating under it would not be recognised in England,[57] to what extent local laws on various private law matters deviated from English ones and what legal implications this might have,[58] and so on.

---

the law of England to rights which, if they exist at all, arise from transactions taking place in countries which are strictly barbarous.

50 ibid., p. 725.

51 ibid.

52 ibid., p. 639, fn. 3 and p. 640.

53 ibid., p. 68.

54 For a biography of Keith's life and work see R.F. Shinn, *Arthur Berriedale Keith, 1879–1944: The Chief Ornament of Scottish Learning*, Aberdeen University Press, Aberdeen 1990.

55 Shinn and Cosgrove, *Dicey-Keith Correspondence*, above n. 47.

56 ibid., p. 18.

57 ibid., pp. 2–5.

58 ibid., p. 22.

But while Dicey's theoretical eclecticism prompted him to *ask* probing questions at the intersection of imperial constitutional law and private international law, very few insights are pulled through in the *Digest*. For example, Dicey cites *Philips v Eyre*[59] – the case involving the prosecution of Edward John Eyre, Governor of Jamaica, for the violent repression of the Morant Bay uprising against colonial rule[60] – for the proposition that English courts have jurisdiction to try a Governor for acts done in a 'foreign country'.[61] Yet he had nothing to say about the court's ruling that failing to apply an indemnity law passed by the local legislature would have been 'an unprecedented and mischievous violation of the law of nations'[62] or about the references in the press at the time that, even if it were possible to ignore a local law in a colony like Jamaica, 'a colony like New South Wales or the Canadian states would ill bear to find its Legislature treated with less courtesy than those of foreign states'.[63] This would have been a key case precisely for the kind of puzzle that he raised on the nature of colonies as civilised because they were *governed by English principles of justice* but 'foreign' jurisdictions for purposes of private international law.[64]

3.2. GENDER

Dicey's reluctant focus on the imperial context brought him into yet another unexpected corner, that of questions about gender. Different parts of the Empire had more or less progressive provisions on gender questions. Some allowed married women following desertion or judicial separation to establish a domicile separate from that of their husbands.[65]

---

59 *Phillips v Eyre* (1870) LR 6 QB 1 (Ex Ch).

60 For a wonderful analysis see R.W. Kostal, *A Jurisprudence of Power: Victorian Empire and the Rule of Law*, Oxford University Press, Oxford 2008.

61 See Dicey, above n. 39, p. 210.

62 *Phillips v Eyre*, above n. 59, 31.

63 *Pall Mall Gazette*, 30 January 1869, p. 2.

64 Shinn and Cosgrove, *Dicey-Keith Correspondence*, above n. 47, p. 4. For example, Dicey asked Keith whether the tendency in 1906 had 'shifted' such that British courts 'construe the powers of colonial legislatures extensively instead of restrictively'. What would have been the tendency at the time of *Phillips v Eyre*? See also an interesting correspondence on whether in colonies like Jamaica, where 'the white population is too small', representative government had led to responsible government: see ibid., p. 18.

65 For example, New Zealand Act No. 18 1904 provided in s. 22(3) that a deserted wife domiciled in New Zealand at the time of the desertion shall be deemed for the purpose of the Act to have retained her domicile, notwithstanding that her husband may have since the desertion acquired any foreign domicile. For a letter exchange with Keith on

The Indian Divorce Act 1869 appeared to allow for divorce jurisdiction based on residence, rather than domicile.[66] In various parts of the Empire, a man could marry a deceased wife's sister; legitimation and adoption were possible. The list could go on.[67] Dicey was, as he confessed to Keith, more than 'a good deal puzzled' about the challenges this diversity of views on gender-related issues throughout the Empire posed to the structure of private international law.[68]

First, gender questions seemed to bring him back to the broader puzzles about the application of private international law principles in relationship to the Colonies. Could rights arising from family relationships that were different from those prevalent in England be recognised throughout the Empire? Were they recognised based on imperial legislation or his general principle of the recognition of vested rights or a bit of both, bringing him back to the positivist dilemma? Could the public policy exception apply to block the application of laws emanating from the Colonies or was there a higher degree of deference? Would a higher degree of deference imply that different parts of the Empire were, after all, not truly 'foreign jurisdictions'?[69] But as with colonial questions, very little is made of these puzzles in the *Digest*. For example, in the second edition, Dicey removed the statement he inserted in his first edition, having taken it from Joseph Story's private international law treatise, that 'a marriage is not valid which is incestuous by the laws of all Christian countries'[70] because he had come to agree with John Westlake that 'no country with which the communion of private international law exists has such marriages'.[71] This in effect

these questions, see SHINN and COSGROVE, *Dicey-Keith Correspondence*, above n. 47, pp. 7–16.

66 Bringing in very interesting reflections on the relationship between colonial laws and private international law rules, Dicey thought the Act must have intended to establish jurisdiction based on residence. See DICEY, above n. 39, Appendix fn. 14, pp. 800–05. However, Keith argued that the Privy Council 'would satisfy themselves that the Act should be so interpreted as to coincide with their own view of private international law, despite the fact that the Legislation no doubt did not so intend': SHINN and COSGROVE, *Dicey-Keith Correspondence*, above n. 47, pp. 9, 14.

67 On legitimation see J.D. WHITE, 'Legitimation by Subsequent Marriage' (1920) 36 *Law Quarterly Review* 255. On marriages with the deceased wife's sister see E.S.P. HAYNES, 'The Colonial Marriages Act' (1908) *Fortnightly Review* 844.

68 SHINN and COSGROVE, *Dicey-Keith Correspondence*, above n. 47, p. 5.

69 ibid., pp. 4–20.

70 ibid., p. 640.

71 DICEY, above n. 39, p. 626. Note how Dicey still ponders on cases where prohibited degree marriages are valid in parts of the British Empire and recognised in England (i.e. marriages with a deceased husband's brother in New Zealand): see p. 626, fn. 2.

seems to cancel out all the richness of his puzzle about the nature of the 'communion' within which private international law operates.

Second, these issues were constantly challenging the usefulness of Dicey's principle of vested rights for 'unsettled' questions, most of which were gender-related. If the principle of the 'recognition of vested rights' was meant, even if it 'does not directly solve new problems in private international law', to at least 'help us in perceiving what are the problems which need solution',[72] what could it highlight about gender questions? Was it helpful only to point to the pervasiveness of conflict of laws conundrums around gender especially in an imperial context (no small contribution on its own)? In the second edition, Dicey seems to recognise that the principle of recognition of vested rights might at least encourage some principled consistency, such that decisions on gender questions involving the Colonies would need to feed back into the broader theoretical and methodological framework of private international law. For example, Dicey recognised that if English courts were to admit the extraterritorial validity of a divorce granted in India based on residence, then they should be 'driven to relax the rigidity of the rule that divorce jurisdiction depends wholly on domicile' and therefore potentially allow women to establish a separate domicile for divorce purposes at least in cases of desertion.[73]

Gender questions were also cornering Dicey into a dilemma about his own role in the intellectual and doctrinal history of private international law. For example, in his first edition, when discussing cases where judges were ambivalent about the implication of their decisions for the ability of English women to establish a separate domicile from that of their husbands following desertion or judicial separation, Dicey leaned towards conservative and narrow interpretations, while other prominent scholars interpreted the cases as significant steps towards gender equality.[74] Allegedly, taking the judges' self-expressed doubts at face value even on some of the key gender questions of the day was acceptable since 'an

---

72 Dicey, above n. 6, p. 62.

73 Dicey, above n. 39, p. 805.

74 Dicey, above n. 6, p. 127. cf. J. Westlake, *A Treatise on Private International Law, or, The Conflict of Laws, with Principal Reference to its Practice in the English and Other Cognate Systems of Jurisprudence*, W. Maxwell, London 1858, p. 42; J.A. Foote, *A Concise Treatise on Private International Jurisprudence*, Stevens & Haynes, London 1878, p. 18. In *A.G. of Alberta v Cook* [1926] AC 444 (PC), the Privy Council confirmed Dicey's narrow interpretation of the jurisprudence on dependent domicile. see also Bartholomew, above n. 2, 258–60.

expositor or commentator is not required to be an apologist'.[75] Deliberately or not, Dicey underestimated his own role and influence in the doctrinal history of the field[76] and there was room for speculation that conservative decisions on gender questions in private international law were emboldened by his own quibbles in the *Digest*.[77]

4. CONCLUSIONS

Perhaps it is time to move past reading Dicey in the abstract, limiting ourselves to the core distinctions he made in his introduction to the *Digest*. Instead, we should try to probe the relevance of his dilemmas on positivism, the recognition of vested rights, territoriality, comity, and many other themes for the concrete and consequential issues of the time.

One of Dicey's main contributions may have been in posing some fundamental questions about the way in which private international law was constructing (sometimes alongside, sometimes oblivious to, colonial laws) the imperial legal space and about the significance of questions of gender in this construction. In his correspondence with Keith, Dicey pressed the point that recurrent fictions (such as the one according to which wills made by Englishmen or Scotsmen in India 'were made in Canterbury', or that a ship in the Royal Navy when sailing out of British waters is considered 'I know not on what authority ... as being in the Parish of Stepney') are really the markers of an imperial checkerboard of authority.[78] Pointing Keith to the sections of his *Digest* in which he discusses the application of private international law rules in relationship to the Colonies as 'foreign' and civilised, he reminds us that 'these absurd fictions sometimes cover curious and important points of law'.[79]

And on gender, in one of the last letters addressed to Keith, Dicey draws Keith's attention to the extremely convoluted private international law case of *Ex Parte Mir-Anwaruddin*,[80] in which Mohammedan law clashed with

---

75 DICEY, above n. 6, p. 20.
76 For example, Keith reminds Dicey that the Australian court 'will quote you [Dicey] for the distinction between residence & domicile': SHINN and COSGROVE, *Dicey-Keith Correspondence*, above n. 47, p. 3.
77 BARTHOLOMEW, above n. 2, 257–59.
78 SHINN and COSGROVE, *Dicey-Keith Correspondence*, above n. 47, p. 24.
79 ibid.
80 *R. v The Superintendent Registrar of Marriages, Hammersmith Ex Parte Mir-Anwaruddin* [1917] 1 KB 634.

English marriage law across colonial borders.[81] The case raised all the difficult issues Dicey focused on, including differences in gender norms in the Colonies, as opposed to England, the difficulty of maintaining domicile as a major connecting factor in private international law in the intra-imperial context and the doctrine of dependent domicile.[82]

It is a real shame, then, that Dicey does not fully trace the implications of his theoretical reflections and of the 'curious' fictions he underscored, to help us understand better the significance of private international law in the imperial project and for gender questions. But in the penumbra of his writings, he offers us entry points into extremely useful questions with which to start revisiting the history of private international law in those corners.

81 For a wonderful discussion, see G. Savage, 'More than One Mrs. Mir Anwaruddin: Islamic Divorce and Christian Marriage in Early Twentieth-Century London' [2008] 47 *Journal of British Studies* 348.

82 Shinn and Cosgrove, *Dicey-Keith Correspondence*, above n. 47, p. 166.

PART IV

DICEY AND POLITICAL THOUGHT

DICEY'S IDEA OF THE RULE OF LAW IN ITS HISTORICAL CONTEXT

James Kirby

1. INTRODUCTION

On 28 April 1884, A. V. Dicey gave the first of the lectures which became his best-known work, *The Law of the Constitution*.[1] He had recently been elected Vinerian Professor of English Law at All Souls College, Oxford, and this first lecture, titled 'a Public Lecture on the True Nature of (so-called) Constitutional Law', was delivered on 28 April 1884.[2] As a public lecture, it was addressed to the University at large. The subsequent 'Six Lectures on some fundamental principles of Constitutional Law' began on 30 April 1884[3] and had a more specialist, legal quality. When Dicey wrote to Macmillan & Co. in June 1884 to propose the publication of all seven lectures together, he said it 'would not be a law book in the strict sense of the term, but would I think have some interest for a wider class than mere

1 A.V. Dicey, *Lectures Introductory to the Study of the Law of the Constitution*, 1st ed., Macmillan & Co., London 1885 ('*The Law of the Constitution*'). The third and subsequent editions were published under the more familiar title of *Introduction to the Study of the Law of the Constitution*, 3rd ed., Macmillan & Co., London 1889. References in this contribution are to the first edition unless otherwise stated.

2 *Oxford University Gazette*, vol. 14, Clarendon Press, Oxford 1884, p. 386.

3 ibid.

lawyers'.[4] So it has proved. The published *Lectures Introductory to the Study of the Law of the Constitution* were received from the outset not merely as a work of legal education, but as a major contribution to political and constitutional thought.

The two main claims which *The Law of the Constitution* has on historians of political thought today are its treatment of the idea of sovereignty and its role in developing the concept of the rule of law. The second is the focus of this contribution. It is a story which cannot be told with reference to just one modern discipline or canon of thought. Dicey himself – in his reading and his writings – moved between legal thought, political thought, and historical thought; we must follow him, even if, in the more fragmented world of the centenary of his death, this requires more effort than it did in his day.

Dicey's idea of the rule of law ('or the security given under the English constitution to the rights of individuals')[5] was a composite of three related ideas: (i) 'the absolute supremacy ... of regular law as opposed to the influence of arbitrary power';[6] (ii) 'the equal subjection of all classes to the ordinary law of the land administered by the ordinary Law Courts';[7] and (iii) the fact that

> the general principles of the constitution (as for example the right to personal liberty, or the right of public meeting) are with us the result of judicial decisions determining the rights of private persons in particular cases brought before the Courts; whereas under many foreign constitutions the security (such as it is) given to the rights of individuals results, or appears to result, from the general principles of the constitution.[8]

Each of these components has its own place in Dicey's intellectual development, and it was only in *The Law of the Constitution* that all three were brought together under the heading 'the rule of law' for the first time. The coinage of this term was (as we shall see) not entirely Dicey's own, but it was sufficiently original that reviewers regarded it as 'enigmatical' or even (in a judgment which has not stood the test of time) 'infelicitous'.[9]

---

4 British Library, Add. MS. 55084, fn. 7.

5 Dicey, *The Law of the Constitution*, above n. 1, p. 168.

6 ibid., p. 215.

7 ibid.

8 ibid., p. 208.

9 Anon., 'Professor Dicey on the English Constitution' (8 Jan. 1886) *The Times*, p. 8 ('enigmatical'); H. Stephen (published anonymously), 'Constitutional Law' (1885) 60

2. NO ARBITRARY PUNISHMENT

The first component – no arbitrary punishment – has obvious and deep roots in the common law and the English constitution: in Magna Carta, the Petition of Right, and the Bill of Rights. This was a tradition in which Dicey had been steeped since his earliest years.[10] Indeed, Dicey's first book – derived from an Oxford prize essay on the history of the Privy Council – already sets up an antithesis between arbitrary power and regular law. Its readers are told that:

> [t]he subjects of Edward III, accustomed as they were to the regular administration of law, beheld in the Council and the Law Courts the contrast between irresponsible power and legal authority.[11]

The Long Parliament is praised above all for its abolition of Star Chamber: its members' 'noblest achievements were the establishment of the rule of regular law, and the abolition of torture'.[12] The contrast between royal and arbitrary authority on the one hand, and parliamentary and legal authority on the other, is what one would expect from a young author raised in a family of Whig politics and legal learning.

Perhaps more surprising is the importance of Ireland in the development of this component of Dicey's idea of the rule of law. Dicey today is remembered as a leading defender of the Union against Home Rule, but his interest in Ireland started before the Union became a critical constitutional question. This may be seen in Dicey's journalism, in which Ireland features as a prominent topic from the first half of the 1870s.[13] In an article for the *Fortnightly Review* on 'How Is the Law to Be Enforced in Ireland?', he noted that Ireland was being ruled 'under a system of arbitrary government'.[14] This was the system known as 'coercion', the

Saturday Review, 849 ('infelicitous'). The latter review is unsigned, but Dicey identified its author in a letter to Bryce of 3 January 1886: Bodleian Library, MS. Bryce 2, fn. 68. H. Stephen may have been Henry St James Stephen, an editor of *Mr. Serjeant Stephen's New Commentaries on the Laws of England*, 9th ed., Butterworths, London 1883.

10 M.D. Walters, *A. V. Dicey and the Common Law Constitutional Tradition: A Legal Turn of Mind*, Cambridge University Press, Cambridge 2020, pp. 23–26.

11 A.V. Dicey, *The Privy Council: The Arnold Prize Essay, 1860*, Macmillan & Co., London 1887, p. 19.

12 ibid., pp. 130–31.

13 See, e.g., Dicey's three unsigned review articles on 'Froude's English in Ireland': (22 May 1873) 16 *Nation* 355; (23 Jul. 1874) 19 *Nation* 59; (30 Jul. 1874) 19 *Nation* 76.

14 A.V. Dicey, 'How Is the Law to Be Enforced in Ireland?' (1881) 30 *Fortnightly Review* 538.

regime introduced by the Liberal government's Protection of Persons and Property (Ireland) Act 1881 (known as the Coercion Act), which had empowered the government in Ireland to imprison without trial on the basis of mere suspicion.[15] W. E. Gladstone, defending the policy of the Act at a speech in Leeds on 8 October 1881, had declared that if

> there is still to be fought a final conflict in Ireland between law on the one side and sheer lawlessness upon the other ... then I say ... the resources of civilisation against its enemies are not yet exhausted.[16]

Dicey's response was to say that Gladstone was not really offering a choice between law and lawlessness, but between 'despotism and anarchy'. This was, he said, merely to pit 'one kind of lawlessness against another'.[17] His preferred policy was not detention without trial, but the reform of criminal procedure, in order to secure convictions by due process of law.[18] The longer the policy of coercion continued, he said, the harder it would be to return to 'the orderly reign of regular law'.[19] He therefore celebrated the so-called Kilmainham Treaty (the deal by which Gladstone abandoned coercion in May 1882) as an 'attempt to substitute in the government of Ireland the rule of strict law for a system of ineffective despotism',[20] and he considered that its effects had shown 'that it is possible by a vigorous effort to enforce the rule of law [in Ireland] by the use of legal methods'.[21]

In *The Law of the Constitution* itself, Dicey's main discussion of the rule against arbitrary power is a standard Victorian contrast between liberty in England and the relatively wide powers of arrest which prevailed in continental countries.[22] But it also comes into his discussion of habeas corpus, where he contrasts the relatively modest degree of arbitrariness which Parliament had authorised in England in times of disorder by suspending the operation of habeas corpus in cases of suspected treason,

15 See s. 1(1) of the Act; and see also Dicey's remarks on the Act in *The Law of the Constitution*, above n. 1, pp. 243–44.

16 J. Morley, *The Life of William Ewart Gladstone*, vol. 3, Macmillan & Co., London 1903, p. 61.

17 A.V. Dicey, 'How Is the Law to Be Enforced in Ireland?' (1881) 30 *Fortnightly Review* 538, 541.

18 ibid., 542, 545, 552.

19 A.V. Dicey, 'The Political Outlook in England' (20 Apr. 1882) 34 *Nation* 333, 333.

20 A.V. Dicey, 'Another View of Lord Derby' (11 Jan. 1883) 36 *Nation* 31, 32.

21 A.V. Dicey, 'Notes on the Relation between Home Rule and English Politics' (26 Jul. 1883) 37 *Nation* 72, 72–73.

22 Dicey, *The Law of the Constitution*, above n. 1, pp. 172–77.

with the far broader authorisation of arbitrary power which was found in the Coercion Act and other legislation applied to Ireland.[23]

The first component of Dicey's idea of the rule of law – the rule against arbitrary punishment – is therefore rooted in the common law and the English constitutionalist tradition. But its expression in Dicey's thought is not confined to conventional constitutionalist nostrums about English liberty versus continental despotism. There is also – and from a very early stage in Dicey's work – a preoccupation with how this idea played out in practice in Ireland.

3. ORDINARY LAW AND TRIBUNALS

The second component of Dicey's idea of the rule of law is that 'every man, whatever be his rank or condition, is subject to the ordinary law of the realm and amenable to the jurisdiction of ordinary tribunals'.[24]

We think of this now as perhaps the most distinctive element of Dicey's conception of the rule of law. But Dicey was not the first person to use the words 'the rule of law' in this sense. William Stubbs, Regius Professor of Modern History at Oxford and the pre-eminent historian of the English constitution, had used the phrase in the introduction to his *Select Charters* (1870), where he declared '[t]he reign of Henry II initiates the rule of law'.[25] This, Stubbs said, was because Henry had taken on the privileges of the barons and the clergy, and so had sought 'to reduce all men to equality before the same system of law'.[26] This notion of Henry II as the ruler who broke down the privileges of class and status in favour of equality before a single system of law (the common law) was highly attractive to Dicey. We know that Dicey was familiar with the *Select Charters*, which he described as 'Professor Stubbs's excellent work on documents illustrating constitutional history'.[27] We also know that the first time Dicey used the exact phrase 'the rule of law' was in a review of Stubbs's *Constitutional History of England* in 1875, in which he declared that 'the essential peculiarity of English

---

23 ibid., pp. 243–45.
24 ibid., pp. 177–78.
25 W. Stubbs (ed.), *Select Charters and Other Illustrations of English Constitutional History from the Earliest Times to the Reign of Edward the First*, Clarendon Press, Oxford 1870, p. 21.
26 ibid.
27 A.V. Dicey (published anonymously), 'Freeman's Growth of the English Constitution: I' (12 Sep. 1872) 15 *Nation* 169, 170.

political development' had been that 'the rule of law was established in England at a time when it was unknown in every other great country of Europe'.[28] Its origin lay in the paradox that the strong central rule of the Normans and Angevins had

> first checked the lawlessness of the nobility, then established a uniform system of law and of direct taxation ... and lastly accustomed the English people to that rule of the severe but always fixed and definite law which is the real glory of English institutions.[29]

There can be no suggestion that Dicey lifted the phrase 'the rule of law' from Stubbs. But Stubbs's historical scholarship was important for the development of Dicey's idea that the rule of law is bound up with a strong sovereign power: in the Middle Ages, the Crown; in modern times, Parliament. Stubbs was a Tory constitutionalist who celebrated the Crown as a champion of ordinary subjects against the oppression and factionalism of the nobility. Dicey himself was no Tory, but his qualified admiration for the tradition of Bentham and Austin meant that he was a firm believer in the need for a single ultimate authority – a sovereign – in a state. What he found in Stubbs was a scholarly historical argument that the strength of the Crown in Norman and Angevin England had been crucial in the establishment of the rule of one law over all classes of person, and that that in turn had been crucial to the development of English liberty.[30] This was an idea which could easily be repurposed by Dicey's more liberal, yet still centralist, conception of English constitutional development.

Indeed, the chapter in *The Law of the Constitution* on the rule of law opens with the words: 'Two features have at all times since the Norman Conquest characterised the political institutions of England'.[31] The first feature was the supremacy of 'central government': the sovereign Crown in the Middle Ages and the sovereign Parliament in modern times.[32]

---

28 A.V. Dicey (published anonymously), 'Stubbs's Constitutional History of England' (4 Mar. 1875) 20 *Nation* 152, 154.

29 ibid.

30 cf. W. Stubbs, *The Constitutional History of England in Its Origin and Development*, Library Edition, vol. 1, Clarendon Press, Oxford 1880, pp. 282–83, 505–06, 509–19, 611–12. Dicey also found the same idea (slightly later) in the work of the German historian Rudolf von Gneist: A.V. Dicey (published anonymously), 'Gneist's History of the English Constitution' (24 Jun. 1886) 42 *Nation* 531, 532.

31 Dicey, *The Law of the Constitution*, above n. 1, p. 167.

32 ibid.

The second feature, 'very closely connected with the first', was the rule of law.[33] The connection was close because there had to be a supreme central power – a sovereign – in order to make the law supreme over the rest of the realm. This is a historical idea which is not quite the same as the early Whiggism of Dicey's *Privy Council* essay, with its Macaulayan struggle between antithesis of liberty, Parliament, and the law on one side and the Crown on the other.[34] It is more of a Stubbsian account in which Crown and Parliament each have their role to play in the building of the English constitution and individual liberty.

Yet it was not from Stubbs alone that Dicey drew his conception of the rule of law as the supremacy of the ordinary law and courts. There was also the comparison Dicey drew between English law and *droit administratif.* Dicey himself acknowledged in the preface to *The Law of the Constitution* that he was 'deeply indebted' to 'three authors in particular', namely W. E. Hearn, S. R. Gardiner, and E. A. Freeman.[35] He went on:

> Mr Gardiner's *History of England* has suggested to me the conclusion ... that the views of the prerogative maintained by Crown lawyers under the Tudors and the Stuarts bear a marked resemblance to the legal and administrative ideas which at the present day under the Third Republic still support the *droit administratif* of France.[36]

Gardiner – a historian who strove to write impartially about the divisive events of the Civil War era – had compared Bacon's attempt to give the Crown a veto on cases touching Crown interests with the modern French provision under which 'no agent of the Government can be summoned before a tribunal for acts done in the exercise of his office, without a preliminary authorisation by the Council of State'.[37] This idea was borrowed by Dicey and incorporated into *The Law of the Constitution*.[38]

Hearn – the first of the three authors to whom Dicey had acknowledged a particular debt – had also drawn on the same passage in Gardiner's *History of England* to draw a comparison between Bacon's Chancellorship

33 ibid., pp. 167–68.
34 cf. J.W. Burrow, *A Liberal Descent: Victorian Historians and the English Past*, Cambridge University Press, Cambridge 1981, pp. 31–33.
35 ibid., p. vi.
36 ibid.
37 S.R. Gardiner, *History of England from the Accession of James I to the Disgrace of Chief-Justice Coke 1603–1616*, vol. 2, Hurst & Blackett, London 1863, pp. 266–67.
38 Dicey, *The Law of the Constitution*, above n. 1, pp. 203–07.

and '*la justice administrative*'.[39] This came in a section of Hearn's treatise on *The Government of England* in which he discussed the principle that '[e]very servant of the Crown is amenable to the ordinary tribunals'.[40] Hearn's work also contained a brief section on how '[t]he supremacy of the law', which surveyed how 'the highest of the realm in his contention with the lowest submits to the undisputed supremacy of the law'.[41] It is on this basis that it has been argued that Hearn was the true author of the idea of the rule of law,[42] but this is to overstate the case. Hearn, in the formation of Dicey's idea, is on the same level as Stubbs: he is an author whose work made a significant impression on Dicey, but he did not combine Dicey's three elements of the rule of law, nor elevate them to be one of the main principles of the English constitution.

Standing behind both Hearn and Gardiner as a source of Dicey's ideas about French administrative law was Tocqueville.[43] He had been a noted opponent of *droit administratif*,[44] and regarded French officials' legal privileges as a relic of the *ancien régime*: a means by which officials could break the law with impunity.[45] Dicey drew on him (together with more specialist French legal treatises) as a principal source on *droit administratif* in *The Law of the Constitution*. In particular, he cited Tocqueville's account of how the immunity of officials was a survival from the days of the *ancien régime*.[46] Thus the French Revolution – in Dicey's eyes – had not broken the supremacy of the state over the ordinary law but had, instead, confirmed it.

Dicey's ideas here bear comparison to those of the historical jurist Henry Maine, for whom 'the movement of the progressive societies has hitherto been a movement *from Status to Contract*'.[47] For Maine, this was

---

39 W.E. Hearn, *The Government of England: Its Structure and Its Development*, Longmans, Green & Co., London 1867, pp. 106–07 ('*The Government of England*').

40 ibid.

41 ibid., pp. 87–89.

42 H.W. Arndt, 'Origins of Dicey's Concept of the "Rule of Law"' (1957) 31 *Australian Law Journal* 117, 117–23.

43 Hearn cited Tocqueville directly: *The Government of England*, above n. 39, pp. 107–08. Gardiner did not cite Tocqueville on the comparison with French administrative law, but he did cite him in support of a comparison between another element of Bacon's system and the modern French constitution: Gardiner, above n. 37, pp. 262–63.

44 H.S. Jones, *The French State in Question: Public Law and Political Argument in the Third Republic*, Cambridge University Press, Cambridge 1993, p. 50.

45 A. de Tocqueville, *The Old Regime and the Revolution*, F. Furet and F. Melonio (eds.), A.S. Kahan (trans.), vol. 1, University of Chicago Press, Chicago 1998, pp. 132–35.

46 Dicey, *The Law of the Constitution*, above n. 1, pp. 193–96.

47 H.S. Maine, *Ancient Law: Its Connection with the Early History of Society, and its Relation to Modern Ideas*, John Murray, London 1861, p. 170.

a movement from the family to the individual as 'the unit of which civil laws take account'.[48] For Dicey, the important development was the gradual abolition of status-based privileges and the reduction of all individuals – including nobles, clergy and state officials – to equality before the law.

Another expression of this individualistic idea of equality before the law was Dicey's belief that private law was a better bulwark against tyranny than any special body of public or administrative law. Some jurists of the time had begun to lament that English law lacked an idea of public law. The analytical jurist T. E. Holland noted in his *Elements of Jurisprudence* that the Roman meaning of public law 'has been accepted, and is in daily use, in the legal speculation and practice of the continent of Europe, but unfortunately finds no equivalent in our insular legal terminology'.[49] The legal historian F. W. Maitland lamented the absence of 'the state' from English law, and the fictitious substitution of 'the Crown' as a corporation sole in its place.[50] (Indeed, it is characteristic that the closest to a practitioner's text on public or administrative law at the time bore the title *The Practice on the Crown Side of the Queen's Bench Division*.)[51]

Dicey was quite conscious of the absence of an idea of administrative law in England:

> *Droit administratif* is a term known under one form or another to the law of most continental states, but it is one for which English legal phraseology supplies no proper equivalent. The words 'administrative law' … are unknown to English judges and counsel, and are in themselves hardly intelligible without further explanation.[52]

This was because 'the principles of private law have with us been … so extended as to determine the position of the Crown and its servants'.[53] It was through the law of tort and the writ of habeas corpus (which lay

48 ibid., p. 168.
49 T.E. Holland, *The Elements of Jurisprudence*, Clarendon Press, Oxford 1880, p. 245.
50 F.W. Maitland, 'The Crown as Corporation' (1901) in F.W. Maitland, *State, Trust and Corporation*, D. Runciman and M. Ryan (eds.), Cambridge University Press, Cambridge 2003, pp. 32–51, esp. p. 38.
51 F.H. Short and F.H. Mellor, *The Practice on the Crown Side of the Queen's Bench Division of Her Majesty's High Court of Justice, Founded on Corner's Crown Office Practice*, Stevens & Haynes, London 1890. This was based on the earlier work by R.J. Corner and A.B. Corner, *The Practice of the Crown Side of the Court of Queen's Bench*, W. Benning, London 1844.
52 Dicey, *The Law of the Constitution*, above n. 1, p. 180.
53 ibid., p. 216.

against officials and private individuals alike) that official misdeeds were to be controlled, not through the development of a special body of law applied by special tribunals.[54] Indeed, he ventured to say that 'English legalism is hardly consistent with the existence of an official body which bears any true resemblance to what foreigners called "the administration"'.[55] Such a body would, Dicey feared, attract privileges which lifted its officials above the status of ordinary individuals, thereby infringing the principle of equality before the law.

4. JUDICIAL DECISIONS NOT DECLARATIONS OF RIGHTS

And so, onto the third and final component of Dicey's concept of the rule of law: that constitutional rights were more secure when they resulted from 'judicial decisions determining the rights of private persons in particular cases' than from 'the general principles of the constitution' established by a code.[56]

This idea drew on the traditional constitutionalist view that freedom was better secured by England's ancient constitution and the accumulated precedents of the common law than by any paper constitution or declaration of natural rights.[57] But Dicey was no ancient constitutionalist. He did not believe in the historical accuracy of claims that the assertion of modern liberties was merely the recovery of the ancient rights of Englishmen: 'that modern constitutional freedom has been established by an astounding method of retroactive progress'. This set him apart from most of the leading historians of the day, including William Stubbs and E. A. Freeman, who successively held the Regius Chair of Modern History at Oxford in Dicey's early years as Vinerian Professor.[58]

---

54 ibid., pp. 221–26 (official orders no defence to a claim in tort), 226–50 (habeas corpus).

55 ibid., p. 398.

56 ibid., p. 208.

57 See e.g., J.W. Burrow, *A Liberal Descent: Victorian Historians and the English Past*, Cambridge University Press, Cambridge 1981, passim.

58 E.A. Freeman, *The Growth of the English Constitution from the Earliest Times*, Macmillan & Co., London 1872, was credited by Dicey as the origin of the distinction between the law and the conventions of the constitution: *The Law of the Constitution*, above n. 1, p. vii (and see *The Growth of the English Constitution*, pp. 106–20). Freeman had told Macmillan in 1872 that 'Dicey is specially taken with the third chapter' (which included the material on constitutional conventions): British Library, Add. MS. 55050, fn. 24.

Yet it was still a distinctly historical conception of the basis of individual liberty, rooted as it was in the gradual accretion of judicial precedent rather than in the promulgation of a single code by a rational lawmaker. So in spite of his undoubted Benthamism, he had none of Bentham's contempt for 'judge-made law'.[59] Instead, he shared the goal of many other nineteenth-century law reformers who believed that the task for jurists was not to replace the common law wholesale, but rather to codify it gradually in statutes and textbooks, reforming and improving it where necessary.[60] This kind of codification would not destroy but fulfil the work of the judges. The only objection he saw to the codification of the constitution was that it would be pointless while Parliament remained sovereign and able to amend the code by ordinary law (which, of course, Dicey believed to be vital).[61]

The common law also shaped Dicey's third component of the rule of law in that it had predisposed him to value remedies, forms, and procedure over the content of substantive rights: to focus on the writ of habeas corpus, for instance, over the right to personal liberty.[62] This formalism is encapsulated in Dicey's declaration that the maxim *ubi jus ibi remedium* (where there's a right there's a remedy) was 'much more important than a mere tautologous proposition', since if there was no remedy, there could be no right.[63] This may be compared with his cousin Mr Justice Stephen's dictum that the maxim 'there is no wrong without a remedy' would be better stated 'if it were reversed, so as to stand, "Where there is no legal remedy, there is no legal wrong"'.[64] The remedy was, for a common lawyer, prior to the right or wrong; this reasoning had a decisive impact upon Dicey's concept of the rule of law.

---

59 cf. J.R. Dinwiddy, *Bentham*, Oxford University Press, Oxford 1989, pp. 56–59.

60 See W. Cornish, 'Sources of Law' in W. Cornish, S. Anderson, R. Cocks, M. Lobban, P. Polden and K. Smith (eds.), *The Oxford History of the Laws of England*, Oxford University Press, Oxford 2010, pp. xi, 55–59; K.J.M. Smith, *James Fitzjames Stephen: Portrait of a Victorian Rationalist*, Cambridge University Press, Cambridge 1988, pp. 73–84. Dicey's treatises on domicile and parties to an action were examples of this approach to the common law.

61 Dicey, *The Law of the Constitution*, above n. 1, pp. 82–84.

62 For the formalism of the common law, see F.W. Maitland, *The Forms of Action at Common Law: A Course of Lectures*, Cambridge University Press, Cambridge 1968, pp. 1–9, 65; J.H. Baker, *An Introduction to English Legal History*, 4th ed., Oxford University Press, Oxford 2007, pp. 67–69.

63 Dicey, *The Law of the Constitution*, above n. 1, p. 212.

64 *Bradlaugh v Gossett* (1884) 12 QBD 271, 285.

5. THE 'RULE OF LAW' IN ITS CONTEXT

If Dicey's concept of the rule of law is considered in its context, two points come into focus.

First, it becomes clear that Dicey's concept is not really an Austinian or Benthamite concept. There is perhaps something Benthamite in Dicey's appreciation of *regularity* in his concept of the rule of law. But *The Law of the Constitution* is not concerned with how the law of the constitution promotes the happiness of the greatest number, but rather with how it protects individuals' rights and freedoms (i.e. the rule of law). Nor is the idea of law in 'the rule of law' an idea of law as sovereign command, or indeed law as *lex*; it is a normative idea of law as a just system for securing individual liberty (or law as *ius*).

Secondly, and relatedly, the origins of Dicey's concept of the rule of law are not – for the most part – the works of Bentham, Austin, or the philosophic radicals. Instead, they are primarily the common law, and the works of constitutional historians and political scientists. So, in spite of Dicey's insistence in *The Law of the Constitution* that law is independent from history, and that one can lecture on *The Law of the Constitution* without lecturing on its history, he was in no sense an ahistorical thinker. He was quite aware that he lived in a profoundly historicist culture, as he joked in *The Law of the Constitution*:

> It were far better, as things now stand, to be charged with heresy, or even to be found guilty of petty larceny, than to fall under the suspicion of lacking historical-mindedness, or of questioning the universal validity of the historical method.[65]

Dicey has sometimes fallen under the suspicion of lacking historical-mindedness, but if we look beneath the surface, it is clear that – whatever his other debts to Bentham and Austin – he was still profoundly shaped by the historicist and comparativist intellectual culture in which he lived.

---

65 Dicey, *The Law of the Constitution*, above n. 1, p. 14.

WORDSWORTH AND DICEY

Poet as Political Prophet

Sally Bushell

This contribution explores A. V. Dicey's political thought from a literary perspective, exploring his strong interest in the poetry and political ideals of William Wordsworth. We will approach Wordsworth through Dicey, and Dicey through Wordsworth, in order to address two questions: first, why did Dicey turn to Wordsworth and what core political principles lie at the heart of that attraction? Second, why *poetry*? What can a poet do with politics that others cannot?

Dicey himself draws links between two periods and corresponding works of Wordsworth that, for him, embody his political ideals as they evolve over time:[1]

> Let it be further noted that Wordsworth's statesmanship was a living policy; it grew and developed gradually between 1802 and 1809, between the publication, that is to say, of his earliest patriotic sonnets and the publication of his *Tract on the Convention of Cintra*, which incidentally sets forth the essence of his statesmanship.

Taking our lead from Dicey, then, this contribution will primarily move across and between Wordsworth's 'Sonnets to Liberty' of 1802 (published 1807) and his prose essay on 'The Convention of Cintra' (1809).

We can begin with one of Wordsworth's most well-known sonnets. In 1802, a brief break in the Napoleonic Wars created by the Peace of Amiens allowed Wordsworth to return to France and to reflect upon his own nation from across the channel. In the well-known sonnet 'London',

1 A.V. Dicey, *The Statesmanship of Wordsworth: An Essay*, Clarendon Press, Oxford 1917, p. 75 ('*Statesmanship*').

Wordsworth looks back to a great poetic predecessor who also lived through difficult times:[2]

> Milton! thou should'st be living at this hour:
> England hath need of thee: she is a fen
> Of stagnant waters: altar, sword, and pen,
> Fireside, the heroic wealth of hall and bower,
> Have forfeited their ancient English dower
> Of inward happiness. We are selfish men;
> Oh! raise us up, return to us again;
> And give us manners, virtue, freedom, power.
> Thy soul was like a Star and dwelt apart:
> Thou hadst a voice whose sound was like the sea;
> Pure as the naked heavens, majestic, free,
> So didst thou travel on life's common way,
> In chearful godliness; and yet thy heart
> The lowliest duties on itself did lay.

At first sight, the sonnet seems an unlikely choice for writing about the value and importance of freedom, since it is formally so tight and constrained, but Wordsworth fully maximises its potential in what Judith Page calls a 'dialectic of liberty and restraint'.[3] As Page points out, 'Wordsworth learnt from Milton's sonnets that potentially explosive material could be contained and controlled within such a limited form'.[4] The first section of the sonnet (the eight lines of the octave) establishes the fallen nature of the nation and concludes with a call to the spirit of Miltonic liberty. The second section (the sestet) describes Milton himself in characteristically Romantic terms of nature – as 'a star', 'the sea', 'the heavens' – but the final three lines return to earth to drive towards the conclusion: the real power of Milton was not in his superior poetic skills but his sense of responsibility to self and others. Milton's own position was based on his Christian belief that liberty resulted from Christ's freeing of humans from the slavery of sin. For Milton, true liberty relies on virtuous self-regulation in an individual who is answerable only to God. This is opposed by him to false liberty or 'license'. Wordsworth gestures directly towards this at the end of the octave

---

2 W. WORDSWORTH, *The Major Works*, S. GILL (ed.), Oxford World's Classics, Oxford 1984, p. 286.

3 J. PAGE, 'The Weight of Too Much Liberty: Genre and Gender in Wordsworth's Calais Sonnets' (1988) 30 *Criticism* 192.

4 ibid., 193.

when he contrasts the 'selfish men' of the present with what they should be – virtuous and thus truly free.

Many of the characteristics that *Wordsworth* finds in Milton, *Dicey* finds in Wordsworth. As Dicey makes clear, one reason for his interest in Wordsworth is the way in which the poet's life was shaped by the period of war he lived through, first by the French Revolution and then in response to the Napoleonic Wars. This led him to develop strong principles in relation to freedom and in opposition to tyranny that, for Dicey, create a parallel with his own time. He was not alone in this, as Nettie Tillett makes clear. She describes a meeting between the British and Americans prior to the latter entering the First World War:[5]

> Grey asked Page his opinion of Wordsworth's war poetry. Grey hastened to comment that he considered Wordsworth's the greatest of all war poetry because it does not glorify war, but has to do with the philosophy of war. Viscount Grey was not alone in falling back upon Wordsworth's poetry as he watched the lights go out over Europe in 1914. Wordsworth's 'Character of the Happy Warrior' was the favourite poem of America's Commander in Chief, Woodrow Wilson.[6]

What all of these figures value in Wordsworth, as Dicey also does, is his prophetic position, in 1802, in proclaiming that the rise of a dictator (in his case Napoleon, in theirs the Kaiser and Hitler) will bring about a corresponding response on behalf of liberty in those opposing him. At the same time though, Wordsworth is self-critical and honest in appraising the situation, calling for the necessary response founded on moral virtues, but admitting his own fears.

Dicey published two books on Wordsworth, both during the period of the First World War. The first was an edition of Wordsworth's *The Convention of Cintra* (1915), a prose essay in response to British capitulation in Portugal during the Napoleonic wars (with an introduction by Dicey).[7]

---

5 N.S. Tillett, 'Poet of the Present Crisis' (1944) 52 *The Sewanee Review* 367, 367, referring to a letter written by Walter Hines Page (US Ambassador to Great Britain) to Edward M. House, on 7 December 1915, following a meeting with Sir Edward Gray (British Foreign Secretary). See B.J. Hendrick, *The Life and Letters of Walter H. Page*, vol. II, Doubleday, Page & Co., Garden City 1922, p. 103.

6 Tillett returns to Wordsworth again, in 1944, in relation to the Second World War: 'not even Churchill has expressed so exactly why England took up Germany's challenge in 1939 as has Wordsworth' (Tillett above n. 5, p. 368).

7 A.V. Dicey (ed.), *Wordsworth's Tract on the Convention of Cintra (Published 1809) with Two Letters of Wordsworth Written in the Year 1811, now Republished*, Humphrey Milford, London 1915 ('*Convention*').

The second was a book-long study: *The Statesmanship of Wordsworth* (1917).[8] In both cases, Dicey makes clear that his interest is in what can be learnt from the past to inform the present situation. He introduces Wordsworth's essay in these terms, praising:[9]

> Thoughts which from their profundity and impressiveness are full of instruction for the men of today and are often as applicable to the world-wide war of 1914–15 as they were to the Great War as it used to be called, of 1803–1815.

Similarly, Dicey's given reason for writing *Statesmanship* is that:[10]

> [T]he thoughts and words of Wordsworth, which cheered and strengthened our grandfathers in their resistance to Napoleonic despotism, might encourage and strengthen Englishmen of today in their determination to destroy an aggressive military despotism far stronger and far more cruel than the tyranny which Napoleon all but imposed on the whole continent of Europe.

It is clear that, for Dicey, Wordsworth's own historicity speaks directly to him.

To understand the historical parallels a little more, it is necessary to contextualise Wordsworth's own position. As a young man, he was a radical sympathiser, strongly aligned with the core principles of the Revolution – *Liberté, Egalité, Fraternité*. Although in later life he became more conservative (and was condemned for this by Romantic poets of the younger generation), this is to simplify the difficulties of living through such a period of flux and turmoil and experiencing it first hand, as Wordsworth did. It is worth aligning key dates and events of this period historically to Wordsworth's life.

- 1770 Wordsworth is born
- 1789 The Fall of the Bastille/start of the French Revolution
- 1790 Wordsworth walks across France during his vacation from Cambridge
- 1792 Wordsworth lives in France and has an affair with a French woman
- 1793 France declares war on England
- 1793–1802 French Revolutionary Wars

8 See Dicey, *Statesmanship*, above n. 1.
9 Dicey, *Convention*, above n. 7, p. vii.
10 Dicey, *Statesmanship*, above n. 1, p. 6.

- 1802 The Peace of Amiens
- 1802 Wordsworth is able to visit France and meet his illegitimate daughter for the first time in nine years. He writes the 'Sonnets to Liberty' during this stay
- 1803 Start of the Napoleonic Wars
- 1805 The Battle of Trafalgar
- 1805 Wordsworth completes his great autobiographical epic, *The Prelude*
- 1808 The Convention of Cintra
- 1815 The Battle of Waterloo and defeat of Napoleon

Like many of his contemporaries, the young Wordsworth embraced the principles of the early French Revolution and the belief that this heralded a new dawn for Europe. In his autobiographical epic, *The Prelude*, which charts both the heady optimism and the destruction of those ideals for those living through the Revolution, he declares: 'Bliss was it in that dawn to be alive/ But to be young was very heaven'.[11] In 1790, Wordsworth chose to undertake a walking tour through Revolutionary France during his vacation from Cambridge, and he returned to live in France in 1792, at which time he fell in love with a French woman (Annette Vallon) and had an illegitimate daughter by her (Caroline). However, when the Revolution turned from an internal civil war into a war of foreign aggression, he was put in an impossible position since he could not side with France against his own country. The decisive moment for Wordsworth, as for many others, was the point at which France declared war on Britain in 1793. As Dicey puts it, this created a 'terrific conflict between the inborn love of England on the one hand and vehement sympathy with France, on the other, as long as she was a defender of liberty'.[12] Wordsworth was forced to return to England and to side against France. This led to a period of great depression and despondency (which Wordsworth describes in detail in *The Prelude*) from which poetry essentially saves him.

Wordsworth returned to France at the first opportunity to see his daughter in 1802 (when he also asked Annette's permission to marry Mary Hutchinson) and this is when he looked back at his own country from France and wrote his 'Sonnets to Liberty'. We can see then that these poems are *both* patriotic expressions of Wordsworth as 'statesman' and

---

11 W. Wordsworth, *The Prelude: 1799, 1805, 1850*, J. Wordsworth, M.H. Abrams, and S. Gill (eds.), W.W. Norton & Co., New York 1979, Book X, lines 692–93.

12 Dicey, *Statesmanship*, above n. 1, p. 58.

charged with strong feelings from an intense period of his own life. This doubled charge (universal/individual) seems to strongly attract Dicey.

To consider further the question of why Dicey is drawn to Wordsworth, I want now to turn to his edition of 'The Convention of Cintra'. Because of the Napoleonic Wars, most of Central and Western Europe was under the oppressive rule of France (see Figure 1). Despite the triumphs of the British Navy, who dominated the seas after the battle of Trafalgar in 1805, Napoleon was still largely considered undefeatable on land. This is why a British victory in Portugal in 1808 was so celebrated at home and the ensuing compromise of the Convention of Cintra that followed was so detested. In Spain and Portugal, Sir Arthur Wellesley (later the Duke of Wellington) was in charge of the Peninsular war, defending Portugal against French invasion. He led the Anglo-Portuguese forces against the French successfully in August 1808 at the Battle of Vimeiro, defeating the French General Junot. At this point, the army was ready to press on to Lisbon and force a surrender of the French. However, bizarrely, Wellesley was replaced by two senior generals (Bullard and Dalrymple) who halted the advance and then came to terms with the French in a dismayingly over-generous settlement. Their agreement – the Convention of Cintra – was made without the involvement of the Portuguese themselves and went so far as to agree safe passage for the French troops back to France by the British (to be redeployed against Britain elsewhere).[13]

A sense of public dismay in response to these questionable military decisions can be gleaned from a cartoon by George Woodward, entitled 'The Convention of Cintra, a Portuguese Gambol for the Amusement of John Bull' (Figure 2). By setting the image to the tune of 'This is the House that Jack Built' Woodward uses the cumulative structure of the nursery rhyme to heap outrage upon outrage as he builds to a climax for his final frame:[14]

> This is John Bull, in great dismay, at the sight of the Ships, that carried away, the gold and silver and all the spoil, the French had plundered with so much toil, after the convention which nobody owns, which saved old Junot's Baggage and

---

13 In fact, as Dicey points out, in the long run this may have been a good decision as it saved the City of Lisbon from damage and removed the French entirely from Portugal (Dicey, *Convention*, above n. 7, p. xvi).

14 The verses appeared in the poem titled 'A Poetical Parody; A Christmas Gambol. As sung at the Priory, by the War Minister' published in 'Select Poetry for January 1809' in S. Urban, *The Gentleman's Magazine and Historical Chronicle for the Year 1809*, John Nichols & Son, London 1809, p. 279.

> Bones, altho' Sir Arthur (whose Valour & Skill began so well and ended so ill) had beaten the French, who took the Gold that lay in the city of Lisbon.

Wordsworth's prose essay on this event is fully aligned with public sentiment as well as being characteristic of his political writing, an example of what Simon Bainbridge calls 'impassioned responses to specific crises'.[15] In this, his longest prose work, Wordsworth condemned the agreement and, again (as in his sonnet above), recalled Milton as he lamented Britain's failure to defend universal principles of freedom:[16]

> O sorrow! O misery for England, the land of liberty and courage and peace … O sorrow and shame for our country; for … her Alfred, her Sidneys, and her Milton; whose voice yet speaketh for our reproach; and whose actions survive in memory to confound us, or to redeem!

Still, it was in and through his response to this act of shameful capitulation that Wordsworth articulated the core principles of nationalism that so attracted Dicey.

Dicey's approach to both of these books is that of a historian rather than a literary critic – unapologetically using the texts in strongly factual ways and posing questions about political principles to which he seeks to find the answers. In *Statesmanship* he is explicit about this:[17]

> My conviction then is that while Wordsworth's eminence as a poet is, in England at least, universally acknowledged, his distinction as a statesman has not received anything like due recognition.

For 'The Convention of Cintra' he asks:[18]

> Why was the Convention of Cintra intensely unpopular? …
>
> [W]hat were the grounds on which [it] was denounced by Wordsworth? …
>
> [W]hat were the results or the effects of Wordsworth's pamphlet?

15 S. Bainbridge, 'Wordsworth's Political Odyssey' in R. Gravil and D. Robinson (eds.), *The Oxford Handbook of William Wordsworth*, Oxford University Press, Oxford 2018, p. 117.
16 Dicey, *Convention*, above n. 7, p. 108.
17 Dicey, *Statesmanship*, above n. 1, p. 5.
18 Dicey, *Convention*, above n. 7, pp. vii–viii.

Figure 1. Map of Europe under Napoleonic Rule in 1812

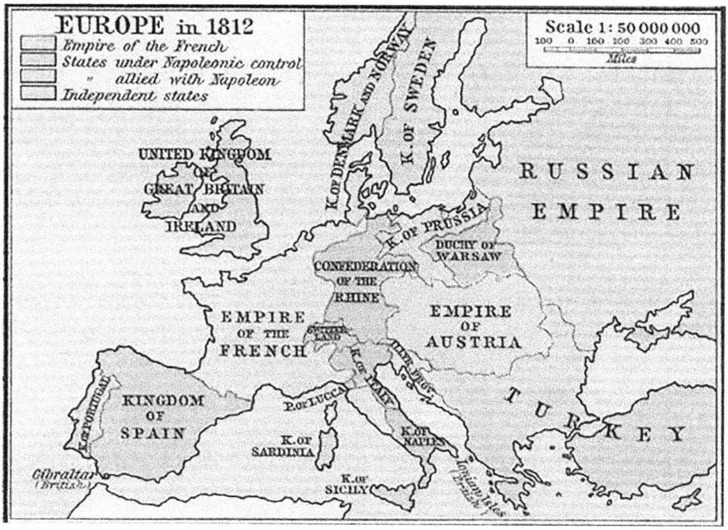

Source: William Robert Shepherd (1911), Historical Atlas. New York: Henry Holt and Company: Wikipedia Commons: https://en.m.wikipedia.org/wiki/File:Europe_in_1812.PNG.

Figure 2. The Convention of Cintra, or a Portuguese Gambol for the Amusement of John Bull

Source: George Woodward (1809), Bodleian Libraries, University of Oxford: https://digital.bodleian.ox.ac.uk/objects/d187bfd5-575a-48de-9d35-fa650195c6d3/surfaces/d187bfd5-575a-48de-9d35-fa650195c6d3/.

It is in addressing the second of these questions that Dicey identifies the grounds of Wordsworthian nationalism. As Dicey makes clear, Wordsworth was less concerned at the incompetence of the military leaders than at the fact that the agreement was made without consulting the government of the country it was meant to be supporting. His outrage was focused upon 'the extent to which the Convention encroached upon the rights of the Portuguese Government, and humiliated and insulted a country to the aid of which [it] had come as its ally'.[19] This led Wordsworth to become what Dicey describes as the 'earliest of English Nationalists',[20] because the ways in which the Convention violated both the principles and feelings of nationalism led him to articulate core statements of his own. These are summarised by Dicey as:

> First. National independence has, to every European State which has become possessed thereof, been the necessary condition or source of the greatest of blessings ... National independence combined ... with the possession of personal freedom.[21]
>
> Secondly. Every independent nation, and above all England, is interested in the maintenance of the national independence of every other country.[22]
>
> Thirdly. No State ought to possess irresistible military power so as to menace the legitimate independence of other countries.[23]
>
> Fourthly. It is desirable to create a new balance of power.[24]

It is in relation to the final point particularly (the combining of a 'remodelling of Europe' with a balance of power centred on a mutual protection of independence) that Dicey's attraction to Wordsworth in the context of his own comparable historical moment is made explicit. It is the combination of the need to retain a balance of power in Europe and the need to defend the independence of each nation against acts of unjustified oppression that fits not only with resistance to Bonaparte in 1802–15, but also to the German Empire in 1915. In anticipating these political ideals, so needed in his own time, Dicey sees Wordsworth as a prophet, envisioning Britain's policy across the whole of the nineteenth century: 'He was at once

19 ibid., p. xvii.
20 ibid., p. xx.
21 ibid., p. xxi.
22 ibid., p. xxiv.
23 ibid., p. xxv.
24 ibid., p. xxvi.

a Prophet, a Nationalist, and a Patriot'.[25] In fact Dicey goes so far as to claim that:[26]

> The policy of our country, in so far as it coincided with the statesmanship of Wordsworth, was during that century markedly successful; in so far as it deviated from his statesmanship it ended in failure …

In the final chapter of *Statesmanship*, entitled 'The Lessons for the Present War of Wordsworth's Statesmanship', Dicey again explicitly draws on Wordsworth to assert a moral basis for political decision-making in relation to the First World War:

> England should pay due respect to nationalism.[27]
>
> Our duty is … to employ the true means of liberty and virtue for the ends of liberty and virtue.[28]
>
> England and her Allies must reject every peace which is not based on complete victory.[29]
>
> [T]he paramount duty [is] of cherishing a noble hopefulness …[30]

To some extent then, we have answered the first question posed at the start of this piece concerning the reasons for Dicey's interest in Wordsworth's political principles, but what of the second question: why *poetry*?

The effect of the democratic principles of the French Revolution upon Wordsworth is deeply social and humanitarian, and this affects his core poetic statements. As a poet he declared himself to be 'a man speaking to men'.[31] He sought to write from the heart in language that could be understood by the ordinary man; he chose to live away from the metropolis and took as his subject the lives of farmers, pedlars, and beggars that he saw around him. What poetry can do, that other forms of writing cannot, is speak to us directly. As Wordsworth puts it in his poem 'The Old Cumberland Beggar', 'man is dear to man' and 'we have

---

25 Dicey, *Statesmanship*, above n. 1, p. 77.
26 Dicey, *Convention*, above n. 7, p. xxxiii.
27 Dicey, *Statesmanship*, above n. 1, p. 119.
28 ibid., p. 121.
29 ibid., p. 129.
30 ibid., p. 133.
31 See R.L. Brett and A.R. Jones (eds.), *Lyrical Ballads: Wordsworth and Coleridge*, Cambridge University Press, Cambridge 1963, Preface, p. 255.

all of us one human heart'.[32] In the end, I think for Dicey it is the way in which Wordsworth's principles are personal, humanised, and grounded that makes him so attractive:[33]

> It is the effort to place himself in harmony with the best and strongest feelings of human nature which makes sentences from Wordsworth's tract ring as true and have as much meaning in 1915 as they had in 1809.

Bearing this in mind, I want to conclude with another of Wordsworth's 'Sonnets to Liberty'. While visiting Annette and Caroline in Calais in 1802, during the temporary peace between England and France, Wordsworth took advantage of his physical distance to look back to England physically, spiritually, and symbolically from across the Channel. Unknowingly, he did so, fearing invasion, from the same beach upon which Napoleon would mass his forces for intended invasion one year later in 1803, when the threat of invasion was at its highest.[34]

> Fair Star of evening, Splendour of the West,
> Star of my Country! on the horizon's brink
> Thou hangest, stooping, as might seem, to sink
> On England's bosom; yet well pleas'd to rest,
> Meanwhile, and be to her a glorious crest
> Conspicuous to the Nations. Thou, I think,
> Should'st be my Country's emblem; and should'st wink,
> Bright Star! with laughter on her banners, drest
> In thy fresh beauty. There! that dusky spot
> Beneath thee, it is England; there it lies.
> Blessings be on you both! one hope, one lot,
> One life, one glory! I, with many a fear
> For my dear Country, many heartfelt sighs,
> Among Men who do not love her, linger here.

As in the sonnet to Milton, Wordsworth manipulates the tight form to move visually downward and inward, across each part. First, he looks up to the star, then to the distant coastline, and finally he moves inward, into the poet's own anxious state. At the same time, we can also see, in the light cast by Dicey, that the poem articulates a proto-nationalist response.

---

32 ibid., p. 202, lines 140, 146.
33 Dicey, *Convention*, above n. 7, p. xl.
34 Wordsworth, above n. 2, p. 281.

The nation is a symbol of freedom, a light beaconing in the darkness, remaining free, off the coast of mainland Europe, 'Conspicuous to the Nations', when so many others have capitulated. At the same time though, England is not just a remote symbol but a real place, a 'dusky spot' that – precisely *because* of the poet's distance from it – can be seen to be unified: 'one hope, one lot, one life, one glory'. All this is abstract and idealised, but the ending of the poem brings it home, fixing its sights on the individual living in and through this particular historical moment.

The conclusion is a strange anticlimax, turning from hope to fear, from unity to isolation and yet it perfectly embodies the complexities of Wordsworth's personal position – torn between one nation and another, between his personal past and future as well as that of his country. J. Hillis Miller describes the ending as a 'blankness of irresolution'.[35] Judith Page sees it as a bringing together of public and private:[36]

> Through the nuptial metaphor … Wordsworth links his personal ambivalence with his public hopes and fears, and thus articulates both in the same breath. Wordsworth's preoccupation with marriage becomes the underlying metaphor of his thoughts about England.

For Dicey, Wordsworth is living through a process at the same time as seeking to make sense of it and to help others in articulating that response, as he himself is then doing through his books *on* Wordsworth. It is this above all that attracts him – Wordsworth as person, poet and prophet, three-in-one:[37]

> Wordsworth is … intensely interested in tracing the connexion between his political beliefs and his moral creed and especially the connexion between these beliefs and the common beliefs and feeling of ordinary men.

---

35 J.H. MILLER, 'The Still Heart: Poetic Form in Wordsworth' (1971) 2 *New Literary History* 297, 303.
36 PAGE, above n. 3, 196–97.
37 DICEY, *Convention*, above n. 7, p. xxxix.

REVOLUTION AND THE RULE OF LAW

Dicey on Irish Home Rule

Marc MULHOLLAND

In 1907, one G. Locker-Lampson published a survey of Irish history since the 1800 Act of Union, *A Consideration of the State of Ireland in the Nineteenth-Century*. Ireland before the Union, he wrote, was a sink of Irish poverty and English corruption, where sinecures were secured for those 'bawds and bastards whom public opinion would have made it dangerous to provide for on the English Pension List'.[1] In 1798, rebellion had been cynically provoked by the government, in a spirit of 'political malignity', so that the peasantry, 'hounded to desperation by a deliberate policy of cruel persecution', could be crushed in arms.[2] In the subsequent 'carnival of butchery' the rebel Irish 'were drowned in their own revolutionary blood'.[3] The Act of Union, 'unconstitutional to the core', was promoted by Prime Minister Pitt's 'cold, formal, stately verbiage' and secured by 'trickery and corruption'.[4] It marked the abandonment of Irish national interests by its land-owning classes, who voted their own parliament out of existence, and thereby became 'traitors'.[5] The Union was a 'farce' and by 1810, relations between Britain and Ireland had become 'well-nigh insufferable'.[6]

---

1 G. LOCKER-LAMPSON, *A Consideration of the State of Ireland in the Nineteenth Century*, A. Constable, London 1907, p. 12.
2 ibid., pp. 49–50, 53, 55.
3 ibid., p. 57.
4 ibid., pp. 104, 70.
5 ibid., pp. 65, 69.
6 ibid., pp. 200–01.

The landed elite, having betrayed their country, 'severed themselves entirely from the native Irish', threw in their lot with England, and resisted all reasonable attempts at reform.[7] The legacy of conquest and confiscations had produced 'perhaps the worst agrarian system the world has ever seen'.[8] The Catholic masses, however, 'after a period of cruelty, anguish, and hopeless combat that would have crushed into the dumb servility of despair any other race of men … rose from their mother soil … unconquered and proud'.[9] They found their champion in Daniel O'Connell, hysterically loathed by the Protestant Ascendancy 'with an execration that was all the more bitter for being tinged with … fear'.[10] O'Connell secured Catholic emancipation in 1829, a concession wrested from his enemies who, 'after years of fighting him tooth and nail for many years … had at length been driven into a corner with their tail between their legs', but who nonetheless insisted on hedging their retreat with provisos 'savouring of petty spite'.[11] O'Connell struggled on, fighting for reform and restoration of the Irish Parliament, only to die defeated and heartbroken in 1847 in the midst of the Famine. He had been 'scoffed at, reviled, hated, shunned, almost spat upon by men who were not worthy to tie his boot-strings', politicians who were 'highly polished on the outside' but 'incurably useless … radically rotten and unsound' on the inside: 'the scum' of British civilisation.[12]

Years of struggle by the Irish peasantry against landlordism wracked Ireland. There was 'no greater indictment' of English misgovernance because 'for several hundred years the rulers of Ireland had been employing every conceivable method of persuasion to enable the landlord to exploit his property in Ireland regardless of the welfare of those who had to live on it'.[13] During the Famine years, 'the land produced ample provision for its own population … without the necessity of importing an ounce of food', but much of it was exported.[14] Repeal of the Corn Laws destroyed Irish tillage and replaced families with cattle and sheep. The Encumbered Estates Act, passed at the tail-end of the Famine, was 'nothing less than an edict of confiscation of Irish land'. Most cases of 'harsh eviction, rack-renting, and other unjustifiable conduct during the next forty years', could be traced to

---

7 ibid., p. 74.
8 ibid., p. 14.
9 ibid., p. 94.
10 ibid., p. 101.
11 ibid., pp. 122, 123.
12 ibid., p. 220.
13 ibid., pp. 225, 235.
14 ibid., p. 272.

the 'brood' of new owners it created.[15] Chronic agrarian crime, 'a system of wild justice', was forced upon the peasantry 'for want of any legal means of redress'. It was 'a symptom of her rulers' own disease'; Ireland's rulers 'lacked the brains and character necessary' to deal with it.[16]

Charles Stewart Parnell, with 'pale face and indomitable courage', stepped forward as 'the mysterious protagonist in the struggle for Irish freedom'.[17] The Land League, of which Parnell was president, led a militant campaign of the peasantry against landlordism from 1879–81, occasioning terrible violence and intimidation.[18] The resultant Land Act of 1881, which severely limited the rights of private property in land, was 'a revolutionary socialistic measure', but the 'landlords had brought it on themselves'.[19] Parnell was on the brink of winning Home Rule for Ireland when he was brought down by a divorce case, the 'incomparable hypocrisy' of the English nonconformist conscience, and the betrayal of his followers in 1889–90.[20] 'This is Ireland', Locker-Lampson concluded, 'this is the country whose rulers deem they have governed wisely … Oh! The vanity, the obtuseness, the vulgar conceit of so supposing'. He called upon his British readers to 'humble yourselves and desperately feel the poignancy of your own failure'.[21]

This, we might reasonably surmise, was an Anglophobic Irish nationalist screed. We would be wrong. Godfrey Locker-Lampson was a Conservative and Unionist Member of Parliament, adamantly opposed to Home Rule. He had no Irish background, was a product of Eton and Cambridge, served in the Foreign Office, and had a long and respectable career as a belle-lettrist and a junior minister. His book on Ireland, moreover, was no eccentricity. Britain's governing incompetence and malignancy in Ireland was standard fare in establishment diagnoses. Disraeli, in 1844, had famously described Ireland as having 'a starving population, an absentee aristocracy, an alien Church, and … the weakest Executive in the world'. The obvious remedy, to its miseries, he admitted, was a revolution that would be amply justified in its own right, even if against the interests of Britain.[22] Gladstone had agreed. 'We admit among ourselves', he had said to

15 ibid., p. 265.
16 ibid., pp. 336, 337.
17 ibid., p. 369.
18 ibid., pp. 380, 381.
19 ibid., p. 391.
20 ibid., p. 446.
21 ibid., p. 459.
22 T.E. Kebbel, *A History of Toryism: From the Accession of Mr. Pitt to Power in 1783 to the Death of Lord Beaconsfield in 1881*, W. H. Allen & Co., London 1886, p. 392.

Parliament when seeking to explain the revolutionary separatist Fenianism of the 1860s, that it was 'the ultimate result of our misgovernment of the country'.[23] Joseph Chamberlain, who would go on to become the leader of the Liberal Unionists, was unsparing in his confession that Ireland was ruled 'on the bayonets of 30,000 soldiers encamped permanently as in a hostile country'.[24]

1. THE PARADOXES OF UNIONIST HISTORY

History, it was clear, provided little sustenance for the unionist cause. James Antony Froude, it was true, had written a massive anti-Irish study, reeking with racial tropes, but his general conclusion was that England had never understood Ireland and persistently misgoverned it:[25]

> All things have their appointed end, and English dominion over Ireland must come to an end also. And yet the cause is so plain that there is scarcely a man in either country who does not know what it is. We have professed to govern, and we have not governed or tried to govern.

If his recommendation of something like despotic rule was hardly in the spirit of Irish nationalism, his diagnosis of British incompetence and selfishness did little to burnish unionist pride. W. E. H. Lecky's histories of the eighteenth century and first half of the nineteenth century damned the cruelty and short-sightedness of England. 'It had been one of the great misfortunes of the English Government', he wrote,[26]

> that during a considerable period of its history, it had been either compelled or persuaded to adopt as its method of managing Ireland, the worst of all expedients, that of endeavouring to inflame the animosities and deepen the divisions between the Protestants and Catholics.

---

23 J. Morley, *The Life Of William Ewart Gladstone*, vol. II, Macmillan & Co., New York 1903, p. 297.

24 *Home Rule: A Reprint from the 'Times' of Articles and Letters*, George Edward Wright, London 1886, p. 329.

25 J.A. Froude, *The English in Ireland in the Eighteenth Century*, vol. III, Longmans, Green & Co., London 1881, p. 558.

26 W.E.H. Lecky, *A History of England in the Eighteenth Century*, vol. VII, Longmans, Green & Co., London 1890, pp. 100–01.

Lecky, like Froude, was a vehement unionist, but nationalists turned first to their works when seeking an indictment of the Union.

It was partly though a reading of such history that Gladstone, in 1885, stunned unionism in Britain and Ireland by adopting the Irish nationalist demand for Home Rule. He was persuaded that the Union had been passed illegitimately and that rule from Westminster had proven itself both inefficient in governing the Irish and unable to win their willing consent. Unionists were now posed with the challenge of seeing off an argument for Home Rule that was solidly based on a history that their own brightest luminaries had largely composed. It was not a historian, therefore, but a legal scholar, A.V. Dicey, who most influentially accepted a challenge, which, as George Boyce puts it, 'welded together' his 'judgement and his passion'.[27]

2. THE LAND WAR AND THE LEAGUES

Dicey wrote his famous riposte, *England's Case against Home Rule* (1886), in the midst of a period of extraordinary tumult. Gladstone's volte-face was not just a shocking adoption of a risky constitutional novelty, but in the eyes of many a perilous retreat in the face of a novel and dangerous socio-political phenomenon widely known as 'Parnellism'. This was based on the 'New Departure', a semi-official alliance of revolutionary Fenianism (represented by John Devoy), agrarian agitation (Michael Davitt), and parliamentary Home Rule nationalism (Parnell). In 1879, Devoy and Davitt had offered Parnell Fenian support if he substituted the Home Rule slogan of federation with that of 'self-government' and endorsed an agitation for peasant proprietorship. Devoy was disowned by the Supreme Council of the Irish Republican Brotherhood ('IRB'), who saw the land issue as a diversion from the republican struggle, but the failure of the 1867 Fenian rising encouraged Fenian militants to emerge from their 'rat holes of conspiracy', as Devoy put it, and engage in mass agitation.[28]

In April 1879, 10,000 people attended a rally in Irishtown, County Mayo, forcing Parnellites to pay attention. In June 1879, the 'New Departure' was

27 D. George Boyce, 'Moral force unionism: A. V. Dicey and Ireland, 1885–1922' in S. Wichert (ed.), *From the United Irishmen to Twentieth-century Unionism: A Festschrift for A.T.Q. Stewart*, Four Courts Press, Dublin 2004, p. 98.

28 J. MacDonald, *Diary of the Parnell Commission*, T. Fisher Unwin, London 1890, pp. 288–89.

formalised, with Parnell apparently giving vague assurances to Devoy and Davitt. The same month, Parnell addressed a demonstration in Westport, also in the west of Ireland, where he called for resistance to high rents and evictions: 'keep a firm grip on your homesteads'.[29] In October 1879 the Irish National Land League was established, with Parnell as its President.

The Land War developed first as mass demonstrations, followed by secret society vigilantism. Evictions were resisted, Land League 'courts' usurped the normal functions of law, and 'boycotting' socially excommunicated landlords, their agents, and land-grabbers. The March–April 1880 general election returned a cohort of Parnellite MPs and a Liberal government led by Gladstone. Back in Ireland, full-time League organisers were appointed in October 1880, their names selected on the advice of Patrick Egan, Treasurer of the League and a Fenian. The four most important were Matt Harris, P. J. Sheridan, Michael Boyton, and James J. O'Kelly: all four were ex- or current Fenians (Harris would remain on the Supreme Council of the IRB until December). All ostensibly urged the Irish faming classes to keep within the law while making clear their approval of local 'moonlighters' using force to maintain solidarity behind the Land League. Harris counselled militant resistance to eviction in a speech lambasting landlord evictions delivered in Galway on 24 October 1880:[30]

> And when I see this extermination, and when I see the weakness of our people, and when I see tyranny triumphing over right and justice, and when I see my fellow-countrymen driven to the four winds of heaven, I say to myself, and I say it here today, that if the tenant farmers of Ireland shoot down landlords as partridges are shot in the month of September, that Matt Harris never would say one word against them.

Gladstone saw the agitation as an invitation to crime, telling the House of Commons on 28 January 1881 that it was 'with fatal and painful precision the steps of crime dogged the steps of the Land League'.[31] Unmoved, Parnell obstructed attempts to introduce repressive legislation at Westminster, and in so doing freely showed his contempt for Parliament. When he denied that 'secret societies' still existed in Ireland, as he later admitted in a rare

---

29 J.E. Pomfret, *The Struggle for Land in Ireland, 1800–1923*, Russell & Russell, New York 1969, p. 143.

30 H. James, *The Work of the Irish Leagues*, Cassel & Co., London 1890, pp. 300–01.

31 *'As It Was Said': Extracts from Prominent Speeches and Writings of the Parnellite Party 1878–1886*, Irish Loyal and Patriotic Union, Dublin 1886, p. 119.

lapse of caution, it was because 'I was trying to mislead the House so as to cut away the ground from the feet' of the government.[32]

Driven to compromise, the government, in October 1881, passed a Land Act which enshrined 'dual ownership' of the land between tenant and landlord. A Land Commission was set up to fix fair rents and evictions were limited to cases of non-payment of these rents. A 'Coercion' Act passed at the same time saw Parnell arrested along with other Land League leaders. In response to this and inadequacies in the Act, a general rent strike call was issued by the imprisoned leaders. In the winter of 1881–82, agrarian 'outrage' erupted as agrarian 'moonlighters' roamed the localities. Parnell and Gladstone were eager for a settlement. In return for the release of the leaders and the inclusion in the terms of the Land Act of those small farmers in arrears with their rent, Parnell, in the so-called Treaty of Kilmainham Gaol of May 1882, agreed to call off the agitation. Parnell's move to respectability was accelerated by the double assassination, on 6 May, of the Chief Secretary and the Permanent Under-Secretary in Phoenix Park, carried out by the Irish National Invincible, a secret strike unit that had been first organised by Matt Harris. Parnell condemned the murders.

In 1882, the National League, a primarily constitutional and electoral organisation with Parnell as president, replaced the Land League. Electoral reform in 1884 tripled the electorate to 700,000. In the 1885 general election, the Parnellite party won complete hegemony over Catholic Ireland with 86 seats. From 1885, the Parnellite Party at Westminster was superbly organised, had a whip applied, and paid its members, many of whom were of a relatively low social class, out of party funds. They behaved as a disciplined, independent Irish Party. Parnell concentrated on winning influence over British politicians. His party tacked and manoeuvred between both of the main British parties. When Gladstone publicly announced his willingness to introduce Home Rule for Ireland, the Conservatives reacted by coming out forcefully against. Parnell, who held the balance of power, combined with the Liberals to drive the Conservatives out of office in January 1886.

The April 1886 Home Rule Bill failed in the House of Commons due to Liberal defections, and the Conservatives were returned with a massive majority in the ensuing election. In the hiatus that followed, land agitation was restarted with the Plan of Campaign (1886–90). This was effectively an attempt at collective bargaining over rents on a limited number of estates

---

32 MacDonald, above n. 28, p. 224.

and a series of rent strikes. The Campaign was always limited and was met by severe coercion from the Conservative government. Parnell, annoyed at the strains put on his alliance with the Liberals, stayed aloof.

Two further Land Acts were passed in 1885 and 1887 which increased loan funds for tenants to buy their farms. Parnell's authority was now at its height. An attempt to associate him with terrorism and extremism, particularly the Phoenix Park murders, collapsed when a series of allegations printed by *The Times* proved to be based upon forgeries. The Conservative government, however, used a Special Commission, established to investigate the allegations, to associate the Irish nationalists with crime, and thus blacken their cause in British opinion. In 1889, Captain William O'Shea cited Parnell's name in divorce proceedings against his wife, Katharine. Parnell and Mrs O'Shea had been closely involved since 1880, probably with Captain O'Shea's connivance. Parnell's public exposure led to his repudiation by the Liberal Party and consequently his rejection as leader by the majority of the Irish MPs. Parnell spent the last year of his life on incessant speaking tours in Ireland, in which he switched back to radical rhetoric. He condemned the Liberal alliance, appealed obliquely to Fenian sympathies, and nurtured an urban and rural working class audience. He died of pneumonia, contracted while attempting to rally supporters in numerous open air meetings over the winter, in 1891, aged only 45, leaving a split party and the myth of the 'lost leader'.

'Parnellism' represented a new and disquieting incursion into the British body-politic. It combined a disdain for Parliamentary protocol, pragmatic disregard for law and order in Ireland, and willingness to tacitly co-operate with dedicated revolutionaries. Parnell, with invincible sang-froid, had been quite clear about this when asked about the 'New Departure' in late 1879:[33]

> As far as I have been able to gather the Fenian organisation and its leaders are opposed, though not hostile, to our movement, the reason being that it is constitutional. A true revolutionary movement in Ireland, should, in my opinion, partake of both a constitutional and an illegal character. … [I]ndeed if we look at the action of the Irish parliamentary leaders since the union, there is ample justification for the views of the physical force party.

A mass movement that partook of 'both a constitutional and an illegal character' was a terror in itself for the establishment political classes, and

[33] 'Report of the Special Commission, 1888', HMSO, London 1890, p. 18.

many feared that it presaged a similar course for proletarian politics in Britain.

Parnellism had recast the Home Rule movement as a potent combination of the revolutionary and the constitutional. Richard Barry O'Brien, himself a Parnellite nationalist Member of Parliament, said of the charges considered by the Special Commission:[34]

> The *Times did* prove that, during the Land League agitation, lawlessness and anarchy prevailed, and that crime and outrage were rampant in many parts of the country. The *Times* did *not* prove that the Irish members were in any way implicated in outrage, though they made no serious effort to stop outrages. ... The *Times* proved that Fenians or ex-Fenians and certain members of Parliament, and certain leaguers were in touch ... but it did *not* prove that any alliance, strictly so called, existed ... In a word, the Parnellite party lived, moved, and had its being in an atmosphere of treason and lawlessness, but no overt acts were brought home to individuals.

Parnell's private response to the Special Commission's final Report, embodying these conclusions, was to say, 'Well, really, between ourselves, I think it is just about what I should have said myself'.[35]

3. DICEY'S REJECTION OF HISTORICISM

Dicey's intervention, therefore, was against the background of a new kind of revolutionary-constitutional agitation. How was he to evaluate it? Though a strain of historicism was evident in English legal scholarship, notably in Austin and Maine, Dicey's point of departure, even while it acknowledged the slow accretions of common law, was essentially rationalist. Commenting on Edward Freeman's *Growth of the English Constitution*,[36] with its mass of involved historical analysis and antecedents, he had remarked placidly:[37]

> All this is interesting, erudite, full of historical importance, and thoroughly in its place in a book concerned solely with the 'growth' of the constitution; but in

---

34 R.B. O'Brien, *The Life of Lord Russell of Killowen*, Smith, Elder & Co., London 1901, pp. 221–22.

35 R.B. O'Brien, *The Life of Charles Stewart Parnell*, vol. II, Thomas Nelson & Sons, London 1899, p. 233.

36 E.A. Freeman, *The Growth of the English Constitution from the Earliest Times*, Macmillan & Co., London 1872 (2nd ed., 1873).

> regard to English law and the law of the constitution … mere antiquarianism. Let no one suppose that to say this is to deny the relation between history and law. It were far better, as things now stand, to be charged with heresy, than to fall under the suspicion of lacking historical-mindedness, or of questioning the universal validity of the historical method. What one may assert without incurring the risk of such crushing imputations is, that the kind of constitutional history which consists in researches into the antiquities of English institutions, has no direct bearing on the rules of constitutional law in the sense in which these rules can become the subject of legal comment. … [A]ntiquarianism is not law, and that the function of a trained lawyer is not to know what the law of England was yesterday, still less what it was centuries ago, or what it ought to be to-morrow, but to know and be able to state what are the principles of law which actually and at the present day exist in England.

This was a position that favoured a presentist and legalist, rather than a historical, response, and was the basis for Dicey's *England's Case against Home Rule.*

The organising balance of Dicey's critique was that between 'revolution' and the 'rule of law' (a phrase he had coined). The 'crises called revolutions', he wrote, 'are the ultimate and desperate cures for the fundamental disorganisation of society'.[38] They are traumatic but often necessary events, sweeping away an accumulation of abuses and clarifying where true sovereign power lies. England had experienced at least two salutary revolutions: that which expelled the Stuart dynasty in 1688, giving a 'death-blow to arbitrary power', and the Great Reform Act of 1832, which 'taught Englishmen, once and for all, that venerable institutions which custom had made unchangeable could easily, and without the use of violence, be changed'.[39] Ireland, under English rule, however, had inevitably been 'prevented from attempting the cure of deeply rooted evils by the violent though occasionally successful remedy of revolution'.[40] The British connection had 'been fatal for Ireland' because it meant that revolution had been suppressed 'at the price of permanent disorganisation',

---

37 A.V. Dicey, *Introduction to the Study of the Law of the Constitution*, Macmillan & Co., London 1885, pp. 14–15 ('*Introduction to the Study of the Law of the Constitution*').

38 A.V. Dicey, *England's Case against Home Rule*, John Murray, London 1886, p. 87 ('*England's Case*').

39 A.V. Dicey, *Lectures on the Relation between Law and Public Opinion in England During the Nineteenth Century*, Macmillan & Co., London 1905, pp. 42, 77 ('*Lectures on the Law and Public Opinion*').

40 Dicey, *England's Case*, above n. 38, pp. 87–88. cf. Dicey, *Lectures on the Law and Public Opinion*, above n. 39, p. 5.

and classes and religious groups in Ireland, mapped onto a historic native/settler divide, had not been able to coalesce into a nation.[41]

The 'rule of law', characteristic of England, meant that 'no man is above the law' and that 'every man, whatever be his rank or condition, is subject to the ordinary law of the realm and amenable to the jurisdiction of the ordinary tribunals'.[42] This rule of law, which had existed from the time of the Norman Conquest,[43] meant that England (and its daughter countries, such as the United States) was spared that class and ethnic acrimony that made revolutions so devastating in other countries. The problem in Ireland, however, was that the 'rule of law' by Dicey's definition did not apply. A succession of so-called Coercion Acts, 'passed both before and since the Act of Union', had regularly established special courts to deal with agrarian and political 'outages' and detained 'suspects' without trial. This, Dicey admitted, gave 'undeniable evidence, if evidence were wanted, of the ceaseless, and as it would appear almost irrepressible, resistance in Ireland offered by the people to the enforcement of the law'.[44] Even the normal exercise of law was popularly seen in Ireland, and was, in reality, a defence of foreign power and of the class interest of the landed elite against popular hostility. No rule of law 'ethic' had ever bedded down.

All serious observers, Dicey found, agreed that:

> the history of the country [Ireland] is a record of incessant failure on the part of the Government, and of incessant misery on the part of the people. … [That British rule] has failed in Ireland of achieving the elementary results of good government is as certain of any fact of history or of experience.[45]

It was this very fact, in Dicey's construal, that justified continuing British rule. 'Due respect for law' was the main justification for the very existence of the British Empire.[46] This primary result of British rule in Ireland, however – the 'greatest evil that misgovernment can cause' – was an ingrained 'hostility to law in the minds of the people'.[47] This hostility to law underpinned everything else that aggrieved Ireland. Self-government requires harmony between the different classes, Dicey insisted. 'The rich

41 Dicey, *England's Case*, above n. 38, p. 88.
42 Dicey, *Introduction to the Study of the Law of the Constitution*, above n. 37, pp. 192–93.
43 ibid., pp. 183–84.
44 Dicey, *England's Case*, above n. 38, p. 93.
45 ibid., p. 72.
46 ibid., p. 207.
47 ibid., p. 74.

must be the guides of the poor, the poor must put their trust in the rich'.[48] This was *not* the condition pertaining in Ireland due to her 'peculiar and calamitous history'.[49] If anarchy was to be avoided, therefore, it could only be by Britain's forceful imposition.

The only possible alternative was to establish a popularly legitimate sovereignty in Ireland. Dicey was rather contradictory on the status of 'nationality' and whether popular sovereignty must result in Irish separation from Britain, but he was realistic enough to incline this way. He implied that the real source of popular discontent was agrarian rather than nationality and at one point would only admit that 'the spirit of nationality has some, though probably a small, part in the production of Irish discontent'.[50] Elsewhere he argued, however, that the British system of aristocracy was foreign to the traditions and opposed to the interests of the mass of people. Even the question of land tenure was secondary: 'The real grievance is our presence in Ireland at all'.[51] Dicey admitted that 'if a fair vote was taken' it was as likely that an Irish majority would vote for separation as it would for Home Rule.[52]

Dicey evinced respect for the virtue and purity of Republican separatism while lambasting the Land War's 'murderous conflict … for the possession of Irish land'.[53] But while pure, honourable and sensible from an Irish point of view, a separatist revolution was simply intolerable from the British perspective: 'By men of all parties and of all views it is practically conceded that England neither will nor can, except under compulsion, assent to Irish independence'.[54] To do so, not least, would be *embarrassing* for Britain, a humiliation of its vaunted constitution in the face of the world. This was the prior datum, to be taken for granted. The question to be considered, therefore, was whether Home Rule, a measure of devolution rather than separation, would in practice imperil the sovereignty of the United Kingdom Parliament.

Dicey's case against Home Rule was that it was neither fish, nor fowl, nor good red meat. It meant neither local self-government nor national independence. It would impose restrictions on Ireland's political liberty

48 ibid., p. 26.
49 ibid., p. 31.
50 ibid., p. 268.
51 ibid., p. 77.
52 ibid., p. 68.
53 A.V. Dicey, *A Fool's Paradise: Being a Constitutionalist's Criticism on the Home Rule Bill of 1912*, John Murray, London 1913, pp. 4–5.
54 Dicey, *England's Case*, above n. 38, p. 196.

'absolutely inconsistent with the principle of nationality' so that a '*bona fide* Home Ruler cannot be a *bona fide* Nationalist'.[55] But from a British perspective, it would be destructively revolutionary. The main problem with Irish Home Rule, so far as Dicey was concerned, would be its British consequences.

Gladstonian Home Rule was half-federalism, half-colonialism. From federalism, as seen for example in the United States, the Bill proposed: restrictions on an Irish parliament's legislative authority; disputes between it and the Imperial Parliament at Westminster to be settled by a court; and Ireland contributing to Imperial expenses. From the colonial model, derived from the white dominions within the Empire, there was an Irish Home Rule government dependent on its own parliament, and the preservation of Westminster's supremacy through a right of veto. Dicey predicted that such a hybrid arrangement, as applied to Ireland, would be neither smooth nor final.

Irish 'colonialism' was not viable because where colonial self-government worked, as it did in Canada, there was a desire to cleave close to Britain for the *gratis* protection it offered, in the form of the Royal Navy. Irish nationalism, however, had no such desire to remain close to Britain and, as Ireland was necessarily in Britain's homeland security zone, there could never be a realistic chance of Britain withdrawing its naval protection from Ireland and so no Irish temptation to curry English favour. Irish *federalism*, on the other hand, would upend the entirety of the British constitution. Britain would lose the secret of its strength, the 'absolute omnipotence' of Parliament.[56] Gladstone's proposed restriction on Westminster's right to legislate was in fact 'the most "revolutionary" proposal' in the entire Bill, 'if the word "revolutionary" be used in its strict sense'.[57] Federalism would act as a solvent, leading to the break-up of the United Kingdom and the British Empire. Dicey stated:[58]

> It revolutionizes the whole Constitution of the United Kingdom; by undermining the sovereignty of Parliament, it deprives English institutions of their elasticity, their strength, and their life; it weakens the Executive at home, and lessens the power of the country to resist foreign attack. The revolution which works these changes holds out no hope of reconciliation with Ireland. An attempt, in short, to impose on England and Scotland a constitution which they do not

[55] ibid., pp. 32–33.
[56] ibid., p. 168.
[57] ibid.
[58] ibid., pp. 196–97.

> want, and which is quite unsuited to the historical traditions and to the genius of Great Britain, offers to Ireland a constitution which Ireland is certain to dislike, which has none of the real or imaginary charms of independence, and ensures none of the solid benefits to be hoped for from a genuine union with England. … Federalism offers to England not a constitutional compromise, but a fundamental revolution, and this revolution, however moderate in its form or in the intention of its advocates, does not offer that reasonable chance of reconciliation with the mass of the Irish people which might be a compensation for a repeal of the Union, and is as much opposed to the interests of Great Britain as would be the national independence of Ireland.

The creation of an Irish Home Rule Parliament 'must be the beginning, not the end, of a revolution' and this would not be limited to the British Isles:[59]

> in the present state of the world it is inconceivable that Irish autonomy – if such be the proper term – should not excite or justify claims for local independence which would unloose the ties which bind together the huge fabric of the British Empire.

The paradox here was that moderate Home Rule was in its effect more revolutionary than the clean break actual Irish independence would involve. The question became, therefore, what kind of revolution did Ireland have a right to?

> If the Irish people are a nation, this may give them a right to independence, but it can never in itself give them a moral claim to dictate the particular term of union with England.[60]

4. CONCLUSION

Dicey wanted to argue that the Irish Home Rule demand was hypocritical. The Irish demanded that their nationality be recognised, but if that really was what was at stake, 'then the demand must be satisfied, if at all, not by Home Rule, but by independence'.[61] Dicey came very close to frankly admitting that British misgovernment and Irish nationality did give Ireland an unimpeachable moral right to revolution, but it had also created

59 ibid., p. 134.
60 ibid., p. 70.
61 ibid., p. 98.

a situation in which the minority (he referred much more to landlords than to Ulster Protestants) would inevitably be mistreated by a vengeful Catholic democracy: 'The problem (it may be said) admits of no solution. This may be so, and is indeed my own conviction'.[62]

In the coming years, the liquidation of Irish landlordism by British legislation, most notably by the Wyndham Land Act of 1903, the secession of the Irish Free State from the United Kingdom following a War of Independence, and the setting aside of the six counties of Northern Ireland by partition, would present a way through for Dicey's problem without a solution. An Irish rule of law was stabilised on the basis of sovereign independence, while the interests of Irish unionism, north and south, were either bought out or laagered behind a border. What Dicey had feared most, a revolutionary disruption of the British constitution by the victory of a Parnellite Home Rule, was averted, if at considerable cost. Paradoxically, it was Irish history that ultimately saved Dicey's beloved supremacy of the Crown-in-Parliament for Britain.

62 ibid., p. 226.

INDEX

ABOUT THE EDITORS AND ASSISTANT EDITOR

Editors

ANDREW DICKINSON is Professor of the Conflict of Laws and a Fellow of St Catherine's College at the University of Oxford, and an Honorary Senior Fellow at the British Institute of International and Comparative Law. Andrew is one of the specialist editors of Dicey, Morris & Collins, *The Conflict of Laws* (16th edition, 2022) and has, since 2006, served as a member of the Mance Committee, the UK Ministry of Justice's advisory committee on private international law matters.

TIMOTHY ENDICOTT is the Vinerian Professor of English Law and a Fellow of All Souls College at the University of Oxford. He writes on constitutional and administrative law and jurisprudence, with special interests in law, and language and legal interpretation. Prior to his appointment to the Vinerian Professorship in 2020, Timothy was a Fellow in Law at Balliol College, and served as the Dean of the Faculty of Law from 2007 to 2015.

WOLFGANG ERNST is the Regius Professor of Civil Law and a Fellow of All Souls College at the University of Oxford, having previously held the chair of Roman and Private Law at the University of Zurich. Wolfgang's main research areas are Roman law and the Roman law-based doctrinal history of civil law, with contributions examining the role of notable figures in the history of legal science.

Assistant Editor

SOPHIE RYAN is a Rhodes Scholar and DPhil in Law candidate at the University of Oxford, having graduated from the University of Queensland (Bachelor of Arts and Laws) and the University of Oxford (Bachelor of Civil Law). Sophie's research examines the interaction of different legal orders in cross-border human rights litigation before the English courts.

www.ingramcontent.com/pod-product-compliance
Ingram Content Group UK Ltd.
Pitfield, Milton Keynes, MK11 3LW, UK
UKHW021844100926
8556IPUK00019B/1036